Building English Skills

Purple Level

Yellow Level

Blue Level

Orange Level

Green Level

Red Level

GOLD LEVEL

Silver Level

Aqua Level

Brown Level

Plum Level

Pink Level

Kindergarten Level

Building English Skills

Gold Level

McDougal, Littell & Company
Evanston, Illinois
New York   Dallas   Sacramento

Authors

Kathleen L. Bell, Assistant Director of Composition, Department of English, University of Miami, Coral Gables, Florida

Donna Rae Blackall, Chairperson, Language Arts Department, Thomas Junior High School, Arlington Heights, Illinois

Kraft and Kraft, Developers of Educational Materials, Stow, Massachusetts

Susan Duffy Schaffrath, Consultant in Educational Materials for the Elementary and Middle Grades, Chicago, Illinois

Mary Ann Trost, Former Elementary Teacher, East Cleveland City School District, East Cleveland, Ohio

Consultants

H. Kaye Griffin, Ed. D., Language Arts Coordinator, Klein Independent School District, Spring, Texas

Thomas C. Holland, Ed. D., Assistant Superintendent, Curriculum and Instruction, McKinney Independent School District, McKinney, Texas

Sue Cox Mays, Ph.D., Instructional Specialist, Fort Worth Independent School District, Fort Worth, Texas

Barbara Wirth Sirotin, Language Arts Coordinator, Arlington Heights Public Schools, Arlington Heights, Illinois

Edmund Sullivan, Supervisor of Language Arts, Evansville-Vanderburgh School Corporation, Evansville, Indiana

Cathy Zollars, Director of Instruction, Grand Prairie Schools, Grand Prairie, Texas

ISBN: 0-86609-005-3

Copyright © 1984, 1980 by McDougal, Littell & Company
Box 1667, Evanston, Illinois 60204
All rights reserved. Printed in the United States of America

Acknowledgments

Simon & Schuster, Inc.: For entries appearing on pages 203, 204, 205, 206 and 208 from *Webster's New World Dictionary of the American Language*, Students Edition; copyright © 1981 by Simon & Schuster, Inc. Macmillan Publishing Company: Chapters 3, 10, 11, 12, 17, 18, 22, 27 and 28 contain, in revised form, some materials that appeared originally in *The MacMillan English Series, Grade 6*, by Thomas Clark Pollock et al., copyright © 1963, 1960, 1954 by The Macmillan Company. Used by arrangement.

(Acknowledgements are continued on page 482.)

Contents

Handbook: The Mechanics of Writing

Special Features of This Text

1. Balanced Coverage. Building English Skills, Gold Level is a comprehensive text that presents balanced coverage of seven areas of language arts:

1. Vocabulary development
2. Speaking and listening skills
3. Grammar and usage
4. Composition skills
5. Study and research skills
6. Appreciation of literature
7. The mechanics of writing

2. Effective Teaching Method. Each chapter develops one topic completely through a combination of clear, readable explanations; examples that appeal to students at this grade level; and numerous exercises, at frequent, appropriate intervals, that directly reinforce the preceding lessons. Chapters of the grammar and usage strand and of the composition strand refer to and build upon what has been taught in the previous chapters of each of those strands. This steady development of grammar and composition concepts not only provides for meaningful maintenance but also makes possible an ever-growing awareness of the nature of language.

3. Emphasis on the Process of Writing. Chapters 5, The Process of Writing; 6, Studying Good Paragraphs; 7, Ways of Developing a Paragraph; 8, Different Kinds of Paragraphs; 15, Writing Compositions; 16, Different Kinds of Compositions; and 20, Writing Reports, help develop and improve writing skills by leading the student through the process of writing. This process consists of three major steps in the development of any piece of writing:

Pre-writing, which includes choosing a topic and planning what to write

Writing, which includes writing topic sentences and developing paragraphs or reports according to a plan

Revising, which includes changing the ideas or organization of a piece of writing to improve its meaning and correcting the capitalization, punctuation, and other mechanics to make the writing more easily read and understood

The text teaches that changing a piece of writing does not mean just correcting mistakes. Rather, it means expressing an idea more clearly or developing the idea more fully. The step of proofreading for mistakes comes after the idea and its expression have been developed as far as the writer can take them.

4. Useful Handbook for Student Reference. Chapters 27, Capitalization; 28, Punctuation; and 29, Spelling, form the Handbook of the Mechanics of Writing. These chapters list the basic rules likely to be needed by a student at this level, with easy-to-follow explanations, examples, and exercises. The Handbook is a practical reference tool for students, who should be encouraged to consult it independently throughout the year. It appears at the back of the book and is printed on lightly tinted pages for easy reference.

The Handbook will be most helpful if the teacher introduces and explains its use early in the year and reminds students of it at strategic intervals. The chapters may also be taught following the usual teacher-directed method, either an entire chapter at a time or one Part at a time.

Chapter 1

How Our Language Grows

The English language is always changing and growing. New words come into our language all the time. There are many ways in which new words are added to our language. Here are seven ways.

1. Words are borrowed from other languages.
2. Words are made from initials.
3. The name of a famous person or place becomes a word.
4. Sounds are imitated and eventually become words.
5. Old words are shortened.
6. Two words are put together.
7. Technical terms from jobs and science become common words.

In this chapter we will talk about these seven ways in which new words come into our language.

Part 1 Words Borrowed from Other Languages

Throughout its history, the English language has taken many words from other languages. Even today English is still borrowing words. Some of the languages that English has borrowed from are American Indian, French, Spanish, Dutch, and German. The following lists give some examples for each.

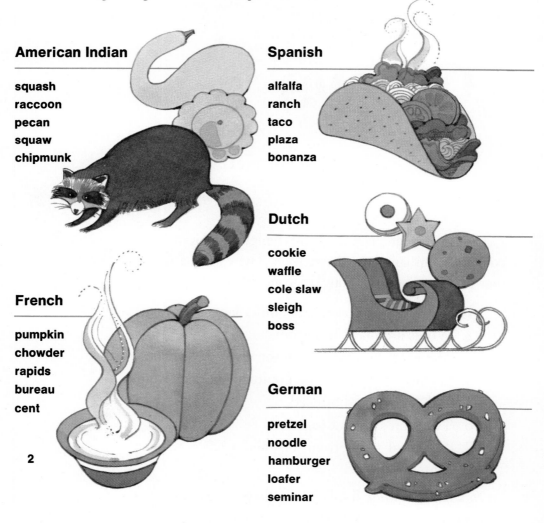

American Indian

squash
raccoon
pecan
squaw
chipmunk

French

pumpkin
chowder
rapids
bureau
cent

Spanish

alfalfa
ranch
taco
plaza
bonanza

Dutch

cookie
waffle
cole slaw
sleigh
boss

German

pretzel
noodle
hamburger
loafer
seminar

2

Exercise Borrowed Words

From what language was each word in the box borrowed? Number from 1 to 10. Write the correct abbreviation after each number.

Algon. = Algonquian (American Indian)
Fr. = French
Sp. = Spanish
Du. = Dutch
G. = German

A dictionary will give you the answers. Practice pronouncing each word you look up.

1. kindergarten
2. chaise longue
3. wigwam
4. sombrero
5. margarine
6. moccasin
7. ersatz
8. snoop
9. patio
10. snorkel

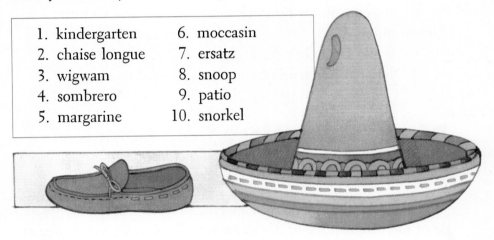

Part 2 Words Made from Initials

Sometimes the initials of a group of words are put together to make a new word. These words are called **acronyms**. They give us shorter ways to say and write things. For example, it is easier to say VISTA than to say Volunteers in Service to America. Acronyms are pronounced as words. However, some groups of initials used to make new words are pronounced as separate letters. For example, UN is a shortened way to write or say United Nations. There are over 12,000 acronyms in our language. More come into use every year.

3

Exercise   Acronyms

Tell what acronym is used as a short form for each of the following names.

1. Strategic Arms Limitations Talks
2. Job Opportunities for Better Skills
3. Fabbrica Italiana Automobili Torino
4. Congress of Racial Equality
5. North Atlantic Treaty Organization
6. Cooperative for American Relief Everywhere
7. Women's Army Corps
8. United Nations Educational, Scientific, and Cultural Organization.
9. People United to Save Humanity
10. National Aeronautics and Space Administration

Part 3   Words Made from Names of People and Places

In 490 B.C. the Greeks won a war against the Persians at the battle of Marathon. One of the victorious Greek soldiers ran twenty-six miles to bring the news of the victory to Athens. Today the word *marathon* usually means a twenty-six mile race. Sometimes it means another type of endurance contest.

The Earl of Sandwich, who lived about 200 years ago, loved to gamble. He did not even want to leave the gambling room for meals. Therefore, he asked for a more portable kind of meal, something he could eat as he played. Eventually, his snack was known as a *sandwich*.

4

Exercise **Words from Names of People and Places**

Look up each of the following words in the dictionary. Find out what name or place each came from. Write the name on your paper.

bloomers   cardigan   hamburger
macadam   tuxedo   magnolia
calico   chesterfield sousaphone
maverick   pompadour   macadamia nut

Part 4 Words Made from Sounds

One way in which language might have begun was by imitating the sound that something made. English has a number of words that imitate actual sounds. These are called **echoic words**. They echo real sounds. Some of them are *pop, buzz,* and *clop.*

Exercise **Echoic Words**

Think of an echoic word that describes or names each of the following sounds. Number your paper from 1 to 12. After each number, write the echoic word.

1. The sound of water when someone jumps in
2. The sound of a person telling secrets
3. The sound of brakes
4. The sound of cloth tearing
5. The sound of a dog
6. The sound of heavy boots
7. The sound of a ringmaster's whip in an animal cage
8. The sound a pencil makes when you break it
9. The sound of scissors
10. The sound of a leaky faucet
11. The sound of a person with a cold
12. The sound of thunder

5

Part 5 Shortened Words

People who speak the English language like to shorten long words. They use only a small part of a word. For example, they say *fan* for *fanatic*, *auto* for *automobile*, and *burger* for *hamburger*. Each short form of such words eventually becomes a new word itself. Using only part of a long word is called **clipping**.

Exercise Clipping

Here are the long forms of some English words. Can you give the clipped form for each?

omnibus gymnasium mathematics
laboratory influenza examination
taximeter cabriolet telephone submarine
advertisement airplane dormitory

6

Part 6   Words Put Together

Sometimes two words are put together to make a new word. The new word is called a **compound word**. English has many compound words. New ones are being made all the time. Some compound words are *bookkeeper, football, outdoors, downtown,* and *input.*

Sometimes when two words are put together to make a new word, some of the letters are dropped. The new word is then called a **blend**. The word *smog* is a blend of *smoke* and *fog. Paratroops* is a blend of *parachute* and *troops.*

Exercise   Compounds and Blends

Each of these words is a compound or a blend. Tell what each word means. Tell what two words it is made from.

bedtime	doorknob	bedspread
motel	skyscraper	chortle
cloudburst	telethon	motorcade
drugstore	bellhop	brunch

Part 7   Technical Words

People who work at a job have a special vocabulary for that job. The special language of a job is called shoptalk. It is made up of technical words. These words have specific meanings that are related to the job. For example, the space agency NASA has such terms as *countdown* and *blastoff.* Athletes have such terms as *tackle* and *hurdle.* Sometimes these words are useful for talking about other things besides the job. Then the words become part of everybody's vocabulary. In other words, a person "tackles" a problem or overcomes a "hurdle." The technical word changes slightly in meaning when it comes out of its original setting. It becomes a common word,

7

a new word in our language. The following chart gives some examples of shoptalk, the job from which it came, its job meaning, and its general meaning.

Word	Job	Job Meaning	General Meaning
southpaw	baseball	left-handed baseball pitcher	a person who is left-handed
grandstand	baseball	seating for spectators	to show off before people
shill	carnival	a helper in the audience permitted to win money so that others will take a chance	a person who works with a gambler, auctioneer, etc., by pretending to bet, bid, or buy so as to lure others
sucker	circus	circusgoer	a person easily cheated
fade-out	movie	picture slowly disappearing	slowly disappearing
third degree	police	harsh questioning of criminals	any harsh questioning
feedback	computers	return of data	reactions between people, answers to questions

Exercise Technical Words

Can you think of examples of technical words that have become common words? Try to think of five such words. Explain their sources and original meanings. Then tell their common, new meanings.

Review Exercise How Our Language Grows

Here are the seven ways that words are added to the English language:

1. By borrowing
2. By making a word from initials
3. By using the name of a person or place
4. By imitating a sound
5. By using part of another word
6. By putting two words together
7. By using technical terms as common words

Decide how each of the following words came into our language. Write each word on your paper. After each word, write the number of the way that applies. Use your dictionary for help.

sunrise	jersey	fizz	camouflage
mike	HUD	roommate	pasteurize
honk	boycott	memo	basketball
raglan	gas	UNICEF	garage
chassis	bookcase	deb	mackintosh

9

Reinforcement Exercises—Review

How Our Language Grows

A. Borrowed Words

Look up each word below in a dictionary. Number your paper from 1 to 10. Write the abbreviation of the language it was borrowed from.

Algon.	= Algonquian	It.	= Italian
Fr.	= French	Du.	= Dutch
Sp.	= Spanish	G.	= German

1. barbecue
2. piano
3. totem
4. frankfurter
5. chocolate
6. woodchuck
7. levee
8. delicatessen
9. balcony
10. alfalfa

B. Acronyms

Tell what acronym is used as a short form for each of the following names.

1. Internal Revenue Service
2. National Organization for Women
3. Very Important Person
4. Extra Sensory Perception
5. Distant Early Warning line

C. Words from Names of People and Places

Look up each of the following words in a dictionary. Find out what name or place each came from. Write the name on your paper.

watt   bayonet
volcano   bobby
gerrymander   atlas

10

D. Words Made From Sounds

Use each of the echoic words below in sentences of your own.

clash	plop	whoosh
crunch	rap	crash

E. Shortened Words

Here are the long forms of some English words. Can you give the clipped form for each?

caravan	penitentiary	memorandum
periwig	champion	promenade
curiosity	askutasquash	graduate
turnpike	drapery	convict

F. Compounds and Blends

Each of the words below is a compound or a blend. Tell what each word means. Tell what two words it is made from.

twinight	earthworm	newsmagazine
bathrobe	backbone	dishpan
candleholder	smog	copyreader
footbridge	handbag	headache

Chapter 2

Developing a Vocabulary of Specific Words

There are two kinds of words: **general** and **specific**. A general word is one that covers a whole range of ideas or feelings. A specific word has a more limited meaning. For instance, *go* is a general word. It means "move along." *Sail* is a more specific word. It means "to be moved forward by means of a sail or sails." He *sailed* across *the river* describes more exactly what he did than *He went across the river*.

Specific words pack a lot of information into a small space. They make writing lively and interesting. They say exactly what you mean.

Six general words are *go, make, big, small, good,* and *bad*. This chapter will show you how to choose specific words for each of these general words. The specific words will express our meaning exactly.

Part 1 Specific Words for *Go*

Think about the general word *go*. It does not give much information. It tells only that something moved. If you say, "Tony went home with his report card," you have told where Tony went. What if the report card was wonderful? Would *went* accurately describe how Tony got home? Maybe *dashed* would be a better word, since it shows that Tony was happy. However, if the report card was bad, *dashed* would be the wrong word. In that case, saying "Tony *trudged* home with his report card" would be better.

Many specific words may be used instead of *go*. Each word will have a slightly different meaning. For example, the word *stampede* has a different meaning from the word *flutter*. You could use *stampede* to describe the "go" of a herd of buffalo. But you could not use *stampede* to describe the "go" of a butterfly. Instead, you would use *flutter*.

Specific Words for *Go*

sail	ride	roll	tumble
run	walk	plunge	trot
skip	trudge	dash	glide
charge	drift	jump	fly
wander	hurry	flutter	race
stampede	rush	streak	plod
hike	march	climb	drive

14 **Exercises** **Specific Words for *Go***

A. Choose the better word for each sentence.

1. Donna (trudged, dashed) into the room shouting, "Fire!"

2. During the fire drill the students (charged, walked) out of the school building in single file.

3. Andy was daydreaming. He just seemed to (wander, trudge) around with his head in the clouds.

4. The old horse (plodded, skipped) along the path.

5. The swimmer was so enthusiastic that he (tumbled, plunged) right into the cold water.

6. The butterfly was not hurt. It (fluttered, rushed) away.

7. She (walked, ran) to get to the store before it closed.

8. I watched the sailboat (skip, glide) over the water.

9. You will have to (jump, fly) over the puddle.

10. The family dog proudly (trotted, trudged) along beside the new baby carriage.

B. Choose five precise words for *go*. List them in order of increasing speed. Start with words that mean "go slowly." For example, *plod* would come before *race*.

C. Replace the italicized word in each sentence. Use a more specific word that fits the idea in the sentence.

1. When the last day of school ended, the students *went* out the door.

2. The wind made the lifeboat *go* off course.

3. After I had delivered the last paper, I *went* home and collapsed into a chair.

4. The car *went* down the race track at nearly 300 kilometers per hour.

5. The dancers *went* lightly across the stage.

6. John and Jim *went* to the shelter on their overnight camping trip.

7. My family is thinking of *going* across the country next summer. **15**

8. Wait till you see the lions *go* through a burning hoop.

9. Diane's homerun blast *went* over the center field fence.

10. If you *go* right in, the water won't feel cold.

Part 2   Specific Words for *Make*

Some words are so general that they can be confusing. The word *make* is a good example of a word that is not clear. Suppose you said that someone *"made* a house." Did someone design the house? Was someone hired to build it? Did someone actually take hammer and nails and put the boards together?

The word *made* does not say exactly what the person did. If you said instead that a person *designed* a house, or *built* a house, your meaning would be clear.

Specific Words for *Make*

create	compose	design
invent	manufacture	concoct
build	construct	fashion
forge	devise	prepare
produce	cause	form

There are many other specific words for *make*. They are words for the work that is needed to make specific things. Do you *make* cloth or *weave* cloth? Do you *make* a picture or *draw* a picture?

Exercises   Specific Words for *Make*

A. Replace the italicized word in each sentence. Use a more specific word that fits the idea in the sentence. You may use words that are not on the list.

1. Hurricanes and tornadoes can *make* destruction.

2. Thomas Edison *made* the electric light bulb.

3. The only tools you'll need to *make* this birdhouse are a hammer and saw.

4. This jacket was *made* to allow easy movement.

5. My aunt spends her evenings trying to *make* a hit tune.

6. Use a spade to *make* a trench around the tent.

7. If I had known you were coming, I would have *made* a cake.

8. Even if you can't thread a needle, I can teach you to *make* your own clothes.

9. In this plant we *make* television antennas.

10. *Make* the dough into a ball.

11. I've *made* a new kind of bubble gum!

12. Donna *made* a watercolor picture of the forest.

13. Can you *make* a meal for two hundred hungry hikers?

14. Juan is always able to *make* some excuse for being late.

15. We watched the spider *make* a web.

B. Choose the better word for each sentence.

1. We (built, fashioned) a fishhook from a safety pin.

2. The Wright brothers (built, formed) the first successful airplane.

3. Directions that are not clear may (manufacture, cause) confusion.

4. Most bicycles are (created, designed) to carry only one person.

5. The United States is (composed, built) of fifty states.

6. With a sharp knife, Dan (carved, concocted) a grinning face in the pumpkin.

7. I (manufactured, concocted) a stew from some leftovers.

8. As a hobby, I (build, invent) model boats.

9. Carol hopes to become a writer; she's good at (creating, preparing) stories.

10. We have to (build, devise) a plan for getting across the river.

17

Part 3 Specific Words for *Big*

Action words are not the only words that you should choose carefully. Descriptive words are just as important.

Big is a general word. *Tall* is more specific; so is *fat*. Each of these words tells in what way something is big. A word like *monstrous* tells even more. Something *monstrous* is frightening as well as big.

Think of different words you might use to describe a house. *Spacious* might fit, or *substantial*, or *huge*. What about *imposing*? That could be used, too. But a word like *fat* would not work.

However, if you were describing a person, *fat* might be a better word than *huge*. The correct word will depend on the particular thing you are writing about.

Specific Words for *Big*

great	hulking	substantial
fat	vast	bulky
imposing	gigantic	massive
spacious	monstrous	heavy
huge	tremendous	strapping

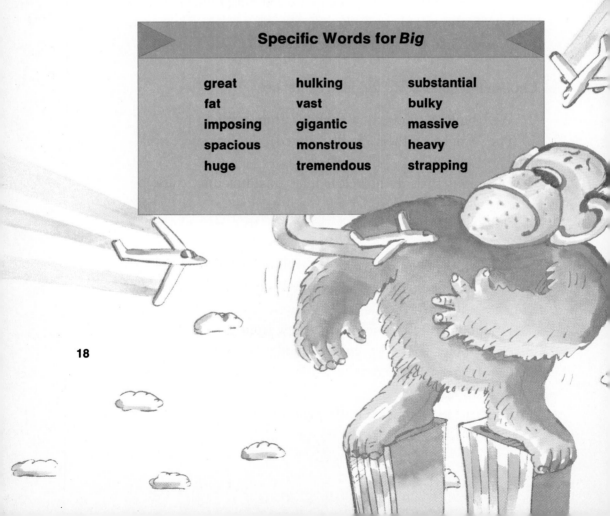

18

Exercises **Specific Words for *Big***

A. Look at the word list. Find the word that matches each definition. For some definitions, more than one word will fit. Discuss your choices with the class.

1. big and solid and strong
2. big and healthy
3. big and scary
4. too big
5. big and hard to move
6. big and full of room

B. Choose the better word.

1. The doorway to the cathedral certainly was (fat, imposing) .
2. We wandered through the airy, (spacious, hulking) rooms.
3. Everyone hoped to get a (huge, heavy) piece of cake.
4. The elephant had (massive, tall) feet.
5. The furniture was much too (spacious, bulky) to move.
6. The circus was held in a (tremendous, strapping) canvas tent.
7. We looked out over a (monstrous, vast) field of wheat.
8. My aunt and uncle have a (strapping, substantial) house in the suburbs.
9. We went to the store during its (gigantic, imposing) clearance sale.
10. The airplane searched over a (vast, heavy) area.

C. Choose at least three specific words for *big* that you might use to describe each of the following things.

1. a big place
2. a big shipping crate
3. a big dragon
4. a big baby
5. a big rock

19

Part 4 Specific Words for *Small*

Many words that describe an object also show how the speaker feels about the object. Take, for instance, the word *small. Small* is a general word that means "not large."

If you said that a cat was *small*, you would merely be describing the size of the cat. If you said the cat was *scrawny*, you would also be telling how you felt about the cat. A listener would imagine a stray cat that looked underfed and unhealthy. A *scrawny* cat does not sound very attractive.

A *delicate* cat describes a prettier cat. *Delicate* still means small. It would be a better word to use if the animal were slender instead of unhealthy.

People have different feelings about what size is the "right" size. If large rooms make you feel lost, you might call a small one *snug*. If large rooms are what you like, you might think a small one was *cramped*.

Some specific words are complimentary. Some are insulting. Your feelings will help determine which you use.

Specific Words for *Small*

tiny	microscopic	modest
petite	dainty	shrunken
miniature	cozy	puny
little	snug	scrawny
cramped	delicate	shriveled

microscopic animals

20

Exercises **Specific Words for *Small***

A. Look at the list of specific words for *small.* Use them to fill the blanks in the following sentences. Choose a word that fits each sentence. More than one word might be correct. Use only one.

1. The _____ golden slippers were beautiful.

2. We felt at home in the _____ living room.

3. It was hot and sticky in the _____ bus.

4. My hobby is collecting _____ car models.

5. The ring was covered with _____ diamonds.

6. The _____ puppy was the last to be bought.

7. The spider wove a _____ web in the corner of the doorway.

8. We won the game by a _____ number of points.

B. Some words are used mostly to describe things that are alive, like people or animals. From the word list for *small,* choose the words that you think might be used to describe a person or animal. Try to list at least five words.

C. List six specific words for *small.* Use words from the list or make up your own. Put a + by each word that makes smallness seem good. Put a − by each word that makes smallness seem bad. Put a 0 by words that do not make smallness seem good or bad.

D. Write two short paragraphs describing a small person. In the first paragraphs, imagine that the person is someone you like. In the second, imagine that he or she is someone you dislike.

Part 5   Specific Words for *Good*

21

Good is a general word we use frequently. It can describe how something looks, how much it is worth, or how well it works. Most often it tells how the writer feels about a person or thing.

Specific words for *good* cover a wide range of feelings. If you said that a party was *passable*, no one who missed it would feel sorry. If you said the party was *perfect*, anyone who missed it would be full of envy. If you said that the party was *proper*, people would have still different feelings about it.

People often use certain words in spoken English to mean "nice" or "fine" or "excellent." Some of these are *okay, terrific, wonderful, great, neat,* and *super.* These words are not specific words for *good.* They are merely other general words that mean the same as *good.* They may be used in speaking. However, they should be avoided in writing.

Specific Words for *Good*

nice	suitable	pleasing
fine	perfect	useful
passable	adequate	satisfactory
excellent	rare	proper
superb	valuable	moral
delicious	sound	enjoyable

22   **Exercises   Specific Words for *Good***

A. Read the word list. Make sure you understand all the words. Then choose a more specific word for *good* in each sentence. You may use a word more than once. You may also use a specific word for *good* that is not on the list.

1. My parents thought the sweater looked good on me.
2. The plump cream puffs dripping with chocolate sauce looked good.
3. That movie was so good that I'm going to see it again.
4. The winner of the race was a good horse.
5. Joe! I haven't seen you since last year! It's good to see you again.
6. Diane is good, honest, and trustworthy.
7. It rained every day, but my vacation was still good.
8. The car isn't in the best shape, but it has four good tires.
9. Here's a coat that's good for rainy weather.
10. My job is to separate the good apples from the bruised ones.

B. Imagine that you are a salesperson. You are trying to persuade a customer to buy Bubbo Soap. What words for *good* would you use to describe Bubbo? List them in a column labeled *Bubbo*. What words for *good* might you use to describe Flubbo, a competitor's soap? List those words in a column labeled *Flubbo*.

C. Choose the better word in each sentence.

1. I'm going to practice this trick until it is (perfect, adequate).
2. Unfortunately, the food at camp is only (proper, passable).
3. Claude's father congratulated us for the (excellent, passable) weeding job we had done.
4. This is the only (superb, suitable) coat I have for winter.
5. My teacher told me that my work is barely (satisfactory, fine).
6. Let's go to see that comedy movie that got such (proper, excellent) reviews.
7. It's not a fancy ring, but I think it's (superb, nice).
8. The museum had a display of (adequate, rare) antique pottery.

Part 6 Specific Words for *Bad*

The word *bad* has as many different meanings as *good* has. It is important to think about exactly what you mean when you use a general word like *bad*. Do you mean *evil?* Or do you just mean *wrong?* Or *defective?* Or *illegal?* Or *dangerous?* Or *harmful?*

Specific words for *bad* range from mild words like *mischievous* all the way to *repulsive* and *disgusting*.

If you were talking about an alarm clock that did not work, would you call it *defective* or *evil?* What about a poisonous gas? Would you call that *unfortunate* or *terrible?* It makes more sense to save strong words like *evil* and *terrible* for serious things. Do not waste strong words on small matters.

Specific Words for *Bad*

poor	worthless	evil
terrible	horrible	harmful
defective	wrong	vicious
shoddy	wicked	inferior
immoral	naughty	dishonest
illegal	vile	devastating

Exercises Specific Words for *Bad*

A. Read the word list. Choose specific words from it to fill the blanks in the following sentences.

24

1. I took a _____ turn somewhere and got lost.

2. The handle on the door was _____ and had to be fixed.

3. We thought the movie was a cheap and _____ job.

4. It is not only dangerous to speed, but also _____.

5. The room has a _____ odor of spoiled meat.

6. People used to think that witches were charmed by _____ spirits.

7. My little brother isn't really nasty, but he can be _____.

8. The tornado left a _____ path of destruction behind it.

9. A balloon is _____ after it bursts.

10. Cigarette smoking is _____ to health.

B. List a specific word for *bad* to match each definition.

1. Not as good as something else
2. Not worth anything
3. Not made correctly
4. Not made well
5. Causing terror
6. Not correct
7. Causing harm
8. Causing horror
9. Showing slightly bad behavior
10. Not honest

Reinforcement Exercises—Review

Developing a Vocabulary of Specific Words

A. Specific Words for *Go*

Number your paper from 1 to 5. Choose the better word for each sentence. Write the word on your paper.

1. The icebreaker (plowed, streaked) through the frozen harbor.
2. The frightened chipmunk (trotted, scurried) into its hole.
3. A hot air balloon (rushed, drifted) over the countryside.
4. John and Linda (skipped, plodded) through the deep snow.
5. A bee (charged, flitted) from flower to flower.

B. Specific Words for *Make*

Number your paper from 1 to 5. Choose the better word for each sentence. Write the word on your paper.

1. Handel (manufactured, composed) the music for *The Messiah*.
2. The colonists learned to (build, manufacture) the goods they couldn't buy.
3. Cuba (produces, constructs) much of the world's sugar.
4. The usher asked the crowd to (devise, form) a line.
5. Lures are (designed, concocted) to look like the food fish eat.

C. Specific Words for *Big*

Number your paper from 1 to 5. Choose the better word for each sentence. Write the word on your paper.

1. This coat is too (bulky, tremendous) to wear skating.
2. The moon landing was a (great, monstrous) accomplishment.
3. A (strapping, vast) area of Russia is still unpopulated.

4. A (gigantic, fat) wave crashed over the sea wall.

5. The truck was too (heavy, vast) to cross the old bridge.

D. Specific Words for *Small*

Number your paper from 1 to 5. Choose the better word for each sentence. Write the word on your paper.

1. Jim has a collection of (shrunken, miniature) trains.

2. My (cramped, scrawny) seat on the plane was uncomfortable.

3. The (tiny, microscopic) bird struggled in the storm.

4. The acrobat lifted his (puny, petite) partner easily.

5. Though the Rands were wealthy, they lived in a (shriveled, modest) home.

E. Specific Words for *Good*

Number your paper from 1 to 5. Choose the better word for each sentence. Write the word on your paper.

1. Greg's touchdown pass was (suitable, perfect)!

2. Bird-watchers enjoy sighting (pleasing, rare) birds.

3. This bread is (delicious, nice). Please give me the recipe.

4. Doris said I did a (fine, rare) job fixing her hem.

5. The (moral, proper) thing to do would be to invite the whole class.

F. Specific Words for *Bad*

Number your paper from 1 to 5. Choose the better word for each sentence. Write the word on your paper.

1. Money is (defective, worthless) on a deserted island.

2. The lumber was (inferior, harmful), so it warped easily.

3. I apologized for dialing a (poor, wrong) number.

4. Some laws protect customers from (dishonest, naughty) salespeople.

5. A warning light shows if the brakes are (wrong, defective).

27

Chapter 3

Learning About Sentences

When you learned to talk, you began slowly. You probably started out with the names of people around you, like *Mama* or *Dada*. Then you added some action words to let others know what you wanted—words like *come* and *give*. Still later you learned words to describe things you saw, like *pretty flowers* or *funny clown*.

Now you know thousands of words, and how to put many of them together to express your needs and ideas. But you may have found that now and then you still have trouble making others understand you. You can still grow in your ability to use your language.

This chapter will describe the rules for arranging words to make good sentences. Learning these rules will help you understand more of the sentences you hear or read. It will also help you to express yourself to others, in speaking or in writing.

29

Part 1 Complete Sentences

A **sentence** is a group of words that expresses a complete thought.

If people hearing you talk do not understand you, they can ask you questions. If they are reading a story, or a report, or a letter you wrote, they cannot ask your paper any questions. Your story, report, or letter by itself must make your thoughts clear.

When you are writing, make sure your sentences answer such basic questions as these: *Who did it? What happened?* If a group of words does not answer these questions, that group is not a complete sentence.

Example 1. His stack of newspapers.

What happened? Did someone do something to the stack of newspapers? Did the stack do something? The example does not give you enough information to answer the questions. It is only part of a sentence, or a **fragment**.

By adding words to a fragment, you can change it into a complete sentence. Here are two sentences that give complete thoughts about the fragment, "His stack of newspapers."

Richard delivered *his stack of newspapers.*
His stack of newspapers fell to the ground.

Example 2. Played in the water.

Who or what played in the water? Again, the group of words does not give a complete thought. Here are two ways you might complete this fragment:

The seals *played in the water.*
Kristen and Gene *played in the water.*

30

Can you add words to the two fragments below to make them complete thoughts?

Threw out the first ball of the season
The TV special yesterday

Exercises **Recognizing Complete Sentences**

A. Number your paper from 1 to 10. Study the groups of words below and decide which of them are sentences. For each word group write "Sentence" or "Fragment."

1. A pocket of my jeans
2. Sold ten tickets
3. Two trucks blocked the intersection
4. The day before the race
5. We visited Mount Rushmore
6. Between the laundromat and the corner
7. Carefully climbed out on the roof
8. Louis was asleep
9. A fountain in Lincoln Park
10. Three pounds of hamburger

B. All but one of the groups of words below are sentence fragments. Add words of your own to make complete sentences. Write the sentences. Copy the one complete sentence just as it is.

1. On Friday
2. All the bus drivers
3. Jill came at six o'clock
4. Half the night
5. The automatic door at the supermarket
6. Across the bridge
7. Exploded in mid-air
8. Cautiously tried the ice on the pond
9. Too much water
10. A block from school

31

Part 2 Four Kinds of Sentences

The girls and boys in the picture above have used four different kinds of sentences. Each kind expresses a complete thought.

1. A **declarative sentence** tells something. It ends with a period (.).

The movie begins at two o'clock.

2. An **interrogative sentence** asks something. It ends with a question mark (?).

Do you like popcorn?

3. An **imperative sentence** requests, instructs, or orders. It usually ends with a period. When it shows strong feeling, it ends with an exclamation point (!).

Sit near the front of the theater.   Don't walk so fast!

4. An **exclamatory sentence** expresses joy, surprise, anger, excitement, or other strong feeling. It ends with an exclamation point (!).

What a huge crowd came to this show!

Begin every sentence with a capital letter.

Exercises   Identifying the Kinds of Sentences

A. The following sentences do not have punctuation marks at the end. Number your paper from 1 to 10. Write *Declarative, Interrogative, Imperative,* or *Exclamatory* to show what kind each sentence is.

1. Measure the length of the table
2. May we watch Channel 11
3. Birds' bones have air pockets
4. Take a break
5. What a scary feeling I got
6. Do you have an eraser
7. Is the pressure in the tires too high
8. Ms. Minden's cat had a rabies shot
9. Does a chipmunk have a white stripe down its back
10. Tell me all about your problem

B. Follow the directions for Exercise A.

1. John Singleton Copley painted portraits of great Americans
2. Turn off the hose, please
3. The melon rolled down the steps
4. Can you lift the 100-pound weight
5. May I come, too
6. What a fast runner Vincent is
7. The ballerina wore toe shoes
8. Wait for the next elevator, please
9. Are you rooting for Peggy
10. Guava is a tropical fruit

33

Punctuating Sentences

When you write sentences, follow these rules of punctuation:

1. Use a period after a declarative sentence.
2. Use a question mark after an interrogative sentence.
3. Use a period after an imperative sentence. If the sentence shows strong feeling, use an exclamation point.
4. Use an exclamation point after an exclamatory sentence.

Exercises Using Correct Punctuation

A. Copy and punctuate these sentences.

1. Which seats are ours
2. Call Debbie to the phone, please
3. Oil floats on the top of water
4. Get off that shaky ladder
5. Have you ever visited the Everglades
6. Place your stamp in the upper right-hand corner
7. How far can you swim under water
8. The Swiss flag is red with a white cross
9. Oil slicks kill hundreds of birds
10. What a lot of questions you ask

B. Follow the directions for Exercise A.

1. Proceed to gate G-7
2. What a great time we had at Disney World
3. Run faster
4. Now, which tooth is loose
5. Elvis Presley Boulevard is a street in Memphis
6. Do twenty push-ups
7. Lauri practices the tuba down in the rec room
8. Does Michael wear his hair in an Afro style
9. Whales are guided by tiny pilot fish
10. What is the Continental Divide

C. Write two declarative sentences, two interrogative sentences, two imperative sentences, and two exclamatory sentences. Begin and end each sentence correctly.

D. Write a paragraph or a story about something exciting, funny, or different that has happened to you. Use the four kinds of sentences.

Part 3   Every Sentence Has Two Parts

Every sentence has a **subject** and a **predicate**.

1.

The old car	lost its tailpipe.
This part is the subject. It tells what the sentence is about.	This is the predicate. It tells what happened.

2.

Our team	won the pennant.
This is the subject. It tells whom the sentence is about.	This is the predicate. It tells what happened.

3.

My friend Sue	hit a home run.
Subject	Predicate

Finding the Subject and the Predicate

Every sentence states a complete thought. A complete thought has two parts: the subject and the predicate.

The **subject** of a sentence tells what or whom the sentence is about.

The **predicate** of a sentence tells what the subject did or what happened.

35

An easy way to understand the parts of a sentence is to think of the sentence as telling who did something or what happened. The subject tells *who* or *what*. The predicate tells *did* or *happened*. You can divide sentences in this way:

Who or What (Subject)	Did or Happened (Predicate)
All my friends	came to my party.
The old elm	was blown down by the storm.

Exercises **Finding Subjects and Predicates**

A. Copy these sentences. Draw one line under the subject of each sentence. Draw two lines under the predicate.

Example: The yellow car was going too fast.

1. Dad locked the house.
2. Thanksgiving will fall on November 28 this year.
3. The first batter struck out.
4. My socks have shrunk.
5. A robin's nest was in the pear tree.
6. Jay's cat eats beetles.
7. The second-string players watched from the bench.
8. We could not see through the water.
9. Lisa took her bathing suit with her.
10. The team can count on Mandy.

B. Follow the directions for Exercise A.

1. Maria found an old gold watch.
2. My little brother swallowed a dime.
3. A pound weighs less than a kilo.
4. My sister's Chevy uses unleaded gas.
5. The sunlight sparkled on the water.

6. Terence's cookies taste best.
7. The final whistle blew.
8. A butterfly struggled in the spider's web.
9. The inventor experimented with the wooden gears.
10. The air conditioner in the family room works.

C. Write an interesting predicate for each of these subjects. Begin each sentence with the words given.

1. The pizza
2. The black hearse
3. My terrier
4. Our front door
5. Stacy's science project
6. The drive-in
7. Charlie Brown
8. The sly old cat
9. The best game
10. The quarterback

D. Write a good subject for each of these predicates.

1. knows all the latest dances
2. is jumping next
3. are going rock climbing
4. has twin engines
5. is allergic to peanuts
6. squeaks a lot
7. saw the movie on Saturday
8. went fishing every day
9. stopped
10. wants to be an engineer

Part 4   The Verb

The subjects and predicates you have been studying so far are called **complete subjects** and **complete predicates**. The complete subject includes all of the words that tell *who* or *what*. The complete predicate includes all of the words that tell *what happened.*

There is one part of every complete predicate that is more important than the rest. This part is the **verb**. It is sometimes called the **simple predicate**. In the rest of this book, we will speak of it as the *verb.*

37

Finding the Verb

The words in italics in these sentences are the verbs.

We *went* to the beach.
Three girls *brought* their goggles.

Some verbs tell of an action:

Charlene *hit* the ball.
The boys *ran* home.

Other verbs state that something is:

The doctor *is* here.
You *are* first.

A **verb** is a word that tells of an action
or a state of being.

Exercises Finding the Verb

A. Copy these sentences. Draw two lines under the verb.

Example: The tornado <u>carried</u> Dorothy to Oz.

1. A pack of dogs runs loose on my street.
2. Reggie does unusual stunts on his skateboard.
3. The first movies were silent.
4. In spring, northern farmers boil maple sap into syrup.
5. The bike marathon lasts all day.
6. The guide told our group about the state capitol.
7. One of my cousins writes for *Newsweek*.
8. A worm was in that apple.
9. Sacajawea guided Lewis and Clark in their exploration of the Northwest Territory.
10. Nobody believed Esther's story.

B. Follow the directions for Exercise A.

1. Queen Elizabeth I ruled England for forty-five years.
2. Water freezes at 0°C or 32°F.
3. All the students went home half an hour ago.
4. The mail arrived early today.
5. Barry rode his bike to school.
6. The baby eats nothing but cereal.
7. Medicine Hat is the name of a town in Canada.
8. My mother once met Pearl Bailey backstage.
9. Alex found a dollar bill in the mall parking lot.
10. The lightning storm caused static on the radio.

Part 5 Main Verbs and Helping Verbs

The verb is often only a single word. Read each sentence below and notice the verb, in italics.

> Eddie *laughed* at the joke.
> Georgia *whistled* a tune.
> The students *cheered.*

Other verbs are made up of more than one word. Notice how you can build a one-word verb into a verb with several words:

> Beth and David *collect* shells.

The verb, *collect,* tells what Beth and David do.

> Beth and David *will collect* shells.

The verb we began with, *collect,* now has another verb, *will,* before it. We call *collect* the **main verb**, and *will* the **helping verb**. The helping verb changes the meaning of the sentence slightly.

> Beth and David *were collecting* shells.

39

The verb *collect* has changed its form now to *collecting*, but it is still the main verb. The new helping verb is *were*. This helping verb changes the meaning of the sentence, too.

Beth and David *have collected* shells.

Here, the main verb is *collected*, another form of the verb *collect*. The helping verb is *have*.

As you have seen in these examples, the main verb may change forms when helping verbs are added to a one-word verb. The endings *-ing*, *-ed*, and *-en* are frequently used on main verbs. Adding helping verbs and changing the ending do not change the basic action of the main verb. However, these changes do modify the meaning slightly.

In the following examples, decide which word is the main verb and which word or words are helping verbs. Then look at the chart to see if you were right.

Grace *was skating*.
The vase *was broken* by accident.
Randy *has combed* his hair.
The old Ford *has been making* strange noises.
The back door *should have been locked*.

Verb	Helping Verbs	Main Verb
was skating	was	skating
was broken	was	broken
has combed	has	combed
has been making	has been	making
should have been locked	should have been	locked

Some words can be used either as verbs by themselves or as helping verbs:

is	was	have	do
are	were	has	does
am		had	did

Examples:

Tomorrow *is* a holiday. (verb)
The pump *is broken*. (helping verb with *broken*)

Ardis *has* a cold. (verb)
She *has stayed* home. (helping verb with *stayed*)

Some words can be used only as helping verbs:

can	may	should
shall	must	would
will	could	might

Examples:

We *may go* with you.
Dad *will finish* the pie.
Jackie's project *might win* an award.

> Some verbs are made up of a main verb and helping verbs.
>
> Some words can be used either as verbs by themselves or as helping verbs.
>
> Some words can be used only as helping verbs.

Exercises **Finding the Main Verb and Helping Verbs**

41

A. Label two columns *Helping Verbs* and *Main Verb*. Find all the parts of the verb in each sentence. Write them in the proper column.

Examples:	Helping Verbs	Main Verb
a. I have enough potato chips for the party.		have
b. Eighteen customers have demanded refunds.	have	demanded

1. I have seen the dinosaur bones in the museum.
2. The blizzard stopped all traffic in the city.
3. The Cubs might beat the Braves.
4. Pennsylvania is the Keystone State.
5. Chris has completed four passes in this quarter.
6. Rick should be waiting for you.
7. Terri can somersault in the air.
8. The chemical had poisoned the fish.
9. My camera needs new batteries.
10. The fireworks in Candlestick Park will begin at eight.

B. Follow the directions for Exercise A.

1. You should have seen the game last Tuesday.
2. Those peppers may burn your tongue.
3. The water in the pool was 26°C.
4. On Saturday the rides will cost a quarter.
5. Seattle was named for an Indian chief, Seathl.
6. The whole house would shake with each new tremor.
7. The Grand Canyon is more than a mile deep.
8. My sister has driven six hundred miles a day.
9. I might show Lion at the pet show tomorrow.
10. You must have taped that noise at the basketball game.

C. Write sentences in which you use the words *do, does, did* as verbs by themselves. Then write sentences using these words as helping verbs with the main verb *go.*

42

D. Use the helping verbs given on page 41 with the main verb *call*. See how many different verbs you can make.

Part 6 Separated Parts of the Verb

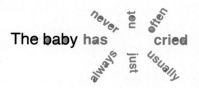

The baby has ... cried (never, not, often, always, just, usually)

The words that make up a verb are not always together in a sentence, like *could have been*, and *might have been*. Sometimes the helping verbs and the main verb are separated by other words that are not verbs:

can hardly wait   could not have come
has always been   didn't understand
is usually found   must have already gone

The parts of the verb are in red. Notice that *not* and the ending *n't* in contractions are not parts of the verb.

Exercises Finding Separated Parts of the Verb

A. Label two columns *Helping Verbs* and *Main Verb*. Find all the parts of the verb in each sentence. Write them in the proper column.

Example: The kitten didn't scratch me.

Helping Verb	Main Verb
did	scratch

1. Jenny has always been my friend.
2. Bruce would often take the bus.
3. Slacks are usually found in the sportswear department.
4. The logs are normally floated down the river.
5. We will probably see the movie this weekend.
6. Judy had just cut the lawn.
7. Lynn is always whistling that song.
8. The carpet is usually vacuumed once a week.

43

9. My brother didn't understand the instructions in the cookbook.

10. Maurie must have already finished his lunch.

B. Follow the directions for Exercise A.

1. My mother was actually looking for a new car.
2. The hot days of July and August are sometimes called dog days.
3. That catbird is always mimicking all the other birds.
4. Ms. Washington doesn't often assign homework.
5. Valerie can really walk a tightrope.
6. Mr. Lang must not have called very loudly.
7. A Venus fly trap can really catch flies.
8. Greg would rather have a corn roast.
9. In Australia, badgers are sometimes called bandicoots.
10. New York was originally named New Amsterdam.

C. The following sentences have main verbs but no helping verbs. On a sheet of paper numbered from 1 to 10, write helping verbs that will fit the blanks.

1. My parents _____ often watched "60 Minutes."
2. Marsha _____ already performed.
3. Jason _____ n't going to the art fair today.
4. Dottie _____ never visited a factory before.
5. Robin _____ surely come tomorrow.
6. Last month the sewing class _____ usually end at three o'clock.
7. The skyscraper _____ probably equipped with eight elevator shafts.
8. The sound equipment _____n't working.
9. Larry _____ not _____ put his ticket on the windowsill.
10. You _____ hardly looked at the geology display.

Part 7 The Simple Subject

In a complete sentence, every verb has a subject.

	Subject	Verb
1.	**Ginny**	ran.
2.	Your **popsicle**	will melt.
3.	The old **man**	laughed.

The most important word in the complete subject is sometimes called the **simple subject** of the sentence. The simple subjects in the sentences above are *Ginny, popsicle,* and *man.* Another name for the simple subject is the **subject of the verb.**

To find the subject of the verb, first find the verb. Then ask *who or what* before the verb.

Examples:

The crowd at the rock concert cheered loudly.

Verb: *cheered*
Who or what *cheered?* the *crowd*
Crowd is the subject of *cheered.*

After dinner my whole family watched television.

Verb: *watched*
Who or what *watched?* my *family*
Family is the subject of *watched.*

Exercises **Finding the Verb and Its Subject**

A. Copy each sentence. Draw two lines under the verb. Then draw one line under the subject of the verb.

1. Carol coached our team.
2. The space shuttle was first tested in 1978.
3. Joel is our next-door neighbor.

45

4. The hornets under the window buzzed angrily.
5. The cows didn't even look at the train.
6. The grandfather clock struck twelve.
7. The treasures of King Tutankhamen were found in Egypt.
8. We were flying over the airport for an hour.
9. All three boys could play the guitar well.
10. The cat's eyes shone in the dark.

B. Follow the directions for Exercise A.

1. Aretha worked the problem easily.
2. In July and August, the Dog Star rises with the sun.
3. Heavy traffic frequently jams the Holland Tunnel.
4. My dog will not chase cars.
5. The steer in that pen was branded at Lazy T Ranch.
6. The fragrance of popcorn filled the theater.
7. Now Carl can dry the dishes.
8. The hedge behind the tennis court was full of flowers.
9. My older sister must have dropped the vase.
10. The lettuce in that salad was grown in my garden.

Part 8   The Subject in Unusual Positions

In nearly all the sentences you have studied so far, the subject comes before the verb. There are many sentences, however, in which the subject comes after the verb. Notice these sentences:

1. The *shark* lingered off the shore.
   (Subject before the verb)

2. Off the shore lingered the *shark*.
   (Subject after the verb)

Sometimes you can find the subject more easily if you turn the sentence around.

Sentence: Through the cloud shot the missile.
Rewritten: The missile shot through the cloud.

Always find the verb first. Then ask *who?* or *what?* before the verb.

The subject always follows the verb in sentences that begin in these ways:

Here is   Where is   There is
Here are   Where are   There are

1. Where are the *keys?* (*Keys* is subject of *are.*)
2. Here is your *guitar.* (*Guitar* is subject of *is.*)
3. There is our *boat.* (*Boat* is subject of *is.*)

Exercises   Finding the Subject in Unusual Positions

A. Copy each sentence. Draw two lines under the verb. Then draw one line under the subject of the verb.

1. There is a funnel cloud in the distance.
2. Into the pool the diver plunged.
3. The girls zipped the tent windows.
4. Where is the key to your locker?
5. Over the haunted house floated strange shapes.
6. There are many irritating commercials on that program.
7. Across the street darted Mr. Walter's cat.
8. Slowly Sandy understood.
9. Up the bank scrambled Patti.
10. Two hours after lights out, Kevin crept from his tent.

B. Follow the directions for Exercise A.

1. Here is my idea.
2. Overhead were all our helium balloons.
3. Up the river glided the barge.
4. Suddenly the rocket backfired.
5. In the tropical waters are many unusual creatures.

47

6. There is room for Miki.
7. In last year's competition, Al's team won easily.
8. Over the plains thundered the herd.
9. Her bracelet is a souvenir from Niagara Falls.
10. Where is a public telephone?

C. Follow the directions for Exercise A.

1. The sand glittered with gold dust.
2. There are already five teams in our bowling league.
3. Into his burrow whisked the fox.
4. Here is the electrician now.
5. Out of the canyon roared the river.
6. Heather collected the carwash money.
7. Down the tower stairs the knight clattered.
8. Time waits for no man.
9. Where is the latest newspaper?
10. In the shed was an old Victrola.

Part 9 Subjects in Interrogative and Exclamatory Sentences

You may have to revise or rethink some interrogative and exclamatory sentences to find the subject. Here are some examples.

| Interrogative Sentence: | Did you see that touchdown? |
| Revised: | You did see that touchdown. |

| Exclamatory Sentence: | Was that movie boring! |
| Revised: | That movie was boring! |

Sometimes you need to drop some words to make a rewritten sentence sound normal.

Exclamatory Sentence:	What terrible weather we're having!
Revised (Awkward):	We're having what terrible weather!
Revised (Smooth):	We're having terrible weather!

48

Exercises Finding the Subjects and Verbs in Interrogative and Exclamatory Sentences

A. Change the word order in each sentence below. You may need to drop some words to make your sentence smooth. Then write the new sentence. Underline each subject.

Example: Will we never get home!
We will never get home.

1. Were you the winner?
2. What a long time you took! (Drop *What*.)
3. Has the dog been fed?
4. How orange the moon looks! (Drop *How*.)
5. Have they painted the library?
6. Did your friend win the calculator?
7. What a dark cave we saw! (Drop *What*.)
8. May I help you?
9. How fast the baby has grown! (Drop *How*.)
10. Won't this snow ever melt!

B. Copy the sentences below. Draw two lines under the verb in each sentence. Draw one line under the subject of the verb. (If you need to, change the word order mentally to find the subject and verb.)

1. Does that hamburger have onions on it?
2. How did you find the right answer? (Drop *How* mentally.)
3. What a noisy bird that crow is! (Drop *What* mentally.)
4. Does Marianne Moore write poetry?
5. Have the Indians played in the World Series since 1970?
6. How ugly you look in your witch's costume! (Drop *How* mentally.)
7. Has Angel ever ridden a horse bareback? (Drop *ever* mentally.)
8. What a feast we had at Thanksgiving! (Drop *What* mentally.)
9. Has Marcia read today's newspaper already?
10. Am I hungry!

49

Part 10   When the Subject Is Not Given

Look at the two sentences on the signs in the picture. *You* is the subject of each of these sentences. In imperative sentences the subject is understood to be the word *you*.

Examples: (You) Keep off the grass.
(You) Do not feed the animals.

Exercises   Telling the Subject

A. Copy the following sentences. Draw two lines under the verb in each sentence. Draw one line under the subject of the verb. If the subject is not given in the sentence, write it in parentheses in the place where it is understood.

Example: Memorize your new phone number.

(You) memorize your new phone number.

1. Play ball.
2. Marianne almost forgot her umbrella.
3. Take another turn.
4. Finish your game before supper.

50

5. Did Joe bring the net?
6. Give me your autograph, please.
7. How bumpy this road is!
8. Is the story true?
9. Proceed with caution.
10. Do you know Steve Fowler?

B. Follow the directions for Exercise A.

1. Wait a minute.
2. Does Rosalie speak Spanish?
3. The violin players had not arrived.
4. Did the explorers come from Portugal or Spain?
5. Listen to that rain.
6. Can everyone hear me?
7. How many legs do insects have?
8. Shop at Fred's.
9. Turn left at the first stop light.
10. Some of my friends play handball every afternoon.

Part 11 Compound Subjects

Look at these two sentences:

	Subject	Predicate
1.	Tom	saw a traffic accident.
2.	I	saw a traffic accident.

Since the predicates are the same, we can join the two sentences together. Here is the new sentence:

	Subject	Predicate
3.	Tom and I	saw a traffic accident.

Now the subject has two parts. When two or more subjects are used with the same predicate, they are called a **compound subject**. The word *compound* means having more than one part.

In sentence 3 the word *and* joins the two parts of the subject. The word *or* is also used to join parts of a subject.

> A word that is used to join words or groups of words is called a **conjunction**.

Simple subject: **Darren** may win.
Simple subject: **Alicia** may win.
Compound subject: **Darren** or **Alicia** may win.

When three or more subjects are combined in a compound subject, use commas to separate them. The conjunction is placed before the last subject.

Example: The *trees*, the *bushes*, and the *flowers* need rain.

Exercises **Writing Compound Subjects**

A. Copy the following sentences. Draw two lines under the verb in every sentence. Then draw one line under each part of the compound subject. (Reminder: Be careful to copy every comma.)

Examples: a. The <u>wind</u> and the sudden <u>rain</u> <u><u>ruined</u></u> the picnic.

b. <u>John Lennon</u>, <u>Paul McCartney</u>, <u>George Harrison</u>, and <u>Ringo Starr</u> <u><u>became</u></u> famous as the Beatles.

1. Emily, Charlotte, and Ann Brontë wrote novels.
2. The Knicks or the Celtics may win the playoffs.
3. Shirley, Della, and Pat are best friends.
4. In *Star Wars*, C3PO and R2D2 aid in the fight against the evil Darth Vader.
5. Radishes, carrots, and potatoes grow underground.

6. That stuffed dog or the rubber duck would be a good gift for the baby.

7. George Burns and Gracie Allen performed in vaudeville, on radio, and on TV.

8. Marisa and Juan tied for first place in the essay contest.

9. Cereal, milk, and toast make a nutritious breakfast.

10. The Mohawks and four other Indian tribes joined forces as the powerful Five Nations.

B. Think of a compound subject for each sentence below. Copy the sentences, filling in the blanks with a compound subject.

Example: _____ and _____ rent canoes at Bow Lake.
Mr. Walker and his daughter rent canoes at Bow Lake.

1. _____ and _____ are the busiest streets near us.

2. _____ or _____ whistled.

3. Gooey _____ or _____ tastes good on ice cream.

4. _____ and _____ are my favorite sports.

5. _____ , _____ , and _____ were coming down Cherry Street.

6. Many _____ and _____ grew in the greenhouse.

7. _____ , _____ , and _____ have thirty days.

8. _____ and _____ clung to the overturned boat.

9. My _____ or my _____ is my oldest relative.

10. Over-ripe _____ and day-old _____ were on sale.

53

C. Think of a compound subject for each predicate listed below. Then write the complete sentence. In some sentences, try to use a compound subject with three parts. Use correct punctuation.

1. suddenly rounded the corner
2. are waiting outside
3. were my best subjects
4. have never been afraid of spiders
5. covered the ground
6. were not ready yet
7. ran for the last bus
8. are in the tool kit
9. were blocking the supermarket driveway
10. tied down the trunk of the car

Part 12 Compound Predicates

When two or more predicates are used with the same subject, they are called a **compound predicate**.

By using a compound predicate and a conjunction you are often able to combine two or more sentences.

Subject	Predicate
1. The dog	growled.
2. The dog	bit the paperboy.

Subject	Predicate
3. The dog	growled and bit the paperboy.

When three or more predicates are combined in a compound predicate, commas are used to separate them. The conjunction is placed before the last predicate.

Example: Katherine saw the bear, dropped the camera, and ran off.

Exercises   Writing Compound Predicates

A. Copy the following sentences. Draw one line under the subject of each sentence. Then draw two lines under each part of the compound predicate. (Reminder: Be careful to copy every comma.)

Examples: a. Chris Evert practiced long hours and became a

top tennis player.

b. My father jacked up the car, took off the flat tire,

and put on the spare.

1. I left the cake in the oven too long and burned it.

2. Ice covered the streets and caused numerous accidents.

3. Lydia's family went to the Grand Canyon, rode burros down the trail, and spent the night at the bottom of the Canyon.

4. The Angels scored four runs in the first inning and stayed ahead during the rest of the game.

5. Frederick Douglass escaped from slavery and became a speaker for anti-slavery groups.

6. Our class rented a bus and visited the Natural History Museum.

7. King Kong broke loose in New York City, climbed the World Trade Center, and fought off fighter planes.

8. On the field trip, you bring your lunch or buy a hot dog at the cafeteria.

9. Mary Pickford starred in silent movies and was called "America's Sweetheart."

10. Ector came to bat, ignored three wide pitches, and smashed the fourth pitch into the stands.

55

B. Think of a compound predicate for each subject listed below. Copy the sentences, filling in the blanks with verbs to complete the compound predicates.

Example: The lean gray cat _____ on the shed, _____ itself, and _____ the sparrows.

The lean gray cat sat on the shed, sunned itself, and watched the sparrows.

1. The photographer _____ for buffalo and finally _____ a herd.

2. The lion cub _____ and _____ his food.

3. The gymnast _____ on the balance beam and _____ a prize.

4. Noisy crows _____ over the field and _____ the corn.

5. A 747 _____ very big and _____ many passengers.

6. My little sister _____ her food, _____ her shoes, and _____ with her toys.

7. A foghorn _____ a loud noise and _____ ships about rocks and other dangers.

8. Benjamin Franklin _____ electricity, _____ bifocal glasses, and _____ *Poor Richard's Almanac.*

9. Satellites _____ the earth below and _____ information about the weather.

10. A huge Christmas tree _____ in the shopping mall and _____ many shiny ornaments.

C. Think of a compound predicate for each subject listed below. Then write the complete sentence. In some of your sentences, try to use a compound predicate with three parts.

1. The catcher
2. A shrewd detective
3. The Statue of Liberty
4. The big band
5. Stars and planets
6. The ice cream
7. Rotten floor boards
8. Forest fires
9. An octopus
10. The snowstorm

Sentence Patterns   Word Order and Meaning

Sentences are made up of words. To make sense, the words must be put together in a special order. Look at the groups of words below. Which group makes sense?

Ralph jumped up.

Jumped Ralph up.

The first group makes sense. The words are in the right order for an English sentence. The second group does not make sense. Our experience tells us that the words are not in the right order for an English sentence.

Sometimes there is more than one right order for a group of words. Each order makes sense and expresses a message, but the messages are not always the same. Read the following pair of sentences.

Elaine saw Hugh.

Hugh saw Elaine.

The words are the same in each sentence. Only the order of the words makes the sentences different. But the difference in order makes an important difference in meaning.

Exercise   Word Order and Meaning

Read each sentence. Then change the order of the words to change the meaning. Write each new sentence on your paper.

1. Tom spotted Phyllis.
2. Cake crumbs covered the dish.
3. The Tigers beat the Lions.
4. Carol knows my best friend.
5. Some insects eat plants.
6. Some men are nurses.
7. Donna heard the cat.
8. That boy is a dancer.

57

Reinforcement Exercises—Review

Learning About Sentences

A. Recognizing Complete Sentences

Number your paper from 1 to 10. Study the groups of words below and decide which of them are sentences. For each word group write "Sentence" or "Fragment." Then add words to the fragments to make complete sentences.

1. Just bought a new ten-speed bike
2. Peanut butter and jelly
3. Many airlines fly to Los Angeles
4. Quickly chose players for their teams
5. The lights of New York
6. Won a prize in the broad jump
7. We have already mailed the boxtops
8. The satellite monitored the weather
9. Cars for rent
10. The Colorado River flows through the Grand Canyon

B. Using Correct Punctuation

Copy and punctuate these sentences.

1. What a good mood you're in
2. Cotton is cooler than polyester
3. From the airplane the thunderheads looked huge
4. Can you repair this cuckoo clock
5. Call me at five
6. Does Kim's jackknife have a can opener
7. Give the baby her bottle at two o'clock
8. Rustler is my cousin's horse
9. How tan you're getting
10. Hit the puck harder

C. Finding Subjects and Predicates

Copy these sentences. Draw one line under the subject of each sentence. Draw two lines under the predicate.

1. Our class hung the posters in the gym.
2. The seaplane revved up its motors.
3. A six-foot drift covers our driveway.
4. The final score for the game was tied.
5. Mr. Lewis will take our class picture next week.
6. A huge brown eagle glided over the mountain top.
7. The book from Japan shows pearl divers.
8. The old apple trees by the barn are loaded with green fruit.
9. The woolly mammoth became extinct in prehistoric times.
10. A heavy fog hid the old lighthouse.

D. Finding the Verb

Copy these sentences. Draw two lines under the verb only.

1. Sequoya invented the first Indian alphabet.
2. All the guests brought birthday presents.
3. Jennifer pitched three scoreless innings.
4. Clothing styles change every few months.
5. Mrs. Figueroa runs a grocery store on West Fourteenth Street.
6. The rug had a lump in it.
7. My pencils are in my desk.
8. Roger Bannister ran the first four-minute mile.
9. The empty car rolled down the hill.
10. Many cats are very independent.

E. Finding the Main Verb and Helping Verbs

Label two columns *Helping Verbs* and *Main Verb*. Find all the parts of the verb in each sentence. Write them in the proper column.

1. Veronica can speak German.

2. The camera had slid under the seat.
3. Gayle has been shoveling snow for half an hour.
4. The maple sap is boiling.
5. My cousins are in Mexico.
6. The White Sox were winning.
7. Janice could read the sign in the moonlight.
8. My brother will be in boot camp for three months.
9. You should taste this mild cheese.
10. Spencer might have taken the short cut.

F. Finding Separated Parts of the Verb

Label two columns *Helping Verbs* and *Main Verb*. Find all the parts of the verb in each sentence. Write them in the proper column.

1. Kirk could hardly avoid the chuckholes.
2. My aunt had just finished that sketch.
3. The arctic bush pilot has already flown a thousand miles today.
4. The weather will very likely be worse in February.
5. My family has always gone to the Octoberfest.
6. Grass will never grow under your feet.
7. Montreal was originally settled by the French.
8. The girls will certainly like these blueberry muffins.
9. I don't often watch the Saturday morning cartoon shows.
10. Corky might have been seriously hurt in that accident.

G. Finding the Verb and Its Subject

Copy each sentence. Draw two lines under the verb. Then draw one line under the subject of the verb.

1. The tallest girl in the class was Nicole.
2. Eric usually takes his flippers with him.
3. The first official flag had only thirteen stars.
4. The joggers circled the field again and again.

60

5. The water is dripping onto the bookshelves.
6. The bus on Euclid Avenue doesn't run after seven o'clock.
7. The high iron gate swung soundlessly on its hinges.
8. Rob can water-ski on one foot.
9. Out of breath, Sara just grunted.
10. A light on the instrument panel flashed on and off.

H. Finding the Subject in Unusual Positions

Find the verb in each sentence. Write it on your paper. Then find the subject of the verb and write it in front of the verb.

1. Here comes Mark.
2. Under the eaves several long icicles formed.
3. Where is the other plate?
4. Here are the statistics for the Yankees.
5. Out of nowhere came a sonic boom.
6. After the argument Holly left.
7. On the Mississippi are many dangerous sandbars.
8. During our vacation we went to Disneyland.
9. In today's newspaper there is an article about our school.
10. Over the city was a double rainbow.

I. Finding the Subjects and Verbs in Interrogative and Exclamatory Sentences

Change the word order of each sentence below. You may need to drop some words to make your sentence smooth. Then write the new sentence. Draw one line under the subject and two lines under the verb.

1. How awfully strong you are! (Drop *How.*)
2. Has Robert found the answer?
3. How delicious that big cake looks! (Drop *How.*)
4. What exciting stories Nancy tells! (Drop *What.*)
5. Did the rabbit get into the garden again?

61

6. Is *The Floorwalker* a Charlie Chaplin comedy?
7. What beautiful flowers you have in your garden! (Drop *What*.)
8. How can I thank you? (Drop *How*.)
9. Doesn't this rain ever stop!
10. Are all the songs from the movie on the record?

J. Telling the Subject

Copy the following sentences. Draw two lines under the verb in each sentence. Draw one line under the subject of the verb. If the subject is not given in the sentence, write it in parentheses in the place where it is understood.

1. Untie the boat.
2. Return these empty bottles for the deposit.
3. There are only five minutes left before liftoff.
4. Did Tandra have the ace?
5. Spin the game dial for your turn.
6. Is Leonard collecting the money?
7. Look at that flash of lightning.
8. What did Luis find inside the box?
9. Come in an hour.
10. Ask the ranger for information.

K. Writing Compound Subjects

Think of a compound subject for each predicate listed below. Then write the complete sentence. In some of your sentences, try to use a compound subject with three parts.

1. hibernate in winter
2. are loaded with calories
3. stopped playing their trumpets
4. were piled on the table
5. have the biggest appetites

6. headed out to sea
7. fluttered around the streetlight
8. graze in the fields
9. are countries in South America
10. should be oiled

L. Writing Compound Predicates

Think of a compound predicate for each subject listed below. Then write the complete sentence. In some of your sentences, try to use a compound predicate with three parts.

1. The garage attendant
2. Abraham Lincoln
3. Rain
4. The Ping Pong ball
5. Three players
6. Early American Indians
7. The elm tree
8. A delivery truck
9. The *Tyrannosaurus Rex*
10. A plumber

Chapter 4

Combining Sentences

A sentence is a group of words that states one main idea. However, some main ideas are made up of smaller ideas. If you write a sentence for each smaller idea, the sentences will sound choppy and boring. Also, your reader may not be able to see how these small ideas work together. Here is an example of such choppy, unclear writing.

> The girls worked together. There were two of them. They worked on the computer. They found the answer to their problem.

All of these ideas can be combined in one sentence.

> The two girls worked together on the computer and found the answer to their problem.

Notice that the new sentence is smoother. It is also clearer, because it shows how the ideas work together.

This chapter will give you practice in writing smooth, clear sentences.

Part 1 Joining Related Sentences

Two sentences may often contain ideas that are alike.

Arthur wrote the music for that song. Anna wrote the words to it.

These sentences are on the same topic. They are *related* by this common topic. The related sentences can be combined into one sentence that states both ideas. They can be joined by a comma and the word *and*. Here is the combined sentence.

Arthur wrote the music for that song, and Anna wrote the words to it.

Sometimes two sentences that are on the same topic contain ideas that are different. These related sentences usually can be joined by a comma and the word *but*.

The pea soup looked terrible. It tasted delicious.
The pea soup looked terrible, but it tasted delicious.

At other times, two related sentences show a choice between ideas. The sentences usually can be joined by a comma and the word *or*.

Will I be warm enough in this sweater? Should I wear a coat?
Will I be warm enough in this sweater, or should I wear a coat?

Part 3 Adding Words

Sometimes the main ideas of two sentences work together, but one idea is more important than the other. There may be only one word in the second sentence that is really important.

Susan dropped the pan. *The pan was* hot.

You can add the one important word to the first sentence. The new sentence will be a shorter and better way of telling the idea.

Susan dropped the hot pan.

When only one word in the second sentence is important, it can often be moved to the first sentence without any change.

Mrs. Gomez held the cat. *The cat was* shivering.
Mrs. Gomez held the shivering cat.

Nat slammed the door. *He did it* suddenly.
Nat slammed the door suddenly.

Barry borrowed my record. *It was* new.
Barry borrowed my new record.

Notice that the words printed in italics were left out.

You may be able to combine several sentences in this same way. One sentence must state the main idea. Each of the others must add only one detail to the main idea. Add the important single words to the main-idea sentence.

Someone left a rag on top of the car. *The rag was* dirty. *The person acted* carelessly.
Someone carelessly left a dirty rag on top of the car.

Be careful to choose the right place in the main-idea sentence for each word that you add.

69

Sometimes you will have to use a comma when you add more than one word to a sentence.

We reached the top after a climb. *The climb was* long. *It was* hard.

We reached the top after a long, hard climb.

A. Combine the sentences in each group. Add the important words to the main-idea sentence. Leave out the words printed in italics.

1. One boy sat in the waiting room. *The boy was* small. *The waiting room was* huge.

2. Danielle slipped into the hall. *She moved* silently. *The hall was* empty.

3. Jean skated onto the ice. *The ice was* smooth. *The ice was* shiny. (Use a comma.)

4. Those raccoons were able to open garbage cans. *Those raccoons were* smart. *The garbage cans were* covered.

5. The lock finally snapped open. *The lock was* battered. *It was* rusty. (Use a comma.)

B. Combine the sentences in each group. Add the important words to the main-idea sentence and leave out the other words. Decide on your own how the sentences should be combined.

1. The watch had a battery. The battery was tiny.

2. Edna bought a costume. The costume was second-hand.

3. The fire started in the warehouse. It started yesterday. The warehouse was abandoned.

4. The bus was full of commuters. The commuters were hot. They were tired.

5. The actor put on the make-up. The actor was young. The make-up was sticky. He put it on carefully.

Part 4 Adding Words That Change

Sometimes you must change the form of a word before you can add it to another sentence. Sometimes you will have to add *-y*.

> Put some oil on those hinges. *They* squeak.
> Put some oil on those squeaky hinges.

Sometimes you will have to add *-ing* or *-ed*.

> I like to hear the thunder. It crashes.
> I like to hear the crashing thunder.

> Ann replaced the window. *It had a* crack.
> Ann replaced the cracked window.

Sometimes you will have to add *-ly*.

> We painted the porch furniture. *We were* careful.
> We painted the porch furniture carefully.

Sometimes the word ending in *-ly* can go in more than one place in the sentence.

> Jess counted the coins. *She was* slow.
> Jess counted the coins slowly.
> Jess slowly counted the coins.

Exercises Adding Words That Change

A. Combine the sentences in each pair by adding the important word to the main sentence. Follow the directions. Leave out the words printed in italics.

1. Around the turn came the horses. *They* galloped. (End the important word with **-ing**.)

2. We enjoyed the bread. *It had a good* crust. (End the important word with **-y**.)

71

3. I bandaged my brother's knee. *It had a* scrape. (End the important word with **-ed**.)

4. Deanna opened the door. *She was* cautious. (End the important word with **-ly**.)

5. The breeze rustled the leaves. *The rustling was* gentle. (End the important word with **-ly**.)

B. Find the important word in the second sentence in each pair. Add it to the first sentence. Decide how to change the word.

1. The faucet was driving me crazy. It dripped.
2. The food should stay fresh in the jars. The jars have covers.
3. We had our picnic in a cool spot. It had shade.
4. Kevin stared out the window. His stare was sad.
5. I will be in front of the drugstore. I will wait.

Part 5 Adding Groups of Words

One sentence may contain a group of words that can be added to another sentence without making any changes.

The people tossed coins. *They tossed them* into the fountain.
The people tossed coins into the fountain.

When the group of words tells more about a person or a thing, add the group near the words that name that person or thing.

The bruise was painful. *It was* on my shoulder.
The bruise on my shoulder was painful.

The boy has practiced for weeks. *The boy is* playing the violin now.
The boy playing the violin now has practiced for weeks.

When the group of words describes an action, add it near the words that name the action.

My dog was waiting. *She was* at the end of the driveway.

My dog was waiting at the end of the driveway.

Sometimes the group of words tells more about the whole main idea of the other sentence. Then it may be added at the beginning or at the end.

A loud crash woke us up. *It woke us* at four o'clock.

A loud crash woke us up at four o'clock.

At four o'clock, a loud crash woke us up.

Exercises   Adding Groups of Words

A. Combine the sentences in each pair. Add a group of words from the second sentence to the first sentence. Leave out the words printed in italics.

1. The locker is Matt's. *The locker is* at the end of the hall.
2. Jane spotted a wallet. *It was* lying by the side of the road.
3. The band was playing yesterday. *They were playing* in the park.
4. All the dishes are clean. *The dishes are* stacked on the counter.
5. The snow was two feet deep. *It was* blocking our door.

B. Combine each pair of sentences. Decide which words to add to the main-idea sentence.

1. Those fingerprints are clues! The fingerprints are on the glass.
2. There is a package of white paper. It is in the bottom drawer.
3. The wind blew the dust. The dust went into my eyes.
4. Jamie hit a long fly. It went to deep center field.
5. The gray car looked suspicious to me. It was parked across the street.

73

Reinforcement Exercises—Review

Combining Sentences

A. Joining Related Sentences

Join each pair of sentences by using **, and** or **, but** or **,or**.

1. My sister is acting in the play. I am working on the scenery.
2. Arlene let her hair grow last winter. Now she has it cut short.
3. A parakeet can sing beautifully. A puppy is more friendly.
4. New Jersey is small in size. It has a large population.
5. Ted and Janet can rush for the noon train. They can wait for the one o'clock bus.

B. Joining Related Sentences

Join the related parts in each pair of sentences by using **and**, **or**, or **but**. Leave out the words printed in italics.

1. The alien ship hummed softly. *It* rose slowly into the sky.
2. Ted thought that he might play first base. *He thought that he might play* shortstop.
3. Chris searched the whole house. *She* never found the missing necklace.
4. You can buy the book at Anderson's Bookstore. *You can* borrow it from the Amesbury Library.
5. Steve collects rare postage stamps. *He* trades *rare postage stamps.*

C. Adding Words

Combine the sentences in each group. Add the important words from the other sentences to the main-idea sentence. Follow any directions in parentheses. Leave out the words printed in italics.

1. Mugs of soup warmed the skiers. *The mugs were* steaming. *The soup was* hot.

2. On each plant were several tomatoes. *The tomatoes were* plump. *They were* juicy. (Use a comma.)

3. We paddled down the stream. *We were moving* slowly. *The stream was* winding.

4. The message was hidden in a book. *The message was* mysterious. *The book was* thick.

5. A glow lit up the sky. *The glow was* strange. *The glow was* yellow. *The sky was* black. (Use a comma.)

D. Adding Words That Change

Combine the sentences in each pair by adding the important word to the main-idea sentences. Follow the directions. Leave out the words printed in italics.

1. We pushed our way through the wind. *The wind* howled. (End the important word with **-ing**.)

2. On the leaf was a caterpillar. *It was covered with* fuzz. (End the important word with **-y**.)

3. Serve the eggs on English muffins. Toast *the muffins*. (End the important word with **-ed**.)

4. Elaine folded the letter. *She did a* neat *job*. (End the important word with **-ly**.)

5. The watchdog snarled. *The snarl was* fierce. (End the important word with **-ly**.)

Chapter 5

The Process of Writing

Have you ever made a statue from clay? First you got an idea. Then you studied pictures and planned what your statue would look like. Finally, you worked and reworked the clay until you were happy with the result.

Creating something out of words is a bit like creating something out of clay. You follow the same basic steps of planning, working, and reworking an idea. This is called the **process of writing**. There are three main steps in the process of writing: **pre-writing**, **writing**, and **revising**. You will learn about these steps in this chapter.

Part 1 Pre-Writing

One of the most important parts of the writing process is the **pre-writing**, or planning, stage. Follow these four pre-writing steps before you begin any piece of writing.

1. Choose a topic.

Sometimes your teacher will assign your topic. At other times you will be asked to select your own.

First think about the purpose for your writing. Is it to explain that you have learned about a topic? Or is it to share your own ideas? Also, keep in mind the people who will be reading your writing. You might choose to write a funny story for your class newspaper or a fact-filled report for a school bulletin to the parents. To find your own topic, ask yourself what you are interested in. Think of places you have been, people you have met, and questions you have wondered about. Make a list of all these ideas. Then select one idea to be your topic.

2. Limit your topic.

The writing you will do may be as short as a paragraph or as long as a report. Make sure that the topic you choose is not too broad or too narrow to be handled well within that length. For example, you might plan to write a composition about a class trip to a state park. Then your topic could be all the interesting things you saw. However, if you were writing one paragraph, you might limit your topic to a cave that you explored there.

3. Gather supporting information.

Make a list of the specific details or examples you could use to develop your topic. Select details that will help your reader picture or understand your topic better.

When you list details, use every source of information available to you. Sometimes your best source will be your own knowledge,

78

ideas, or experience. Sometimes you will use the library. List as many details as you can.

4. Organize your ideas.

Read your list of details. Cross out any that are not directly related to your topic. Add details that will make your writing clearer or more interesting. You may even decide to change your topic.

Finally, put your details into a logical order. If you are telling a story, you might put your details in the order in which they occurred. If you are describing a scene or an object, you could arrange your details in the order in which you noticed them. In later chapters, you will learn more about how to organize your ideas.

Study this example of pre-writing notes.

List of Possible Topics

the Halloween party
camping out in winter
the first time I played goalie
why I stopped loving horses
meeting a computer
pets *

Narrowed Topic   problems with my pet chameleon

List of Details

My chameleon is an escape artist.
leaps off high tables
travels fast
eats only live prey, such as crickets
I bought him a heat lamp.
My chameleon doesn't do much except sit on a rock.
Frogs are also difficult, unrewarding pets.
chameleon's name — Houdini

Part 2 Writing the First Draft

Now you are ready to begin writing. At this point in the process of writing, don't be too concerned with spelling and punctuation. You will have a chance to correct your writing later. Just get your ideas on paper and try to make them flow smoothly. Leave space between the lines of writing to make corrections later.

As you write, don't be afraid to use new ideas that occur to you. Remember, you can constantly rework your writing, just as you would a clay statue. Just be sure that the ideas are related to your topic.

Here is the writer's first version, or first **draft**, of the paragraph written from the pre-writing notes on page 79.

> I felt very lucky when I got a chamelon for my Birthday. I decided to name him Houdini. I had figured that a chamelon would be no trouble. I was wrong. A chamelon is an escape artist. He jumped out, jumped off the table, and went under a radator it took me a long time to catch him. From that time on, he tried to get out every time I feed him. I tried to make him feel better. I bought him a new cage and a lamp. It didn't help Houdini just sits on his rock, looking for a way out.

Part 3 Revising

A piece of writing is seldom perfect after the first draft. It usually needs **revising** or editing. Read your draft. Consider the following:

Effectiveness. Are you satisfied with what you have written? Is it interesting to you? Do you think others will find it interesting?

When you started writing, you hoped to do something with the topic. Did you achieve your goal? If your writing is a description, can you see the topic clearly? If it is a story, does it have a satisfying ending? If it is meant to persuade someone, does it present solid reasons in a logical order?

Organization. Look at the organization of your writing. Do the paragraphs or details follow an order that is reasonable?

Is each paragraph organized well? Does it have a topic sentence that expresses its main idea? Do all the sentences stick to that idea? Are they in the best possible order?

Have you covered your topic well? Should you add anything?

Sentences and Words. Be sure that every sentence is a good sentence, expressing a complete thought. However, it should also express that thought in a pleasing way. Read your writing aloud to hear whether the sentences sound good together.

Also examine your words, keeping in mind the purpose of your writing. Is every word the best choice? Does it have the right meaning? Does it have the right effect?

As you reread your writing, mark any changes you think of. Make notes on your rough draft. If your paper gets too messy, copy it and continue to revise on the copy.

Proofreading

81

It is important to make your writing correct as well as interesting. After you have revised your work, proofread it for grammar, capitalization, punctuation, and spelling. Mark any corrections.

The following symbols may be useful.

Proofreading Symbols

$\wedge$	Add letters or words.	—	Take out letters or words.
$\odot$	Add a period.	¶	Begin a new paragraph.
$\equiv$	Capitalize a letter.	$\wedge$	Add a comma.
/	Make a capital letter lowercase.	$\sim$	Trade the position of letters or words.

Here is the first draft of the Houdini paragraph marked for corrections. What changes have been made? Why?

I got more than I asked for
I felt very lucky when I got a chamelon for my
received
Birthday. *That's when* I decided to name him Houdini. I had
figured that a chamelon would be no trouble. *such a small pet* I was
wrong. *Little did I know that* A chamelon is an escape artist. *When I opened the door to his cage,* He jumped
out, jumped off the table, and went under a *raced* *leaped*
radator, it took me a long time to catch him. *an hour*
From that time on, he tried to get out every time *has* *make a getaway*
I feed him. I tried to make him feel better. I *'ve fed* *'ve* *more content by*
bought him a new cage and a lamp. It *buying* *big* *heat*
didn't help Houdini just sits on his rock, *hasn't helped.* *all day,*
looking for a way out. *the nearest exit*

82

Preparing the Final Copy

When you are satisfied that your writing is the best you can make it, write your final copy. Make it as neat as possible. Leave good margins around your writing.

When you have finished your final copy, proofread your work again. Read it aloud. Sometimes your ears catch errors that your eyes have missed.

Here is the final copy of the paragraph. Compare it with the rough draft. What further changes have been made? Why?

I got more than I asked for when I received a chameleon for my birthday. I had figured that such a small pet would be no trouble. Little did I know that a chameleon is an escape artist. When I opened the door to his cage, he leaped out, jumped off the table, and raced under a radiator. It took me an hour to catch him. That's when I decided to name him Houdini. From that time on, he has tried to make a getaway every time I've fed him. I've tried to make him feel more content by buying him a big new cage and a heat lamp. It hasn't helped. Houdini just sits on his rock all day, looking for the nearest exit.

83

Guidelines for the Process of Writing

Pre-Writing

1. Select a topic and narrow it.

2. Make a list of details that you could use to develop your topic. Decide on your main idea. Check for unrelated details.

3. Put your details into a logical order.

Writing the First Draft

1. With your topic in mind at all times, begin to write. Use the details you listed. Follow the order you chose.

2. Continue to write. You may add new details, but make sure they fit your topic.

Revising

1. Read your rough draft. Keep questions such as these in mind:

   a. Do you like what you have written? Is it interesting? Will others want to read it?

   b. Does your writing make sense? Does it do what you want it to do?

   c. Is your writing organized well? Are the paragraphs well written? Does each have a topic sentence?

   d. Are all your sentences on the topic? Are they arranged correctly? Should any sentence be moved?

   e. Should any details be left out? Should any be added?

   f. Does every sentence express a complete thought? Is every sentence easy to understand?

   g. Is there variety in the sentence patterns? Do the sentences flow smoothly from one idea to the next?

   h. Is every word the best possible word?

2. Mark changes on your paper as you think of them. Keep making changes until you are happy with what you have.

Proofreading

Proofread your revised draft. Consider questions such as these.

GRAMMAR AND USAGE

a. Is every word group a complete sentence? (See pages 30 to 31)
b. Does every verb agree with its subject? (Pages 343 to 351)
c. When you use a pronoun, is it clear about whom you are writing? (Pages 185 to 194)
d. Is the form of each adjective correct? (Pages 270 to 271)
e. Is the form of each adverb correct? (Pages 279 to 280)

CAPITALIZATION

a. Did you capitalize the first word in each sentence? (Page 425)
b. Did you capitalize all proper nouns and adjectives? (Pages 420 to 424)
c. Did you capitalize titles correctly? (Pages 428 to 429)

PUNCTUATION

a. Does each sentence have the correct end mark? (Pages 433 to 437)
b. Did you use these punctuation marks correctly: commas, apostrophes, hyphens, colons, question marks, underlining? (Pages 438 to 453)

SPELLING

a. Did you check unfamiliar words in a dictionary? (Pages 199 to 207)
b. Did you spell plural and possessive forms correctly? (Pages 146 to 151 and 444 to 445)

Preparing the Final Copy

1. Make a clean copy of your writing. Make all changes and correct all mistakes. Then check your work, asking the following questions.

   a. Is your handwriting easy to read?
   b. Is your paper neat?
   c. Did you leave wide margins?
   d. Is every paragraph indented?

2. Proofread your final copy, reading aloud. Correct any mistakes by erasing neatly and writing in the changes.

85

Chapter 6

Studying Good Paragraphs

Think about the last thing you read. Maybe it was a story or a magazine article. Maybe it was directions for how to make something. You were probably so interested in *what* you were reading that you didn't even notice *how* it was written. How something is written can make a big difference, however. It can help you understand what you are reading.

One of the most important things a writer does is to arrange ideas into paragraphs. In this chapter you will learn about things that make a good paragraph. Later, you will use what you learn. You will write good paragraphs of your own.

Part 1 What Is a Paragraph?

A **paragraph** is a group of sentences that work together to explain one idea. Here's an example of a paragraph. As you read it, ask yourself: What is this paragraph about?

> Ramo's eyes were unusual. They were black like a lizard's and very large and, like the eyes of a lizard, could sometimes look sleepy. This was the time when they saw the most. This was the way they looked now. They were half-closed, like those of a lizard lying on a rock about to flick out its tongue to catch a fly.—SCOTT O'DELL

The first sentence tells you that Ramo's eyes were unusual. This is the main idea. Each sentence after the first tells you something about Ramo's eyes. The second sentence, for example, tells you that they were black and large and could look sleepy. The third sentence tells you that this is when they saw the most. The last sentence tells you that now they were half-closed, like a lizard's eyes.

Sticking to the Main Idea

Here is another paragraph. The first sentence tells you the main idea of the paragraph. The rest of the paragraph contains one sentence that does not help to explain the main idea. See if you can pick out that sentence.

> Baseball is truly an international sport. The major U.S. leagues include two teams in Canada. The sport is popular in Latin American countries, such as Venezuela and Panama. Our Little League team won the division championship last year. Baseball is also a major sport in Japan, where games sometimes attract over 30,000 fans.

88

The paragraph explains that baseball is played in many countries. This is the main idea. However, the sentence "Our Little League team won the division championship last year" does not tell about baseball in different countries. It tells about the writer's Little League team. Now go back and reread the paragraph. This time omit the sentence that does not fit. See how much better the paragraph sounds.

You may have noticed that the first line of a paragraph is indented. It is moved a few spaces to the right. This is the way to signal the beginning of a paragraph. It is the way that is used in this book.

Writing About One Main Idea

The next group of sentences looks like a paragraph. However, it is not really a paragraph at all. See if you can figure out why.

Pigeons are good at living in the city. Some pigeons are brown, some are gray, and some are black. Once my brother caught a pigeon and tried to train it. Carrier pigeons have flown thousands of miles.

This group of sentences does not have one main idea. It has four. One idea is that pigeons are good at living in the city. Another is that pigeons come in different colors. A third is that the writer's brother tried to train a pigeon. A fourth is that carrier pigeons have flown thousands of miles. Each one of these sentences could be the main idea of a separate paragraph.

Look at the following paragraph. The first sentence tells the main idea. All the rest of the sentences tell something about that main idea. The whole paragraph sticks to one idea.

Pigeons are good at living in the city. They can live in just about any sheltered place—under railroad tracks, tucked under the edges of roofs, in gutters, in garages. Loud city noises don't scare pigeons a bit. People don't frighten them, either. In fact, they like living near people because people often feed them.

Notice how each one of the sentences tells about why pigeons are good at living in the city. The sentences all work together to explain that one idea.

Exercises Studying Paragraphs

A. Here are five paragraphs. Tell what each paragraph is about. Then pick out any sentences that do not explain the main idea. Two of the paragraphs do not have any extra sentences.

1

Ice hockey has changed since its early days. Then, the game was played with seven rather than six players. Most of the games were played on outdoor rinks. The rinks did not have sideboards. This meant that players often went flying into the crowd of spectators. Goal judges were not protected either. They didn't wear special padding, and they didn't have goal nets.

2

To make a snack-sized pizza, first toast and lightly butter half an English muffin. Spread a thin layer of spaghetti sauce or canned pizza sauce on the muffin. Add extras such as hamburger, onions, olives, and mushrooms. Food that is good for you can be tasty, too. Lay a slice of mozzarella cheese on top. Broil from three to five minutes or until the cheese is melted.

3

Flapjack has strange habits for a parakeet. For instance, she likes to sleep late in the morning. In fact, she's crabby all day if someone wakes her before ten. Each morning she carefully inspects her cage. Then she settles down for her usual breakfast. It's always one pancake spread with a thin layer of peanut butter. Melvin, our cat, has strange habits, too.

4

We went to the shoe store to buy some sneakers. Anthony chose white ones with blue stripes. Nick chose red ones with white stripes. When I chose blue ones with red stripes, the shoe man said, "We're all sold out." I had to buy plain old white ones.

90

5

The first thing you need to start your own business is some ideas. First, sit down and make a list of your own ideas. Then ask your relatives, neighbors, teachers, and friends for their ideas. Beth Brown's cookie stand became very successful. Don't worry about having too many ideas. Just get as many as possible on your list.

B. Here are six groups of sentences. Four of the groups are paragraphs. All of the sentences work together to explain one main idea. Two of the groups do not stick to one idea. Pick out the four good paragraphs. Be ready to explain why you think they are good paragraphs.

1

Early in 1978 the United States released the names of its first women astronauts. All trips to other planets have so far been made without humans on board. The Space Center at Cape Canaveral has the world's longest runway. A Russian woman took part in one of her country's space missions.

2

The young boy turned over on the thin mattress as the summer sun edged its way over the East River. The sun moved slowly. It spread a soft, gray light down into the canyons between the buildings. It touched the boy's face, and he was awakened. His eyes opened quickly, hurrying sleep away. He lay still a moment, smelling and hearing the morning all around him.

3

When Manolo was nine he became aware of three important facts in his life. First, the older he became, the more he looked like his father. Second, he, Manolo Olivar, was a coward. Third, everyone in the town of Arcangel expected him to grow up to be a famous bullfighter, like his father.

4

Salmon are powerful fish. At spawning time they leave the ocean and swim upstream. Sometimes they swim for 2,000 miles. They battle swift currents and swirling rapids. They leap over waterfalls that are often ten feet high. When they reach their spawning grounds, they have no time to rest. They must dig holes for their eggs.

5

Wearing braces on your teeth has some good points. Three students in Mr. Chen's math class got braces the same week. New metals and ways of putting on braces mean that they work better in a shorter time. People with braces often feel shy about them at first. My Mom says it's better to have braces for a few years than to have crooked teeth your whole life.

6

No other dog had a voice like Sounder's. It came out of the great chest cavity and broad jaws as though it had bounced off the walls of a cave. It mellowed into half-echo before it touched the air. It was louder and clearer than any purebred's voice. Each bark bounced from slope to slope in the foothills like a rubber ball. It was not an ordinary bark. It filled up the night and made music.

Part 2   The Topic Sentence

As you know, a paragraph is a group of sentences. The sentences work together to explain one idea. A paragraph should have one sentence called a **topic sentence**. A topic sentence states the main idea. It tells what the entire paragraph is about.

Usually the topic sentence is the first sentence in a paragraph. It lets the reader know what the rest of the sentences are going to be about.

Seeing How Topic Sentences Work

Let's look at two examples of paragraphs. The first sentence is the topic sentence in each paragraph. In the first example, the topic sentence tells you that winter is staying too long. Notice how each sentence in the rest of the paragraph adds something to that main idea.

Example 1

Winter had come and was overstaying its welcome. January had borrowed the winds of March and was using them overtime. Ice spewed out of the ground. Rags and paper were wrapped around faucets to keep them from freezing. Broken window panes were stuffed with rags. Window cracks were jammed with paper. Beds were weighted down with homemade quilts and old overcoats and clothes. Men and boys wore two pairs of trousers. Girls and old ladies bundled up like babes.—SYLVESTER LEAKS

In the paragraph about winter staying too long, the second sentence tells about the wind. The third sentence tells about the ice. The fourth sentence tells how people used rags and paper to protect faucets. The fifth and sixth sentences describe other ways that people used rags and paper to keep out the cold. The seventh sentence describes the covers that people piled on their beds. The last two sentences tell about the clothes people wore to keep warm. All of these sentences work together to create a vivid picture of winter. They explain the main idea stated in the topic sentence.

Example 2

The next morning was a morning of no caterpillars. The world that had been full to bursting with tiny bundles of black and brown fur trundling on their way to green leaf and trembling grass blade, was suddenly empty. The sound that was no sound, the billion footfalls of the caterpillars stomping through their own universe, died. Tom, who said he could hear that sound, looked and wondered at a town where not a single bird's mouthful stirred.

—RAY BRADBURY

The topic sentence, "The next morning was a morning of no caterpillars," begins the paragraph. The next three sentences tell more about that morning. Each sentence adds something to the main idea.

Sticking to the Idea in the Topic Sentence

94

Here is another paragraph. It starts out with this topic sentence:

The removal of the Cherokees from Georgia during the winter of 1838–39 is called the Trail of Tears.

This sentence leads you to think that the whole paragraph is about the Trail of Tears. Read the other sentences in the paragraph to see if this is true.

> The removal of the Cherokees from Georgia during the winter of 1838–39 is known as the Trail of Tears. That winter U. S. troops forced seventeen thousand men, women, and children to march through snow and bitter cold. Most were barefoot. All were hungry. One famous Cherokee named Sequoya invented a system for writing the Cherokee language. The California redwood trees are called sequoias in honor of this leader. Almost a fourth of the Cherokee people died on the Trail of Tears.

In this paragraph the second sentence does add to the main idea. It says that seventeen thousand Cherokees were forced to march through snow and cold. The third and fourth sentences add more information. The fifth sentence, however, has nothing to do with the Trail of Tears. It introduces a Cherokee leader named Sequoya. The next sentence is not about the Trail of Tears either. It also tells something about Sequoya. These two sentences do not work with the others to explain the main idea. The last sentence in the paragraph returns to the main idea. It tells how many Cherokee people died on the Trail of Tears.

Exercise Studying Paragraphs

Here are three topic sentences. Each contains a main idea. Choose one of the topic sentences. Then list three or four more sentences that tell about that main idea. Make sure that all your sentences explain the main idea in the topic sentence.

1. Entertaining a four-year-old isn't as hard as you might think.
2. The paper bag is one of the most useful things ever invented.
3. Certain smells set autumn apart from the other seasons.

Part 3   Writing Good Topic Sentences

You now know what a topic sentence is. You also know that topic sentences help both writers and readers. The next thing to learn, then, is how to write good topic sentences.

Telling What the Paragraph Is About

A good topic sentence tells what the entire paragraph is about. Look at these five sentences. Try to pick out the topic sentence.

1. She applied it to everything from making soup to planting her garden.

2. Sometimes she'd say it barely loud enough to hear, and I'd stop and think about what I was doing.

3. Other times she'd write it on a piece of paper and put the paper where I'd be sure to find it.

4. "An ounce of prevention is worth a pound of cure" was my great-grandmother's favorite saying.

5. I used to tease her about her "all-purpose" advice, but I never questioned the wisdom of that advice.

Sentence 4, of course, is the one sentence that tells what all the rest of the sentences are about. Read that sentence first; then read sentences 1, 2, 3, and 5. Each of these sentences tells about the main idea.

Here is another group of sentences. This time the topic sentence is missing. Read the sentences and decide what all of them are about.

1. _____ (topic sentence) _____

2. Three popular ways are in a dish, on a cone, or frozen on a stick.

3. Another is on a piece of cake or on a brownie.

4. A scoop of ice cream might be placed on a piece of pie.

All three sentences describe ways to serve ice cream. This main idea must be stated in the topic sentence. Here are two possible topic sentences for this paragraph:

> There are many ways to serve ice cream.
> Ice cream can be served in many ways.

When you are writing a topic sentence, try to think of it as an umbrella. It is the one sentence that covers, or takes in, all the other sentences in a paragraph.

Making Topic Sentences Interesting

A topic sentence should do more than just tell what a paragraph is about. It should make the reader want to read the rest of the paragraph. In other words, a topic sentence must *catch the reader's attention.*

Here are three pairs of topic sentences. Notice how the second sentence in each pair does a better job of making you want to read further.

1. I'm going to write about Samantha, who was good at solving mysteries.
   Samantha was a super sleuth.

2. We heard the sound of a werewolf.
   Part wolf, part man, the werewolf howled at the full moon.

3. Newspapers sometimes have interesting articles.
   This morning's *News* printed a fascinating article on active volcanoes.

The following paragraph needs a topic sentence. Below the paragraph are two sentences to choose from. Each one tells what the paragraph will be about. Read the paragraph, using the first sentence. Then read the paragraph again, using the second sentence. Which topic sentence is more interesting? Can you explain why?

_____(topic sentence)_____. Smooth, thick shakes are not really shaken. They are machine-mixed. At the soda fountain, the mixer looks like a long rod with a small ruffled disk on the end. At home, the small blades of the blender do the best job. They blend the shake and make it fluffy. The big blades of an egg beater can't make a good shake. —CAROLYN VOSBURG HALL

1. The secret of great shakes can now be revealed.

2. Here is how to make a good milk shake.

Narrowing the Topic

A topic sentence should state a main idea that can be covered adequately in one paragraph. Consider, for example, this topic sentence:

Cereal makers have a responsibility to children.

You might wonder how the writer could possibly cover this idea in a few sentences. He or she would have to write about using less sugar in cereals, the safety of toys packed in cereal boxes, telling the truth in advertisements, and giving money to projects that help children. All these ideas would have to be covered in one paragraph!

The idea in the topic sentence, then, needs to be narrowed. Just one of those ideas would make a good paragraph. For example:

Manufacturers should add less sugar to breakfast cereals.

The paragraph could then go on to explain why this would be a good thing to do.

Here is another topic sentence that needs to be narrowed:

As a boy, Arthur Mitchell enjoyed many good times with his family.

98 All of these good times could not possibly be described in one paragraph. Notice how the writer of the following paragraph has narrowed the basic idea of good times. She tells only about the family's Sunday mornings.

The best times in the Mitchell household were Sunday mornings. Arthur's father got up early and cooked. He made crisp fried chicken or juicy pork chops and cornmeal pancakes. Delicious smells filled the crowded apartment. Everyone sat around the kitchen table, talking and laughing together. Those were the times Arthur could really feel the love in his family. —TOBI TOBIAS

Points To Remember

As you write topic sentences, keep the following important points in mind:

1. A topic sentence should tell what the paragraph is about.

2. A topic sentence should be interesting enough to catch the reader's attention.

3. A topic sentence should present an idea that is narrow enough to be covered in one paragraph.

Exercises **Working with Topic Sentences**

A. Here are eight topic sentences. Five of them make you want to read the rest of the paragraph. The other three do not. Decide which sentences are interesting and which are not. Then rewrite the dull sentences to make them more interesting.

1. Half-crazed with hunger, the only survivor made his way through the dense jungle.
2. Merle stared out the window at the rain-swept street.
3. I'm going to tell you about my best friend.
4. *Incredible* is the only word to describe Kareem Abdul-Jabbar.
5. I have a pet dog that I'm going to tell you about.
6. The sudden silence was frightening.
7. This paragraph is about camping.
8. Down, down into the black depths the diver descended.

99

B. Here are eight more topic sentences. The main idea in some of them can be covered in one paragraph. The ideas in the rest are too broad. Find the sentences that are narrow enough. Rewrite those that are too broad so that they, too, can be covered in one paragraph.

1. The United States produces more food than it can use.

2. The tree-lined Paseo de la Reforma cuts through the heart of Mexico City.

3. The usefulness of computers is almost unlimited.

4. Sixth graders should take part in after-school activities.

5. The twelve-month school year has good points and bad points.

6. Many immigrants to the United States have become successful.

7. Pablo described the hunting trip to his cousin.

8. A deck of cards is made up of four suits.

C. Here are three groups of sentences. Make them into paragraphs by writing a topic sentence for each group. Be sure that each topic sentence tells what all the rest of the sentences in the group are about.

1. _____(topic sentence)_____. The food of Mexico has become popular in all parts of our country. Many Mexican words have become part of the English language. Mexican music has influenced American music. Mexican designs have been used in American houses, especially in the Southwest.

2. _____(topic sentence)_____. His coat and mane were soft gold. He stood, straight and proud, looking over the grasslands. He gave a long, powerful roar. He was the master of his kingdom.

3. _____(topic sentence)_____. Long ago the people of East Africa used jewelry as weapons. The Aztecs of Mexico used it to show a person's place in society. Certain jewelry has been worn for its magical powers. Other jewelry has been worn to remember people. For example, in the 1800's the British wore bracelets made of the braided hair of dead relatives.

Reinforcement Exercises—Review

Studying Good Paragraphs

Use these two paragraphs to answer the questions below.

1. Pueblo boys learned many things from their fathers. They learned to grow corn, squash, and beans. The Pueblos lived on the desert lands of the West and Southwest. The boys learned to weave beautiful designs into cloth and to paint designs on pottery. They learned to weave baskets for harvesting corn.

2. One howl shows that a wolf wants to "talk". Another is a warning that danger is near. A much wilder, more primitive howl signals the beginning of a hunt. A wolf howls sadly when a loved one dies or is injured.

A. Studying Paragraphs

1. What is the main idea of paragraph 1? of paragraph 2?
2. One of the paragraphs has a sentence that does not explain the main idea. Which paragraph has this sentence? Which sentence is it? Why doesn't it work with the others?

B. Studying Paragraphs

1. One of the paragraphs does not have a topic sentence. Which paragraph is it?
2. What is the topic sentence of the other paragraph? List the ideas that explain the main idea.

101

C. Working with Topic Sentences

Write a topic sentence for the paragraph that does not have one.

Chapter 7

Ways of Developing a Paragraph

You know that a good paragraph must have a topic sentence that presents the main idea. A topic sentence, though, is just a beginning. A good paragraph must also have sentences that explain the main idea. Adding "explaining" sentences to the topic sentence is called **developing the paragraph**.

There are many ways to develop a paragraph. One way is to add sentences with many details. Another is to give one example. Still another is to give several examples of what you are talking about. In this chapter you will learn three ways to develop a paragraph:

1. By using details

2. By using an example

3. By using several examples

Part 1 Using Details

Details are the little things that make a person, place, or thing what it is. The excited shouts of boys playing basketball, the swishing sound of the ball as it flies through the net, the untiring energy of the boys as they play are all details.

Creating a Clear Picture

In a piece of writing, details are specific bits of information. They create a clear picture for the reader. For instance, the sentence "The cat walked down the street" doesn't create much of a picture in your mind. However, if the writer adds specific details about what the cat looks like, about how it walks, and about the place where it is walking, the picture comes alive.

The lame tomcat dragged haltingly down the rain-swept sidewalk.

With these details, the writer has even made you feel sorry for this sad-looking cat.

The writer might have used different details. Then your mental picture would have been different, too. Look at the following sentences:

1. The beautiful Angora strutted proudly down the middle of the empty street.

2. The perky white kitten rolled gaily on the green lawn.

3. The wary Siamese crept quietly under the hedge.

These sentences all describe the same thing—a cat. However, each contains a completely different set of details. Therefore, your mental picture is entirely different in each description.

Adding Details

Some paragraphs are developed by using details. The topic sentence tells what the paragraph is about. The rest of the sentences add details. Little by little, a complete picture is created. The writer of the following paragraph uses many details. Notice how they help you to get a clear mental picture of the man.

He was rather fat but in a round, hard, not unpleasant way. His head was completely round. His teeth were very white under the trim mustache. His skin was darkish, and the features of his face formed a pleasant, round, cheerful image. He wore, naturally, a delivery boy's coat. Underneath he wore nice-looking gray flannel pants. His brown shoes were shined within an inch of their lives.

—LOUISE FITZHUGH

The writer includes all these details:
1. That the man has a round head
2. That he has very white teeth and a trim mustache
3. That he has darkish skin and a pleasant, round face
4. That he is wearing a delivery boy's coat, gray flannel pants, and highly shined brown shoes

The writer has arranged these details so that she describes the man from head to toe.

Developing a Paragraph by Using Details

If you are going to develop a paragraph by using many details, it is a good idea to begin by getting a picture in your own mind. Think about what you are going to write about. Examine every part of your mental picture. Then make a list of details that you want to include in your paragraph. These pre-writing steps give you a good start.

Let's take a look at how one writer followed these steps. The assignment was to describe a painting. The writer chose to describe one called *Kid Stuff*. It showed a pile of old, worn tennis shoes. First, she studied the painting carefully. Later, she pictured it in her mind. She then made the following list of details:

20 worn-out tennis shoes in a pile
faded red
faded blue
gray-white
holes in soles
split seams
tattered edges
broken and knotted laces
frayed linings
grass green background
background paint that looks like blades of grass

She arranged the details. Then she wrote this paragraph.

The painting called *Kid Stuff* uses tennis shoes to show the active life led by children. In the middle of the large, square painting is a pile of twenty worn-out tennis shoes. Some are faded red. Some are faded blue. The rest are a dirty-looking white. The shoes are piled every which way. You can see holes in soles, tattered edges, split seams, broken and knotted laces, and frayed linings. The area around the pile of shoes is grass green. The paint is put on so that, close up, it looks like blades of grass.

First, in her topic sentence, the writer explains the main idea of the painting. She next gives the overall shape of the painting. She then describes the tennis shoes in detail. Finally, she talks about the background. She has arranged her details in the order in which she "sees" the painting in her mind.

Using All of the Senses

So far, all the examples have used details about what things *look* like. Suppose, though, that you were asked to describe something like eating popcorn. It wouldn't be enough to include only details about what popcorn looks like. You'd have to include details about how it smells, sounds, feels, and tastes. That's the only way a reader would get a clear idea of what eating popcorn is like. Here is a list of questions and answers about all the senses. These questions can guide a writer in arranging details. Below, the details are about popcorn.

How does it look?	white, puffy, slightly yellow from butter, exploding from a shiny brown shell
How does it smell?	a little like corn, warm oil, butter
How does it feel?	light, warm
How does it sound?	crunches as it's bitten
How does it taste?	a little like corn, salty, buttery, becomes soft as it's chewed

Here is the paragraph that was written, using these details.

Eating popcorn is one of life's greatest pleasures. When I look at a bowl heaped with those white, exploded puffs of corn, my mouth begins to water. As I breathe in the warm, buttery smell, my hand is drawn to the bowl. I pick up a handful of the warm, light corn and ease it into my mouth. I make the first crunch, then another. As the heavenly corn, butter, and salt flavors blend, the popcorn softens. I sigh with happiness. Would you be surprised if I told you I never can stop at one handful, or two, or three?

Pre-Writing Steps for Paragraphs Using Details

1. Get a clear picture in your mind of what you want to describe.

2. Examine your mental picture. You can do this in any order, such as from top to bottom or from left to right. Ask yourself: How does it look? How does it sound? How does it feel? How does it smell? How does it taste?

3. Make a list of details.

4. Arrange the details. As you plan the paragraph, keep in mind that you want the readers to see in their minds the same picture that you see in yours.

Exercise   Writing a Paragraph Using Details

Here is a list of ideas for paragraphs. Choose an idea that interests you or use one of your own. Write a topic sentence that tells what the paragraph is about. Try to make it interesting, and narrow enough to be covered in one paragraph. Then develop a paragraph using details. Follow the Pre-Writing Steps for Paragraphs Using Details above and the Guidelines for the Process of Writing on pages 84 and 85.

1. The setting for a science fiction movie
2. The animal you'd least like for a pet
3. An unusual Halloween costume
4. Your best friend
5. Your favorite food
6. The most unusual place you've ever been
7. Your special hideaway
8. A cartoon character
9. A box full of something valuable
10. Your bike

Part 2 Using an Example

Some paragraphs can be developed by using an example. The topic sentence again presents the main idea. The rest of the paragraph explains the main idea by using an example.

Explaining the Main Idea

Let's say you're going to write a paragraph about Pecos Bill, the cowboy folk hero. You might begin with this topic sentence:

Pecos Bill was totally fearless.

You might then describe an incident that shows his fearlessness. You would be giving an example of the idea in the topic sentence.

Sticking to One Example

One writer begins with this topic sentence:

Even as a young girl, Maria Mitchell was a skilled astronomer.

She then developed the following paragraph about this famous nineteenth-century astronomer.

Even as a young girl, Maria Mitchell was a skilled astronomer. One night a ship's captain arrived at the Mitchells' house. He wanted Maria's father to set his chronometer. This was a special clock used to tell time by the stars. Maria's father was away, and the captain needed the clock right away. Fourteen-year-old Maria offered to set it for him. The captain agreed to give her a chance. Maria worked long into the night. She measured the positions of the stars. She figured distances. By dawn she had fixed the chronometer. The amazed captain paid her the same fee he would have paid her father. He praised her for the fine work she had done.

This paragraph sticks to one example. The example illustrates the main idea in the topic sentence.

Exercise Writing a Paragraph Using an Example

Here are five topic sentences. Choose one that interests you or one of your own. Then write a paragraph that uses one example to illustrate the main idea. You can use a personal experience or your imagination. Follow the guidelines on pages 84 and 85.

1. My younger brother (or sister) deserves to be called a menace.
2. My attempts at cooking have often been a disaster.
3. Some days it just doesn't pay to get out of bed.
4. Important lessons don't always come from books.
5. Some "firsts" are more memorable than others.

Part 3 Using Several Examples

You have learned that a paragraph can be developed by using one example to explain the main idea. Another type of paragraph can be developed by using several examples to explain the main idea. Here is a topic sentence:

> Jeannette Henry, a Cherokee, and her husband, a California Cahuilla, have worked tirelessly to gain rights for Native Americans.

You could develop this idea into a paragraph. You would probably want to include several examples of how this couple has helped Native Americans. These examples would illustrate the main idea that the Henrys have worked hard to assure the rights of Native Americans.

110   The following topic sentence could also be developed by using several examples.

> Several outstanding leaders of Mexican and Spanish descent have served in the Congress of the United States.

You'd probably complete the paragraph by telling of the contributions of these leaders. You'd be giving examples to illustrate the main idea.

Developing a Paragraph by Using Several Examples

The following paragraph begins with the topic sentence, "The happiest and noisiest Jewish holiday is Purim." The rest of the paragraph gives several examples of what makes the holiday happy and noisy.

> The happiest and noisiest Jewish holiday is Purim. There are parties and plays, Purim songs and costume parades, and lots of *hamantashen*—delicious little triangular cakes. Sometimes gifts are given to friends. That is called *schlach manot*. Sometimes money is given to people in need. The old story of Queen Esther and wicked Haman is read aloud in the synagogue. Esther is the heroine of the Purim story. She protected her people, the Jews, when Haman was trying to hurt them. When the name *Haman* is read in the synagogue, children stamp their feet. They whirl or bang their noisemakers, called *graggers*, so no one can hear his name. The children dress up like characters in this story, and prizes are given for the best costumes. At Purim parties there are always *hamantashen*, so called because they are shaped like Haman's hat.
>
> —WENDY LAZAR

The paragraph gives several examples of why Purim is a happy, noisy Jewish holiday. It explains that the story of Queen Esther and Haman is read. It describes how the children stamp their feet and bang or twirl noisemakers during the reading. It tells about the plays and costumes and prizes. It describes the special food called *hamantashen*. All of these examples explain the main idea in the topic sentence.

Using Examples in a Firsthand Experience

Often a paragraph written from firsthand experience will include many short examples. Look at the following paragraph.

> Martha Mae was the best at just about everything. She could send a ball farther than anyone on her team. She could weave a skateboard down a busy sidewalk and make it look easy. She could swim better and faster than anyone in the neighborhood. She could also make perfect dives off the high board. She could blow the biggest bubbles, draw the straightest lines, and sew on the tightest buttons. She won every card game, board game, and word game she played. To us, Martha Mae seemed unbeatable.

The writer has given many short examples of what Martha Mae did. These examples illustrate the main idea that Martha Mae was the best at just about everything.

Exercise   **Writing a Paragraph Using Several Examples**

Here are ten topic sentences. Choose one or write one of your own. Then write a paragraph that uses several examples. You can use your own personal experience or your imagination. Follow the Guidelines for the Process of Writing on pages 84 and 85.

1. Who says people aren't superstitious?
2. As winter changes to spring, lots of other things begin to change, too.
3. _____(name)_____ is the bravest person I have ever met.
4. A carnival has something for everyone.
5. I am an incurable people-watcher.
6. I have a most unusual group of relatives.
7. Living in a city has many advantages.
8. Some people's names don't fit them at all.
9. My favorite places are all small.
10. It seems that most of the good TV programs are quickly taken off the air.

Reinforcement Exercises—Review

Ways of Developing a Paragraph

A. Writing a Paragraph Using Details

Make a list of the things summer means to this writer. After each detail, tell the sense or senses that it appeals to.

Summer is many things. Summer is birds singing. Summer is bare feet and daisies and dandelions and roses full on their stems. Summer is swimming at the beach and the sun hot and the sand hot from the sun. Summer is porches and cold lemonade and dogs sleeping in the shade. Summer is whirring lawn mowers on still afternoons and ice cream cones and watermelon. Summer is long nights and the stars low in the sky. —CHARLOTTE ZOLOTOW

B. Writing a Paragraph Using an Example

Choose one of the following topic sentences. Develop a paragraph using an example from your own experience. Follow the Guidelines for the Process of Writing listed on pages 84 and 85.

1. My best friend and I argue sometimes. One time...
2. I've always admired _____. One day . . . .
3. I enjoy playing _____. During one game . . . .
4. I remember most of my birthdays. My favorite . . . .

C. Writing a Paragraph Using Several Examples

For each topic sentence, explain whether you would develop the paragraph by using details, an example, or several examples.

1. I was alone in a dark, silent cave.
2. Alexander is the perfect pet.
3. A city is no place for a Great Dane.
4. Watch out for the poison ivy plant.

113

Chapter 8

Different Kinds of Paragraphs

Most paragraphs have certain things in common. For one thing, they're made up of sentences. These sentences work together to explain the main idea in the topic sentence.

Sharing things in common, though, does not mean that all paragraphs are alike. In this chapter you will learn about different kinds of paragraphs. You will study paragraphs that tell about things that happened. They are called **narrative paragraphs**. You will study paragraphs that paint pictures in your mind. They are called **descriptive paragraphs**. You will also study paragraphs that explain how to do something, and paragraphs that explain why a writer holds a certain opinion. They are called **explanatory paragraphs**.

Part 1 The Narrative Paragraph

If you read a paragraph that begins with "Once upon a time . . ." or "Something unexpected happened the day we went windskating," you expect the rest of the paragraph to tell you what happened. This kind of paragraph is called a narrative paragraph. In a narrative paragraph all the sentences work together. They tell about something that happened either to the writer or to someone else.

Telling Things in Order

The following is an example of a narrative paragraph. The writer is telling about something that happened to someone else. She describes what happened in the order that it happened.

> Tyrone took the flashlight and ran toward the darkest part of the alley. It opened into another, wider alley that was really a small street of vacant houses. On his way he stumbled over something round and hard. The flashlight dropped out of his hand and went out as he fell. He could tell his knees were skinned and probably bleeding, but he did not cry out from the pain. He lay there and felt around in the dark till he found the flashlight. It was lying near the piece of broken pipe that had tripped him. Fortunately it still worked. —KRISTIN HUNTER

You can make a list of what happened in this paragraph. Your list might look something like this:

1. Tyrone took the flashlight.
2. He ran toward the darkest part of the alley.
3. He stumbled and fell.
4. The flashlight dropped out of his hand and went out.
5. Tyrone felt around in the dark and found the flashlight.

These events form a **time sequence**. They tell what happened in the order that it happened. Time sequence is the way most narrative paragraphs are organized.

Describing Personal Experiences

The next paragraph is also a narrative paragraph. It, too, is organized in time sequence. The topic sentence tells you that the paragraph is about the writer's first experience with book knowledge. The word *I* lets you know that it is going to be about something that happened to the writer personally.

> The first thing I ever learned in the way of book knowledge was while working in a salt-furnace. Each salt-packer had his barrels marked with a certain number. The number given to my stepfather was *18*. At the close of the day's work the boss of the packers would come around and put *18* on each of our barrels. I soon learned to recognize that figure wherever I saw it. After a while I got to the point where I could make that figure. I knew nothing about any other figures or letters, though. —BOOKER T. WASHINGTON

Here is another narrative paragraph. The topic sentence, "We decided to write our own television show," begins the paragraph. The word *we* lets you know right away that the writer of the paragraph was personally involved. The rest of the paragraph tells what happened in the order that it happened.

> We decided to write our own television show. We called it "Dr. Sickbee at Your Service." It was the story of an orthodontist who moonlights in a rock band. He lives next door to a weird family and has a younger sister who ran away to join the roller derby. In his spare time he solves mysteries. We put the show on videotape and wrote some commercials to use with it. Some of the other English teachers let their classes see it.—PAULA DANZIGER

Using Details

Here is another narrative paragraph. It is a good example of a paragraph with many details.

I remembered how much I used to like being alone. At times, instead of going home from school, I used to go into the bush to listen to pretty little birds quarrel in their harsh voices. One day I walked around the village. Then I climbed the highest hill. I lay looking down at people moving beneath me like so many insects. Soon I forgot time as I let my gaze play around the green of the trees, the bright reds of fruits, the pale blues and pinks of flowers. Then I watched as the wind wove everything into different patterns from one minute to the next. —ROSA GUY

The details are so vivid that you can almost hear the sounds of the birds. You can practically see the people moving around like insects, the green trees, the bright red fruits, the blue and pink flowers, and the changing patterns caused by the wind. These details help you, the reader, share the writer's experience.

Exercise   Writing Narrative Paragraphs

Following is a list of topic sentences. Choose one or write one of your own. Then write a narrative paragraph. Remember to organize your paragraph in a time sequence. Use as many details as possible. You can either write from your own experience or create an imaginary experience. Follow the Guidelines for the Process of Writing on pages 84 and 85.

1. I'll never forget the night my sister had her first date.
2. We took the wrong turn to the park.
3. One night the electricity went off in our apartment.
4. A group of us set out to decorate a wall.
5. _____ was just about the happiest day of my life.
6. The day I changed my mind about _____ is a day to remember.
7. One day I received a surprise package in the mail.
8. My first day of school was a nightmare.
9. We had a funny experience on our class trip.
10. My cat would not come down from the tree.

Part 2   The Descriptive Paragraph

You know that narrative paragraphs tell what happened. Descriptive paragraphs, however, have very little action. That's because the purpose of a descriptive paragraph is to paint a picture with words.

A descriptive paragraph appeals to one or more of the senses. It is written so that a reader sees what the writer sees, smells what the writer smells, hears what the writer hears, tastes what the writer tastes, or feels what the writer feels. In this chapter you will study only one type of descriptive paragraph. It is the type that appeals to the sense of sight.

Using Details

The writer of a descriptive paragraph must include many details. You have learned that details are the specific bits of information that create a clear picture for the readers. Without specific details, whatever the writer is describing never seems to come alive for the reader.

Let's take a look at a paragraph with many details. The topic sentence tells you that the paragraph is going to describe an ocean scene. The rest of the sentences contain many details. They work together to help you see the scene the way the writer sees it.

Example 1

The heaving ocean sprawled under the vast blue sky. Both sea and sky were shimmering with light. It seemed as if the sky poured it into the sea and the sea poured it back into the sky again so rapidly that they were both continually awash with light and never for a moment cold. The sun was tossed from sea to sky like a golden ball. The gulls ranged restlessly backward and forward, up and down, round and round. They searched endlessly, never finding, lighting a moment on the gleaming water, but never at peace.

—ROBERT AYRE

119

The writer of the paragraph includes many details that appeal to the sense of sight. He uses phrases like "heaving ocean," "vast blue sky," "shimmering with light," "awash with light," "golden ball," "ranged restlessly backward and forward," and "gleaming water." These specific details help to paint a vivid picture of the scene.

The next descriptive paragraph also includes many sight details. It paints a picture of a street scene. Pick out the specific details that help you see the street as the writer sees it.

Example 2

James stood for a while in front of his building. He looked at the street and the cars and the people walking or running or hobbling or moving like bits of paper in a high wind. He looked at the trash basket, a new silver one. It was sitting in the middle of the trash that was spread out all around it. He looked at two policemen walking down the middle of the street between the cars. He looked at a man with one arm. He was hurrying along the curb talking to himself and waving the stump of the other arm that was hidden in his sleeve. It looked like a puppet in the puppet show James had seen at a school assembly. What was the arm saying?

—PAULA FOX

Logical Order

In the lesson on using details in Chapter 7 you learned how to arrange them into logical order. You learned four pre-writing steps involved for developing a paragraph with many details:

1. Get a clear picture in your mind of what you want to describe.

2. Examine your mental picture.

3. Make a list of details.

4. Arrange the details. As you plan the paragraph, keep in mind what you want your readers to see.

120

Top-to-Bottom Order

When you do pre-writing step 4, it is important to follow some order. For instance, if you are describing a person, the natural place to begin would be the person's overall size and shape. That's what you would probably notice first about someone. You would then examine the person's head and face and move downward, looking at arms, hands, and clothing. The following paragraph is arranged in top-to-bottom order. The writer describes a newly hatched creature from head to tail.

I thought at first that it was a rat or something that had broken the egg and eaten it. After I got a good look, though, I could see that it wasn't any rat. It was about the size of a squirrel. It didn't have any hair, and its head—well, I couldn't believe my eyes when I saw it. It didn't look like anything I'd ever seen before. It had three little knobs sticking out of its head and sort of a collar up over its neck. It was a lizardy-looking critter. It kept moving its thick tail slowly back and forth in the nest. The poor hen was looking pretty upset. I guess she hadn't expected anything like this. Neither had I. —OLIVER BUTTERWORTH

Bottom-to-Top Order

Some paragraphs are organized so that a thing is described from bottom to top. The following paragraph is like that. It describes a skyscraper from bottom to top. This is the way you would most likely examine a tall building.

The skyscraper was set in a cluster of buildings. Brightly painted benches, and trees and flowers in redwood pots surrounded the building at ground level. The display windows of elegant shops circled the first and second levels. The rest of the building was covered with huge, vertical slabs of gray stone. Between the slabs were long, narrow windows of tinted gray glass. Three antennas rose into the sky from the flat roof.

Moving from One Object to Another

This next descriptive paragraph is organized in yet another way. It moves from one main object to another in a room. This is a logical order. It is the way a person would probably examine a room.

In the kitchen was an old-fashioned black stove, with six round iron lids and a chimney pipe going up to and through the ceiling. The sink was tin, now blackened with age, and there was a ridged wooden drainboard. Through a big hole in the rotting floor you could see to the cellar below. Things were piled high down there. There were wooden boxes with old, musty, mildewed dresses and hats spilling out. There were funny trunks with strips of tin and brass on top and leather handles on the sides. —MARY CHASE

The writer of the paragraph has first described the stove and then the sink. She next describes the hole in the floor and the cellar under it. She has picked out these objects as the most important parts of the kitchen.

As you can see from the examples, a good way to arrange the details in a descriptive paragraph is according to the way you would notice things. This is called a **natural order**. It is one of the most common, and easiest ways to organize a descriptive paragraph.

Exercises Writing Descriptive Paragraphs

A. Below is a list of topics. Write down some of the details you would include in a descriptive paragraph for each. Then decide on the way you would arrange the details. They could be in top-to-bottom order, in bottom-to-top order, or in an order moving from one object to another.

1. A person you like
2. Someone you have seen on TV
3. A basement recreation room
4. An unusual plant or flower
5. A tree

B. Here are eight topic sentences. Choose one or write one of your own. Then write a descriptive paragraph. Follow the four pre-writing steps for developing a paragraph with many details and the Guidelines for the Process of Writing on pages 84 and 85. Be sure that all of your sentences work together to explain the main idea in the topic sentence.

1. Lake _____ is one of the most beautiful places I've ever seen.
2. The decorating committee had changed the gym into an alien environment.
3. Tangled hedges enclosed a tiny, secret garden.
4. My new brother is a beautiful little baby.
5. Traug was an ugly creature.
6. On the table was every kind of food imaginable.
7. _____ is a landmark in our town.
8. The room was a mess.

Part 3 The Explanatory Paragraph

The explanatory paragraph is one of the most useful paragraphs you will learn to write. You will most likely write more of them in your life than any other kind. The word *explanatory* means "to explain." That's exactly what these paragraphs do. They explain **how** or **why**.

The "How" Paragraph

The "how" paragraph explains how to do something. It is the most common type of explanatory paragraph. In fact, you've probably read hundreds of explanatory paragraphs. Every time you read directions for a card game, or for putting together a model, or for feeding a hamster, or for operating a radio, or for planting seeds, you are reading explanatory paragraphs.

Time Sequence

All "how" paragraphs have one important thing in common. They explain something in a step-by-step way. The steps are organized in a time sequence. They explain what should be done first, what should be done next, and so on. The language and organization of a good explanatory paragraph are so clear that a person reading the paragraph knows exactly what to do and when to do it.

Let's take a look at a paragraph that explains how to use an apple to print a T-shirt.

> You can create your own T-shirt design by using a plain T-shirt, a piece of cloth, an apple, a stiff paintbrush, and textile paints in any colors of your choice. Begin by slicing an apple in half lengthwise. Brush a thick layer of textile paint over the cut side of one of the apple halves. Press the apple, paint side down, on a piece of cloth. Keep practicing until you have it just right. Then print your T-shirt.

A person following these directions would be able to start out with a plain T-shirt and end up with a T-shirt printed with an unusual design. That's because the directions are clear. They are organized so that a reader can follow them step by step.

Organizing Ideas

The readers of the next paragraph will be confused. The writer is trying to explain how to do a simple trick with a pencil. Each sentence uses clear language. However, the sentences are so mixed up that the trick is just about impossible to do.

> This trick is called the rubber pencil trick. Move your hand up and down. Hold the pencil lightly between the thumb and forefinger of your right hand. To do it, all you need is one full-length sharpened pencil. The pencil will look as though it's bending, or made of rubber. The pencil should be parallel to your fingers. You should hold the pencil about a third of the way down from the eraser end.

In the next paragraph, see what a difference it makes when the sentences are organized in the right time sequence.

> This trick is called the rubber pencil trick. To do it, all you need is one full-length sharpened pencil. Hold the pencil lightly between the thumb and forefinger of your right hand. Hold it about a third of the way down from the eraser end. The pencil should be parallel to your fingers. Now move your hand up and down. The pencil will look as though it's bending, or made of rubber.

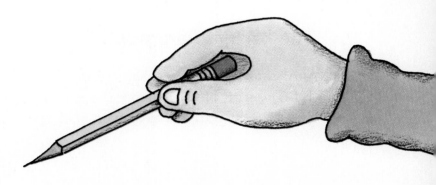

Exercise   Writing a "How" Paragraph

Following are some topics for "how" paragraphs. Choose one of them. Narrow the topic so that it can be covered in one paragraph. List your directions for the activity. Arrange them in the right time sequence. Then write an interesting topic sentence and the rest of your paragraph.

After you have completed the paragraph, ask a friend to try out your directions. Your friend's suggestions will help you when you revise your directions to make them clearer. Last, proofread your paragraph and make a final copy.

1. How to prepare a super special cat dinner
2. How to dress for subzero weather
3. How to get from _____ to _____
4. How to plan a party
5. How to play _____
6. How to grow _____
7. How to cook _____
8. How to make a mobile
9. How to make a puppet
10. How to turn a cardboard box into a _____
11. How to teach a dog to sit up
12. How to win at _____
13. How to make perfect _____
14. How to save energy right at home
15. How to train for _____
16. How to pass a test

The "Why" Paragraph

A second type of explanatory paragraph is the "why" paragraph. It begins with a topic sentence that gives an opinion. The rest of the sentences give reasons to support that opinion.

Giving Reasons

A "why" paragraph might begin with a topic sentence like this:

> Every neighborhood needs a special place that's off-limits to adults.

This is an opinion. The rest of the paragraph would then give reasons to support that opinion. The reasons might include the following:

1. A special place would give kids a chance to take care of something on their own.

2. In a special place, kids could work or play or read without interruption.

3. A place like that would give kids a chance to plan surprises for adults.

The next paragraph is an explanatory paragraph that begins with the topic sentence, "Rocks make great pets." The rest of the paragraph explains why the writer believes that.

> Rocks make great pets. First of all, rocks are just about the cheapest pets to own. They don't need special food, clothes, beds, toys, or shots. Rocks are also clean and well behaved. They never leave half-eaten dog biscuits, scattered seeds, or old bones around. They wouldn't think of climbing on a bed, chewing a slipper, or running into the house with muddy paws. Rocks are independent, too. Their owners can leave them for days at a time and never have to worry about feeding or exercising them. Most important, though, is that rocks are always there when their owners need them. That's because they never get sick, run away, or get into bad moods. Rocks may be a little hard, but they're completely faithful.

Order of Importance

The writer of the paragraph on rocks has given four main reasons for believing that rocks are great pets:

1. Rocks are cheap.
2. Rocks are clean and well behaved.
3. Rocks are independent.
4. Rocks are there when their owners need them.

The writer has not organized these reasons in a time sequence. She has arranged them in their order of importance. The fact that rocks are cheap is the least important reason. The fact that rocks are there when you need them is the most important reason. The usual arrangement of a "why" paragraph is from the least important reason to the most important reason.

Exercise   Writing a " Why" Paragraph

The following topic sentences give opinions. Choose one of these sentences. Revise it to make it as interesting as possible. Then develop the topic into a "why" paragraph. Be sure to arrange your reasons in an order from least important to most important. Follow the Guidelines for the Process of Writing on pages 84 and 85.

1. _____ is the best friend a person could have.
2. Big cities are the best/worst places to live.
3. Rainy days are the worst kind.
4. _____ is my favorite food.
5. It would save time if we could just take a pill every day and never have to eat.
6. Everyone should know how to swim.
7. No child should grow up without a pet.
8. _____ is the best movie I've ever seen.
9. It's important for families to have traditions.
10. Taking part in class discussions is helpful for students.

Reinforcement Exercises—Review

Different Kinds of Paragraphs

A. Writing Narrative Paragraphs

Rewrite the following paragraph so that it is in a time sequence.

The present was a book all right, but it wasn't about secret codes. The birthday present from Uncle Charlie was inside a small, flat box. I eagerly ripped off the paper expecting to find a magic trick or a book about secret codes or a Superman T-shirt. I thanked Uncle Charlie weakly and put it aside. It was called *Me* and it contained nothing but blank pages. I didn't know that that book would become my favorite present of all time.

B. Writing Descriptive Paragraphs

Complete this paragraph by describing the dummy. Arrange the details in top-to-bottom order. Follow the Guidelines for the Process of Writing listed on pages 84 and 85.

The dummy sat stiff and straight on the ventriloquist's knee.

C. Writing an Explanatory Paragraph

Reorganize these sentences so that they are in a time sequence.

Here are five easy steps to great photographs. Then examine the subject through your camera's viewfinder. Put yourself at least four feet away from the subject. Finally, press your shutter button, while holding the camera steady. First you must choose an interesting subject. Next aim your camera carefully.

129

Chapter 9

Improving Study Skills

Study skills can help you in every subject area. They can help you to read chapters in your social studies book and to complete worksheets for health class. They can help you to remember math assignments and to plan science projects.

In this chapter, you will learn a set of study skills that will guide you in planning your school work. You will learn other study skills that will help you make the best use of study time.

Part 1   Understanding the Assignment

To complete any assignment successfully, you must first understand exactly what you are expected to do. You must be able to answer four key questions.

1. **What type of assignment is it?** Are you being asked to read? to answer questions? to write a paragraph? to build a model?

2. **What should the final product be?** Should it be a written report? a skit? a set of answers?

3. **What materials are needed?** Do you need textbooks? tools? art supplies?

4. **When is the assignment due?** Is the work due right away? Do you have time to complete it in stages?

Listening to Directions

To answer the four key questions about an assignment, you must listen closely to the directions. The following guidelines will help.

Guidelines for Listening to Directions

1. Focus attention on the person giving the directions.

2. Listen for helpful words such as *read*, *answer*, and *write*.

3. Ask questions about any directions that are unclear.

4. Repeat the directions to yourself.

5. Write the directions in your own words.

Recording an Assignment

When you get an assignment, write it immediately in a special section of your notebook or in a separate assignment book. Record these facts about each assignment:

1. The subject
2. The exact assignment along with any special instructions
3. The date the assignment is given
4. The date the assignment is due

Here is a sample page from an assignment book. Notice the four columns, one for each item of information.

Subject	Assignment	Date Given	Date Due
Social Studies	Study map on page 104; answer questions on page 105	November 9	November 10
Science	Research the life cycle of one insect (fly, moth, mosquito); show the life cycle on a chart	November 10	November 13

Exercises   **Understanding and Recording Assignments**

Imagine that your teacher is giving you the following assignments. Read each set carefully. Then complete Exercises A and B.

1. "Today you studied the importance of colorful, precise verbs. For homework, look for lively verbs in newspaper headlines. Copy each headline and underline the verb. You should find at least ten examples. This assignment is due tomorrow."

2. "Here is a worksheet that will test your skill at multiplying fractions. The worksheet gives directions for making invisible ink. It lists how much of each ingredient you need. Next to the list,

133

write the amount of ingredients you need to make half the basic recipe. Then list the ingredients you need to make one-and-a-half times the recipe. Today is Wednesday. Have the worksheet finished by Friday."

A. For each assignment, answer the four questions on page 132.

B. Draw four columns on a sheet of paper. Use these headings: *Subject, Assignment, Date Given, Date Due.* Then record the important facts from the two assignments, as you would in an assignment book.

Part 2 Preparing To Study

Recording an assignment accurately is just one part of studying well. There are also other steps you can take to be sure that you get the most out of your study time.

Finding a Place To Study

You will find that you study better if you have a good place to work. At the public library, you would look for a quiet corner or a separate study room. At home, you might study at a table or desk in your room or in another quiet place.

Make sure that your study area meets the following requirements:

1. **The area is quiet.** The area should be free of distractions, such as television, radio, and the telephone.
2. **The lighting is good.** Poor lighting strains your eyes and can give you headaches.
3. **The area is neat and well-organized.** You should not have to search for papers, books, and supplies.
4. **The area is properly equipped.** Pencils, pens, paper, and a dictionary should always be on hand.

Setting Goals

Every year, your assignments will increase in number and in difficulty. In order to finish each assignment by its due date, you must learn to plan your study time wisely. The first step in planning is learning to set short- and long-term goals.

Short-term goals are assignments that can be completed in one day. At the end of each class day, review the assignments that you recorded in your notebook or assignment book. Identify those that are due the following day. Set aside a block of time each day to do these assignments.

Long-term goals are projects that cannot be completed overnight. To complete a large project, divide the work into smaller tasks. These tasks then become short-term goals. Figure out how much time you need for each task. Then develop a study plan for completing them.

Making a Study Plan

A study plan is a tool for showing when you will work on each task in a project. It also shows the time you set aside for your daily homework and for your usual chores and activities.

Suppose you have one week to do a report on Native American legends. You might divide the assignment into these tasks:

1. Go to the library and find books about the legends.
2. Take notes.
3. Organize the notes.
4. Write the first draft of the report.
5. Revise the first draft.
6. Make a final copy.

Once you have identified the tasks, you should fit them into a study plan. Your plans might look something like this.

Monday	Tuesday	Wednesday	Thursday	Friday	Saturday	Sunday
After school— go to library for books Take notes	Piano Lesson 3:30	Practice piano 4:30-5:30 → 4:00 Dentist		Help decorate for J.J.'s party	Clean porch J.J.'s party 1:00-4:00 Revise first draft	Dinner at Grandma's Make final copy
Homework— 6:30-7:30	Take notes	Organize notes	First draft			Homework— 6:30-7:30

Notice how this student scheduled regular blocks of time for daily assignments. The study plan also shows other chores and activities that have to be considered. The student carefully planned work time around the other activities.

Exercise   **Making a Study Plan**

Follow these directions.

1. Read this language arts assignment.

"Your next project is to talk with an adult about his or her memories of school. To prepare for your interview, make up at least five questions. During the interview, take notes.

"Write a report based on your interview. Include at least two quotations. This project must be finished one week from today."

2. Make a study plan like the one at the top of this page. Put this information on the study plan:

Every evening: do homework, finish chores
After school on Monday, Wednesday, Friday: basketball
   practice
Saturday afternoon: go roller-skating with Maria

3. Set up a study plan for the language arts assignment.

Part 3   Using Your Study Time Wisely

For most of your assignments, you need to read and study written information. One way to help yourself learn the material is to use a study method called the SQ3R method. SQ3R stands for the five steps of the method: Survey, Question, Read, Recite, and Review.

Study this explanation of these steps:

Survey. Quickly look over the material to get a general idea of the contents. Read the titles and subtitles. Look at any pictures, maps, tables, or graphs. Read the introduction or the first few paragraphs. Look at the final paragraph. Does it sum up the material? If so, read it too.

Question. Look at any study questions presented at the end of the material or given to you by your teacher. These questions will help you pick out important information as you read.

Read. Read the material thoughtfully. Identify the main ideas in each section. As you read, look for the answers to the study questions.

Recite. After reading, recite the answers to the questions. Make brief notes to help you remember the answers and any other important ideas.

Review. Read the questions again. Try to answer them without looking at your notes. If you can't, review the material to find the answers. Then study your notes so that you will be able to recall the information at a later date.

The notes you take as you study should be in your own words. They should consist of key words and phrases that relate to main ideas. Notes need not be written in complete sentences, but they should be clear enough for you to understand later.

Keep your notes in a notebook with sections for each subject. Write the subject and the date at the top of each page of notes. Add other headings that will help you to locate your notes easily. These notes will provide you with a brief summary of everything you study. They can be used when you need to find information quickly or when you are reviewing for a test.

Survey, Question, Read, Recite, and Review

Exercise Using a Study Method

Read and study the following article, using the SQ3R method described in Part 3. Look at the questions below before you begin the article. They will help you study correctly. Answer each question when you have finished reading.

1. Where should you look for clues about the contents of the article? What clues do you find?

2. Are you given any review questions?

3. Take notes as you read. What are the main ideas in the article?

4. What are the answers to the review questions?

ROLLER SKATES

Joseph Merlin, a Belgian musician, invented the roller skate about 1760. James Plimpton, an American inventor, designed an improved roller skate in 1863. Plimpton's "rocking skate" enabled people to roller skate in a curve by simply leaning to one side. Skating in curves had previously been possible only on ice skates.

Most roller skates have two major parts, the *boot* and the *skate assembly.*

The Boot is made of leather. Boots worn for recreational and artistic skating have high tops and are laced up the front to a point above the ankle. Speed skaters wear boots with low-cut tops. The boots of all roller skates should fit snugly and hug the heel firmly.

The Skate Assembly is a metal structure attached to the sole of the boot. The main parts of the assembly are the *plate,* two *truck assemblies,* the *toe stop,* and four wheels. The plate is a long, flat piece of aluminum fastened to the boot. The truck assmblies, which are mechanisms attached to the front and back of the plate, contain movable parts that enable skaters to turn corners. The toe stop is a device at the front of the skate that allows skaters to stop quickly and to perform maneuvers.

Two wheels are attached to axles at the front and two at the back of the skate. Early roller skate wheels were made of clay or wood. In the mid-1970's, roller skating was revolutionized by the introduction of wheels made of a hard plastic called *polyurethane.* Such wheels are lighter and quieter than those made of clay or metal, and skaters can move faster on them. Polyurethane wheels also provide smoother, more comfortable skating.

Some people wear *clamp-on skates,* which are skate assemblies that they attach to their shoes.

For Your Review
1. When was the first roller skate invented? One hundred years later, the design was improved. How?
2. What two parts make up most roller skates?
3. Why are polyurethane wheels superior to clay or wood wheels?
—Excerpt from *World Book Encyclopedia*

139

Chapter 10

Using Nouns

Part 1   What Are Nouns?

Who are you?

You are a person, a human being, a student. You are a girl or a boy, a daughter or a son, perhaps a sister or a brother. You may be a cyclist, a clarinet-player, a cook. You are a friend.

All of these answers are different names for you. They are all **nouns**.

Nouns are words that are used to name persons, places, or things. Here are a few more examples of nouns:

Naming Persons	Naming Places	Naming Things	
man	city	fence	spinach
woman	country	acorn	robot
dancer	ocean	dinosaur	Eiffel Tower
Juanita	Mexico	curb	boat
Paul	Africa	Peace Bridge	skateboard

> A **noun** is a word that names a person, place, or thing.

Nouns may name things you can see, such as *desk* and *bicycle*. There are many things we talk about that we cannot see or touch —such as *kindness, honesty, skill,* and *courage.* The words that name these things are also nouns.

Exercises Finding the Nouns

A. Number your paper from 1 to 10. Write the nouns in each sentence below.

> Example: In the Arctic, reindeer live on lichen.
>
> Arctic, reindeer, lichen

1. Texas is the second largest state.
2. The rules for this game are easy.
3. The tip of my ski is stuck under the log.
4. Mrs. Holmes kept her promise to the boys.
5. Which contest did the twins win?
6. An alert lifeguard sat on the platform at the beach.
7. Detroit has a problem with pollution.
8. My older sister moved to Massachusetts because of her job.
9. Three porpoises jumped out of the water beside Amy.
10. Does Betty know the title of that song?

B. Follow the directions for Exercise A.

1. Alaska and Hawaii are the newest states.
2. The cheese on this cracker tastes funny.
3. Pepper is a little dog with black spots.
4. A foil is a sword with a button on the point.
5. The prices of the coats are marked on the tags.
6. Sally was in Frontierland, looking at the old streets and houses.

7. People from Brazil speak the Portuguese language.
8. Buttercups and daisies were growing in the long grass.
9. The baby has the cutest smile.
10. Mr. Martin won't take any nonsense or excuses.

C. In this exercise, you will write only nouns.

1. Write the names of four persons you know.
2. Write the names of four places you have visited.
3. Write the names of four things you can see at this moment.
4. Write the names of four things you cannot see or touch, such as *kindness, honesty,* and so on.

Part 2   Common Nouns and Proper Nouns

If you call yourself a student, you are giving yourself a name that you share with all the boys and girls in your class. If you call yourself a boy or a girl, you share that name with about half your classmates. *Student, boy,* and *girl* are names common to whole groups of people. They are **common nouns.**

Playground, town, and *lake* are words that name members of whole groups of places. They are common nouns. Many nouns name whole groups of things, like *book, tool,* or *animal.* These are all common nouns.

> A **common noun** is the name of a whole class of persons, places, or things.

You are not simply any person. You have a name that is specifically yours. James D. Watson, Beverly Sills, and Captain James T. Kirk are specific people. These names of specific people are called **proper nouns**.

143

Proper nouns can also name specific places, like Houston and Lake Erie, or specific things, like the Liberty Bell and a Big Mac.

> A **proper noun** is the name of a particular person, place, or thing.
> A proper noun always starts with a capital letter.

Common Nouns	Proper Nouns
Groups of Persons	**Particular Persons**
doctor	Dr. Jonas Salk
children	Jane Banks, Michael Banks
lawyer	Barbara Jordan
Groups of Places	**Particular Places**
street	Jefferson Street
park	Yosemite National Park
city	Richmond
Groups of Things	**Particular Things**
bridge	George Washington Bridge
country	Canada
religion	Christianity

You can see that a proper noun may be a group of words. *George Washington Bridge* is one noun because it is the name of one bridge. Capitalize all words in a proper noun. Do not capitalize the words *a, an,* or *the* before a proper noun.

144

Exercises **Finding Common and Proper Nouns**

A. Label two columns *Common Noun* and *Proper Noun*. Number from 1 to 20 down the left-hand margin of your paper. Opposite each number, write its noun in the proper column. Be sure to capitalize proper nouns.

1. chair
2. maria
3. colorado
4. mountain
5. rocky mountains
6. miss parsons
7. school
8. woolworth's
9. hudson river
10. actor
11. country
12. lake erie
13. elizabeth
14. daughter
15. cowboy
16. atlantic ocean
17. green river
18. martin luther king
19. elmwood elementary school
20. harbor

B. Follow the directions for Exercise A.

1. bridge
2. france
3. cleveland
4. man
5. chicago black hawks
6. europe
7. philadelphia
8. the white house
9. windsor palace
10. high school
11. world war I
12. policewoman
13. south america
14. crossword puzzle
15. lemonade
16. saint theresa
17. the jefferson memorial
18. horse
19. chess
20. fortress

C. Copy these sentences. Capitalize the first word in the sentence and each proper noun.

1. bob mackey drove his car to florida last winter.
2. doctor moore told us about islands in the pacific ocean.
3. a great many potatoes are grown in the state of idaho.
4. my uncle knew the famous actor lawrence olivier.
5. brenda's birthday is in january.

145

D. Write a proper noun to match each of these common nouns.

Example: island—Cuba

1. teacher 4. lake 7. school 10. country 13. canyon
2. street 5. city 8. ocean 11. doctor 14. supermarket
3. bridge 6. river 9. store 12. governor 15. actor

Player

Players

Part 3 Singular and Plural Nouns

Look at the two nouns in the picture above. They are exactly the same except for the last letter.

The noun *player* refers to one person. It is called a singular noun. A **singular noun** names just one person, place, or thing.

The noun *players* ends in *s*. It refers to several persons. It is called a **plural noun**. The word *plural* means more than one.

146

A **singular noun** names one person, place, or thing.

A **plural noun** names more than one person, place, or thing.

Here are seven rules for forming the plurals of nouns:

1. **To form the plural of most nouns, just add -s.**

   hats   streets   hamburgers   animals

   tables   miles   shakes   movies

2. **When the singular ends in *s, sh, ch, x,* or *z,* add -es.**

   gases   brushes   boxes

   dresses   matches   buzzes

3. **When the singular ends in *o,* add -s.**

   radios   solos   banjos   Eskimos

   Exceptions: For the following nouns ending in *o,* add *es*:

   echoes   heroes   potatoes   tomatoes

4. **When the singular noun ends in *y* with a consonant before it, change the *y* to *i* and add -es.**

   pony—ponies   baby—babies

   lady—ladies   daisy—daisies

5. **For most nouns ending in *f* or *fe,* add -s. For some nouns ending in *f* or *fe,* however, change the *f* to *v* and add -es or -s.**

   belief—beliefs   thief—thieves   leaf—leaves

   roof—roofs   knife—knives   half—halves

   dwarf—dwarfs   wife—wives   shelf—shelves

   cuff—cuffs   life—lives   elf—elves

147

6. **Some nouns are the same for both singular and plural.**

   deer   sheep   trout   salmon   bass

7. **Some nouns form their plurals in special ways.**

mouse—mice   man—men   tooth—teeth

goose—geese   woman—women   foot—feet

child—children

Forming Plurals

A. Number your paper from 1 to 10. Write every plural noun in each sentence. After each noun, write the number of the rule that tells how the plural was formed.

Example: Representatives from three countries signed the treaty.

Representatives—1, countries—4

1. The children heard echoes in the cave.
2. The flies were killed by the sprays.
3. On the fishing trip, I caught two bass and several trout.
4. In some countries even adults believe in witches and elves.
5. There are rushes and bushes in the marshes.
6. The farmer set the potatoes and tomatoes on the tables.
7. If I help you win the prize, will you go halves with me?
8. Three deer and some foxes investigated the sheepfold.
9. Do mice and geese have teeth?
10. The dairies in the cities suffered losses.

B. Write the plural form of these nouns.

1. watch	5. foot	9. leaf	13. mouse	17. robot
2. city	6. sheep	10. hero	14. wife	18. porch
3. half	7. tomato	11. potato	15. woman	19. tooth
4. company	8. life	12. candy	16. wish	20. cry

148

C. Look around your room. In a column, write a noun for every object you see. Then write the plural of each noun in another column.

A dog

Tom's dog

Part 4 How Nouns Show Possession

When you speak of a dog that belongs to Tom, you want a short way of expressing that relationship. You do not want to say, "The dog that belongs to Tom" every time you refer to it. In English, the shortcut is the **possessive form** of the noun. The possessive form of *Tom* is *Tom's*. The fast way to refer to the dog Tom owns is to say *Tom's dog*.

Possessive nouns show possession of the noun that follows.

Forming Possessives of Singular Nouns

The difference between *Tom* and the possessive form *Tom's* is the ending. *Tom's* has an apostrophe and an *s*.

To form the possessive of a singular noun, add an apostrophe and *s*.

Singular Noun	Possessive Form
grandfather	grandfather's
baby	baby's
Charles	Charles's
Mrs. Wills	Mrs. Wills's

149

Forming Possessives of Plural Nouns

There are two rules to remember for forming the possessive of a plural noun.

1. If the plural noun ends in *s*, simply add an apostrophe after the *s*.

Plural Noun	Possessive Form
teachers	teachers'
pirates	pirates'
cats	cats'
doctors	doctors'
students	students'

2. If the plural noun does not end in *s*, add an apostrophe and an *s* after the apostrophe.

Plural Noun	Possessive Form
men	men's
women	women's
children	children's
Hopi	Hopi's

Notice how changing the place of the apostrophe changes the meaning of the possessive.

The student's pencils means pencils belonging to one student.
The students' pencils means pencils belonging to two or more students.

If you are not sure how to write the possessive form of a noun, do this:

Write the noun first. Then follow the rules.

When writing *'s* in cursive, you should not connect the *s* following the apostrophe to the last letter before the apostrophe. The apostrophe should separate the two letters.

Peg's skates   James's mother

Exercises   Writing the Possessive Form

A. Write the words in italics to show possession.

> Example: That is *Curtis* music stand.
>
> Curtis's

1. The trainer took the *runner* pulse.
2. Is that the *manager* phone number?
3. The new *girl* hair was long and curly.
4. Follow your *mother* advice.
5. A parade honored the *astronauts* homecoming.
6. We could see the *raccoon* tracks.
7. The *sailors* waterproofs protected them from the spray.
8. The *actress* smile looked real.
9. My *dog* ears perked up.
10. *Tess* butterfly collection has two dozen specimens.

B. Write the possessive form of each of the following nouns. Then write another noun after each possessive form to show what the first noun might possess.

> Example: Thomas Edison
>
> Thomas Edison's invention

1. a beaver
2. the mechanic
3. a pollywog
4. Louise
5. an Arab
6. Albert Jones
7. the fishermen
8. the secretaries

151

9. some steel workers
10. a chicken
11. Ms. Lopez
12. that cook
13. the ducks
14. your neighbors
15. my aunt
16. the whale
17. the puppets
18. an ostrich
19. those babies
20. the clown

C. Copy these sentences. Underline the person, place, or thing that belongs to someone or something else. Place the apostrophe where it belongs to show who or what possesses the underlined noun.

1. The childrens presents are in Noras closet.
2. Manuels store sells maps.
3. The mens golf bags are in my fathers car.
4. That architect's designs for homes won an award.
5. Many campers tents were destroyed in the forest fire.
6. We used Megans scarf as a bandage.
7. Andreas painting was sold!
8. The mices whiskers twitched nervously.
9. The governors mansion was lit by floodlights.
10. Ms. Conways desk has a no-smoking sign.

D. Follow the directions for Exercise C.

1. The kings charger reared, his eyes flashing.
2. Ma Barretts pies are known all over Grimsby County.
3. The boys faces looked stunned.
4. Mr. Whites garden always had sunflowers.
5. Aunt Frans car has reclining seats.
6. Both wrestlers muscles bulged and strained.
7. Those look like Anitas earmuffs.
8. Suddenly the referees whistle stopped the game.
9. Barneys cats were yowling again.
10. A horned owls feathers make points like ears.

Sentence Patterns The N V Pattern

Every sentence has a subject and a verb. The subject is usually a noun. In this chart, N stands for the noun in the complete subject. V stands for the verb in the complete predicate.

N	V
Margie	cheered.
Carl	ate quickly.
The baby	smiled.
The red balloon	popped.

The word order in these sentences follows a pattern. That pattern is noun-verb, or N V. This pattern is called the **N V pattern**.

Exercises The N V Pattern

A. Make a chart like the one above. Label one column *N* and the other *V*. Write these sentences on the chart.

1. Clouds formed.
2. Jenny skates every day.
3. The teams struggled.
4. Strong winds howled.
5. The dogs barked loudly.
6. Alex whistled.

B. Copy this chart. Complete each sentence in the N V Pattern.

N	V
1. _____	shouted
2. The thunder	_____.
3. _____	stood up.
4. Nick	_____.
5. _____	slept late.

153

C. Make a chart of your own for the N V pattern. Write five sentences in the N V pattern.

Reinforcement Exercises—Review

Using Nouns

A. Finding the Nouns

Write the nouns in the sentences below.

1. The corn was stored in the silo.
2. My sister Tanya invited her classmates to a picnic in the park.
3. Robin Hood led the fight against the Sheriff of Nottingham.
4. Directions are on the back of the package.
5. A diesel uses oil for its fuel.
6. Barbara brought the class some delicious candy made from pecans and caramel.
7. Spring is my favorite season.
8. This thermometer is for the oven.
9. The librarian found the book about Tibet on the top shelf.
10. The chain on my bicycle keeps coming off.

B. Finding Common and Proper Nouns

Copy these sentences. Capitalize the first word in the sentence and each proper noun.

1. a french explorer named cadillac founded detroit.
2. memorial day is a national holiday.
3. my cousin ellen can change that tire.
4. vickers' drive-in theater was showing a double feature.
5. walkerville public library is the biggest library in the county.
6. we visited carlsbad caverns.
7. morning glory pool in yellowstone national park looks like a blue morning glory.

154

8. we got this maple syrup from vermont.

9. the drugstore was running a special on sunglasses.

10. death valley in california receives less than three inches of rain yearly.

C. Forming Plurals

Write the plural form of these nouns.

1. party	6. goose	11. army	16. buoy
2. witch	7. man	12. trout	17. dress
3. deer	8. radio	13. lobby	18. roof
4. switch	9. lady	14. day	19. daisy
5. thief	10. knife	15. dwarf	20. echo

D. Writing the Possessive Form

Write the words in italics in the correct possessive form.

1. *Darcy* math book was on the table.
2. My *uncle* cabin is in New Jersey.
3. The bus *driver* left-turn signal was stuck.
4. The *ladies* coats are in the next room.
5. My *dentist* office is on Shirley Street.
6. A goose was in the *magician* hat.
7. Can you find your *puppy* leash?
8. My *grandfather* business is closed during July.
9. The *boys* appetites were huge.
10. *People* opinions vary.

155

Chapter 11

Using Verbs

Read the following words. Do you understand what they are saying?

Becky _____ the cat.

The words above almost express a message. We can try to complete the message by putting various words in the blank.

Becky *pencil* the cat.

Does this set of words give you a complete idea? No, because *pencil* does not tell what Becky did.

Becky *orange* the cat.

Again, *orange* does not tell what Becky did. We still do not have a sentence.

Becky *petted* the cat.

157

This time the words express a clear message. The word *petted* tells what Becky did, and gives the connection between her and the cat.

Are there any other words that could be placed in the blank to complete the sentence? Perhaps you thought of these:

Becky *fed* the cat.
Becky *held* the cat.
Becky *owned* the cat.

The words *petted, fed, held,* and *owned* all belong to a group of words called verbs. As you have seen, no sentence is complete without a verb. This chapter will tell you about verbs and how to use them.

Part 1 Kinds of Verbs

There are two kinds of verbs.
Some verbs tell about action. They are **action verbs**.

Sue *hit* the ball.   Bill *ran* to the window.

Some verbs name action that you cannot see. That is, there is no physical movement taking place.

Barbara *thought* about pets.   She *wanted* a puppy.

Some verbs are not action verbs. They simply state that something is. They express a state of being. They are **state-of-being verbs**.

Your book *is* on the table.
The slacks *were* the right size.

The most common state-of-being verbs are these:

is	are	were	being
am	was	be	been

Exercises Finding Action Verbs and State-of-Being Verbs

A. Copy these sentences. Draw two lines under each verb.

1. Our school held an art fair.
2. Students displayed their artwork.
3. Colorful ceramic pots lined the tables.
4. A band played music in the gym.
5. The mood at the party was joyful.
6. I took my dog to obedience school.
7. We reward Scamp with dog biscuits.
8. Sharon remembered her umbrella.
9. Last Sunday the weather was hot and humid.
10. Rosario missed the bus this morning.

B. Make two columns on your paper. Head one column *Action Verbs* and the other *State-of-Being Verbs.* Find the verb in each sentence and write it in the correct column.

Examples: a. Willie plans all our camping trips.

b. Debra was in my class during second grade.

Action Verbs	State-of-Being Verbs
a. plans	b. was

1. The rabbit's big, velvety ears twitched.
2. This old dress is still in style.
3. Judy loves dill pickles.
4. Listen to the crickets.
5. The fourth question on the test was tricky.
6. Suddenly Sean's dark eyes flashed.
7. I know the names of all the lifeguards.
8. Valentina Tereshkova was the first woman in space.
9. The kingfisher swallowed a frog and two fish.
10. Richard's bike accident happened last June.

159

C. Follow the directions for Exercise B.

1. In 1927, Charles A. Lindbergh flew from New York to Paris.
2. He was alone.
3. He faced many hardships.
4. After many hours in flight, he was successful.
5. The French people welcomed him.
6. He came home on a United States cruiser.
7. The American nation gave him many honors.
8. His solo flight was a great event.
9. It greatly aided the development of aviation.
10. Lindbergh will always be an aviation hero.

D. Each of the following groups of words would be a sentence if a verb were added. Think of a verb to complete each sentence. Write your sentences and underline the verbs. Add the correct punctuation at the end of every sentence.

1. A northwest wind
2. He the skateboard contest
3. The sleek car smoothly
4. Chris Evert tennis
5. The referee his whistle
6. During autumn the colors of the leaves
7. Three languages French, Spanish, and German
8. A snow skier poles, boots, and skis
9. Giraffes the tallest four-legged animals
10. The gardener the roses and marigolds

Part 2   Main Verbs and Helping Verbs

160

You already know that many verbs are made of more than one word. They are made up of the main verb and helping verbs.

Verb	Helping Verbs	Main Verb
am going	am	going
is going	is	going
can go	can	go
will go	will	go
has gone	has	gone
has been gone	has been	gone
could have gone	could have	gone

The most common of the helping verbs are these forms of *be, have,* and *do.*

be—am, is, are, was, were
have—have, has, had
do—do, does, did

These words can be used by themselves as main verbs.

Used as Helping Verb	Used as Main Verb
Bob *is* going.	Bob *is* the pitcher.
Sally *has* gone.	Sally *has* a moped.

There are several other helping verbs that you will often use with main verbs:

be	may	would	will
being	can	should	shall
been	could	might	must

A **verb** is a word or group of words that tell about action or express a state of being.

A verb with more than one word is made up of a **main verb** and one or more **helping verbs**.

161

Separated Parts of the Verb

The main verb and helping verbs are not always together. They may be separated by other parts of the sentence.

The batter *was* not *watching* for signals.
Andrea *has* never *missed* a band practice.
Did the kindergartners *make* popcorn today?
Frankenstein *couldn't control* his monster.

Notice that *not* and the ending *n't* in the contraction are not verbs.

Exercises **Finding Main Verbs and Helping Verbs**

A. Number your paper from 1 to 10. Make two columns. Head the first column *Helping Verbs.* Head the second *Main Verb.* Write the verbs for each of these sentences in the correct column.

Example: The books could not be found anywhere.

Helping Verbs	Main Verb
could be	found

1. I was expecting a phone call.
2. The old chestnut tree was hit by lightning.
3. Where can we find a book about marine life?
4. You should have seen the flames.
5. This contest entry might be too late.
6. The beachball had completely collapsed.
7. Skip has never had the measles.
8. That bottle could have floated here from Greenland.
9. We have already eaten our sandwiches.
10. The team had been hoping for a sunny day.

162

B. Follow the directions for Exercise A.

1. The red wolf is becoming extinct.
2. Coach Perez had called a time-out.

3. The Bears are beating the Vikings, 7–0.
4. People should always eat a nutritious breakfast.
5. Cartoons can sometimes be violent.
6. Did Momoko bring her skateboard?
7. Have you ever written a poem?
8. Curt might be joining the hockey team.
9. Computers will soon be performing many household tasks.
10. The President may not be elected more than twice.

Part 3   Verbs and Direct Objects

In many sentences the thought is complete when there are only a verb and its subject:

Subject	Verb
The audience	applauded.
Mary Ann	coughed.
Donald	worked.

In other sentences the thought is not complete until other words have been added.

Paul polished _____.
Lucy dropped _____.

So far, you don't know *what* Paul polished and *what* Lucy dropped. We need to complete the sentences.

Paul polished the *silverware.*
Lucy dropped her *book.*

In the first sentence, the word *silverware* receives the action of the word *polished.* It is the **direct object** of the verb.

In the second sentence, *book* receives the action of *dropped.* It is the **direct object** of the verb.

163

The **direct object** tells what receives the action of the verb.

Recognizing Direct Objects

To find the direct object in a sentence, first find the verb. Then ask *what?* after the verb. If you cannot answer the question *what?* there is not a direct object.

Examples:

Christy likes math.
Christy likes *what? math*
The direct object is *math.*

Julio reads quickly.
Julio reads *what?*
You cannot answer the question *what?* so there is no direct object.

Julio reads magazines quickly.
Julio reads *what? magazines*
The direct object is *magazines.*

Exercises   **Adding Direct Objects**

A. Number your paper from 1 to 10. Write objects that will complete each of the following sentences.

1. Hamid planted _____ in his front yard.
2. The Cardinals scored a _____.
3. Newspapers littered the _____.
4. Jolita rode the _____ with ease.
5. The reporter wrote a sensational _____.
6. After the concert Andy Gibb left the _____.

7. Leroy wore a bright yellow _____.
8. Kristin put the _____ in her wallet.
9. My favorite radio station plays good _____.
10. Did you close the _____?

B. On a sheet of paper, write sentences using the following verbs. Put a direct object in each sentence. Draw a circle around the direct object that you have added.

1. have caught
2. filled
3. would have stopped
4. was twisting
5. painted
6. will open
7. has invented
8. ruined
9. should limit
10. might use

Exercises Finding Direct Objects

A. Copy the following sentences. Underline the verb twice. Draw a circle around the direct object.

Example: The policeman stopped all (traffic.)

1. The scuba diver found a shipwreck.
2. Bruce Jenner won the decathlon.
3. The pilot steered his craft onto the airfield.
4. I am studying science now.
5. The children have built a huge snowman.
6. The Bureau of the Mint manufactures all coins.
7. Kathy will repair the brakes on her bike.
8. Delores likes ice cream with celery on top.
9. The United States exports grains to the Far East.
10. On Thanksgiving Day we eat turkey with gravy.

165

B. Number your paper from 1 to 10. Find and write the direct objects in these sentences.

1. A. J. Foyt drives racecars.

2. Jody will answer the telephone.
3. Our girl's basketball team won its first game.
4. In 1785 Jean Pierre Blanchard invented the parachute.
5. Tonia made pizzas for the party.
6. The sailors unfurled the mainsail.
7. The teacher wrote the assignment on the blackboard.
8. The zookeeper fed raw meat to the lions.
9. Did you drop the carton of eggs?
10. Beth placed the saddle on the horse's back.

Part 4 Linking Verbs

State-of-being verbs are often called linking verbs.

Here are some examples.

Carrie *is* tall.

Carrie *is* hungry.

Carrie *is* musical.

Linking verbs connect the subject with a word in the predicate. In the examples, they connect *Carrie* with *tall*, with *hungry*, and with *musical*.

The words *is, am, are, was, were, be,* and *become* are often used as linking verbs. The words *seem, look, appear, smell, taste, feel,* and *sound* are sometimes linking verbs.

The words that follow linking verbs and tell something about the subject are either adjectives or nouns.

Examples of adjectives: I *feel* ill.
These cookies *taste* delicious.

Examples of nouns: Angela *is* my best friend.
A goat *became* the team mascot.

Do not confuse nouns following linking verbs with direct objects of verbs. In the examples just given, you can see that *friend* and *mascot* tell something about the subject of each sentence. They do not receive action of the verbs, and are not direct objects. To identify a linking verb, decide whether the noun following the verb tells something about the subject of the sentence. If it does, the verb is a linking verb.

Exercises Finding Linking Verbs

A. At the top of three columns write: *Subject, Linking Verb,* and *Word Linked to Subject.* Find the three parts in each sentence. Write them in the proper columns.

Example: The contestants in the marathon appeared weary.

Subject	Linking Verb	Word Linked to Subject
contestants	appeared	weary

1. A young kangaroo is a joey.
2. That clown's hat looks ridiculous.
3. My friend Jane will be an actress someday.
4. The banana nut cake smells delicious.
5. Don't bullfights seem brutal?
6. Samuel's story sounds unbelievable.

167

7. That roller coaster looks scary.
8. Under water, straight lines will appear wavy.
9. Big Bird is a character on "Sesame Street."
10. Should we be quiet during the rehearsal?

B. Follow the directions for Exercise A.

1. The edge of this knife is dull.
2. My skates are becoming rusty.
3. The chili tastes fiery.
4. The fastest animal is the cheetah.
5. I don't feel sleepy.
6. The sequoia trees in California look huge.
7. Our country's oldest national park is Yellowstone.
8. The Vikings were Scandinavian pirates.
9. Mother must be very angry.
10. The most popular breed of dog is the poodle.

C. Some of the verbs in the following sentences are linking verbs and the others are verbs with direct objects. Copy each of the sentences. Draw a circle around the linking verbs. Draw two lines under the verbs with direct objects.

Examples: a. Emmett Kelly (is) a famous clown.

b. Congress approved the treaty.

1. The campers carried firewood to the campsite.
2. Bobby Orr is a famous athlete.
3. Vacations always seem too short.
4. The police detective felt the damp earth.
5. A down quilt feels very cozy.
6. The golfer was driving balls.
7. According to legend, Betsy Ross made the first flag.
8. The bill may soon become a law.
9. Mopeds use gas efficiently.
10. Mopeds are efficient vehicles.

168

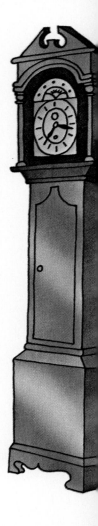

Part 5   Verb Tenses

Verbs are time-telling words. They do more than tell of an action or a state of being. They also tell *when* something takes place. By changing their forms, verbs tell whether the action or state of being is past, present, or future. These changes in form to show time are called **tenses**.

The **present tense** indicates an action or state of being happening now.

I *work* at school. I *am* a student.

The **past tense** indicates an action or state of being completed in the past.

I *worked* all last summer. I *was* a library aide.

The **future tense** indicates an action or state of being happening in the future.

I *will work* at the pool next year. I *will be* a lifeguard.

These three tenses are called the **simple tenses**. They are three of the most important tenses.

Tense changes are made in three ways:

1. By a change in spelling: *know, knew, known*
2. By a change in ending: *look, looked*
3. By a change in helping verbs: *did work, will work*

169

Forming the Tenses

Present Tense

In general, the **present tense** of the verb is the same as the name of the verb: *race, call, do, think.* An *-s* or *-es* is added to produce the form *he races, she calls, it does, she thinks.*

Past Tense

The **past tense** of most verbs is formed by adding *-d* or *-ed* to the present tense:

race   call
rac*ed*   call*ed*

These verbs are called **regular verbs**.

The past tense of other verbs, called **irregular verbs**, is usually shown by a change of spelling:

do   think
did   *thought*

Future Tense

The **future tense** is formed by using the helping verbs *will* or *shall* with the present tense:

will race   *shall think*

Exercises   **Recognizing and Using Verb Tenses**

A. Number your paper from 1 to 10. Write the verb in each of the following sentences. Name the tense of each verb.

Example: Clayton Moore played the Lone Ranger. *played, past*

1. Alison does crossword puzzles.
2. Sir Edmund Hillary climbed Mount Everest.

3. Our class will plan a school carnival.
4. We saw a porpoise show.
5. The fans cheered loudly.
6. "The Muppet Show" is hilarious.
7. Students will take a bus home from school.
8. Tracy Austin plays fine tennis.
9. I will return this book to the library.
10. Indians first explored this wilderness.

B. Number your paper from 1 to 10. Write the form of the verb asked for in each of the following sentences.

Example: The runner (past of *cross*) the finish line. *crossed*

1. I (future of *read*) all of the Hardy Boys mysteries.
2. The lawyer (past of *argue*) her case.
3. We (present of *roast*) chestnuts in the fireplace.
4. Tyrone (past of *make*) a lamp for his room.
5. The airplane (future of *land*) in a few minutes.
6. Scott O'Dell (past of *write*) *Island of the Blue Dolphins.*
7. Evan and Teresa (past of *pick*) raspberries.
8. A cricket game (present of *confuse*) most American spectators.
9. Sponges (present of *live*) in the deep seas.
10. The track team (future of *run*) in a meet tomorrow.

C. Write a sentence for each of the verbs below. Use the verb in the tense indicated.

1. hurry (future)
2. think (past)
3. litter (present)
4. develop (past)
5. remove (past)
6. frame (future)
7. justify (past)
8. promote (present)
9. drain (past)
10. bring (future)

171

Part 6 Pairs of Verbs That Are Often Confused

Study the sentences to see how the following pairs of verbs are used. Study the difference in the meanings to avoid making mistakes when you use these words.

Can and May

1. Can you see me?
2. Tina can swim like a fish.

1. May I go with you?
2. You may go to the party.

1. Use *can* when you are talking about being able to do something.
2. Use *may* when you are asking or giving permission.

Exercise Using the Right Verb

Number your paper from 1 to 10. Choose the right verb from the parentheses. Write it on your paper.

1. (May, Can) you write backwards?
2. (May, Can) I blow the balloons up for the party?
3. You (can, may) turn the pancakes now.
4. (Can, May) that little stove heat this whole room?
5. (May, Can) Melina and I go out in the canoe?
6. (May, Can) you read the bottom line without glasses?
7. A catbird (can, may) imitate other birds.
8. (May, Can) I please be excused?
9. (Can, May) Eduardo go to the park with us?
10. Stevie (may, can) count up to forty-nine.

172

Leave and Let

1. Leave the room.
2. Did you leave a book?

1. Let me see your ring.
2. Don't let the puppy follow us.

1. *Leave* means to go away from.
2. *Let* means to permit or allow.

Exercise Using the Right Verb

Choose the right verb from the parentheses. Write it.

1. Betty (let, left) me see her stamp collection.
2. (Let, Leave) Jim have the spoon to lick.
3. (Leave, Let) Woof alone.
4. The fishing net (leaves, lets) all the minnows through.
5. Don't (let, leave) the baby fall backwards.
6. Who (let, left) the lid off the paint can?
7. (Leave, Let) your umbrella on the porch.
8. That licorice (lets, leaves) a nice taste in my mouth.
9. (Leave, Let) me take your coat.
10. Somebody must have (let, left) the light on.

Lie and Lay

1. I like to lie on the floor.
2. Is there a place where I can lay my books?

1. *Lie* means to rest in a reclining position.
2. *Lay* means to put.
   Lay also means to produce eggs. (A hen *lays* eggs.)

Exercise   Using the Right Verb

Number your paper from 1 to 10. Choose the right verb from the parentheses. Write it on your paper.

1. Elena likes to (lay, lie) on the rug.
2. My dad always (lays, lies) his ties over the doorknob.
3. (Lay, Lie) your cards face up.
4. The trainer can make the lions (lie, lay) still.
5. Those hens (lie, lay) only brown eggs.
6. (Lay, Lie) on the dock and get a good sun tan.
7. Alfalfa's cowlick wouldn't (lie, lay) down.
8. Don't ever (lie, lay) plastic dishes on the hot stove.
9. Mr. Ware was (laying, lying) on the sofa.
10. Papers were (laying, lying) all over the ball diamond.

Review Exercises   Using the Right Verb

A. Number your paper from 1 to 10. Choose the right verb from the parentheses. Write it on your paper.

1. You're (laying, lying) on my towel.
2. (May, Can) Marcia and Fred really read that fast?
3. Certainly Jean (may, can) leave her bike in our garage.
4. (Leave, Let) the needle of the compass settle.
5. A sea turtle will crawl ashore and (lie, lay) her eggs in the sand.
6. (May, Can) we take Trudy to the boat races tomorrow?
7. Cindy always (lets, leaves) the icing till last.
8. Bricklayers never (lie, lay) bricks without a trowel.
9. The bus (lets, leaves) from Fountain Square every half-hour.
10. (May, Can) you hold all the groceries?

174

B. Follow the directions for Exercise A.

1. The explorers (left, let) their camp during the snowstorm.

2. (May, Can) we try shooting the Green River Rapids?

3. Are you (laying, lying) the spoons on the right side of the plates?

4. (Can, May) you see what's inside the box?

5. The brake will not (leave, let) the wheels spin freely.

6. You and she (may, can) take a copy of the play home.

7. My cat was (lying, laying) on top of the pumpkins.

8. You (can, may) often see forty miles from this lookout.

9. (Leave, Let) Wagger sleep.

10. Were you (lying, laying) in the sun?

Teach and *Learn*

1. I learned to do this trick after much practice.
2. Would you like me to teach you how to do it?

1. You *learn* to do something with practice.
2. You *teach* somebody how to do something.

Exercise   Using the Right Verb

Number your paper from 1 to 10. Choose the right verb from the parentheses. Write it on your paper.

1. Can you (learn, teach) me to swim?
2. Fay is (teaching, learning) her parakeet to talk.
3. My little brother is (learning, teaching) the alphabet.
4. Jarilyn will (learn, teach) her nephew about traffic rules.
5. I am just (learning, teaching) to play chess.
6. Will you (learn, teach) me to braid my hair?
7. Juanita is (learning, teaching) us Spanish.
8. Patti would like to (teach, learn) to fly.

175

9. The pioneers (taught, learned) their children to be independent.

10. I can't (learn, teach) my puppy any tricks.

Rise and Raise

1. The rooster rises early to greet the sun.
2. She raised the baby from the floor.
3. The farmer raises many crops.

1. *Rise* means to get up or to go up.
2. *Raise* means to lift.
   Raise also means to grow something.

Exercise   Using the Right Verb

Number your paper from 1 to 10. Choose the right verb from the parentheses. Write it on your paper.

1. All the ducks (raise, rise) into the air at once.
2. (Raise, Rise) your foot while I straighten the rug.
3. In every vampire movie, Count Dracula (raises, rises) from the dead once more.
4. Is the temperature in the engine room still (raising, rising)?
5. The Kellogg boys are (rising, raising) rabbits.
6. Turn off the burner when steam (rises, raises) from the kettle.
7. Marcy and Clare will (raise, rise) the curtain at eight sharp.
8. Is the moon (rising, raising) earlier or later?
9. It's not at all hard to (raise, rise) strawberries.
10. Did the drum major (raise, rise) his baton?

Sit and *Set*

1. Set the wheelbarrow down.
2. Then sit and rest awhile.

1. *Set* means to place or put.
2. *Sit* means to rest.

Exercise   Using the Right Verb

Number your paper from 1 to 10. Choose the right verb from the parentheses. Write it on your paper.

1. Muffer perked his ears and (sat, set) up.
2. Elizabeth (sat, set) out the milk for the cats.
3. I found Jud (setting, sitting) in the Egyptian room.
4. (Set, Sit) the baby in his high chair, Jan.
5. The baby (set, sat) there chewing his spoon.
6. Mary climbed up the rock and (sat, set) down.
7. Billy Wong (set, sat) out food for the birds.
8. Come in and (set, sit) down for a while.
9. (Set, Sit) down the groceries and help me.
10. (Set, Sit) the fudge out in the snow to cool.

Review Exercises   Using the Right Verb

A. Number your paper from 1 to 10. Choose the right verb from the parentheses. Write it on your paper.

1. (Teach, Learn) me how to make a real cake.
2. Jeff (sat, set) the alarm for 5 A.M.
3. Kathy should (rise, raise) next and take her place on stage.
4. (Set, Sit) still while I measure your arm.
5. I (learned, taught) the basic swimming strokes from Ron.

177

6. Do they (raise, rise) only corn in Kansas?
7. (Learn, Teach) Jessica and me how to throw a lasso.
8. The box was (sitting, setting) right where I left it.
9. He was (teaching, learning) us to eat with chopsticks.
10. Did Jill (raise, rise) the flag this morning?

B. Follow the directions for exercise A.

1. In a standing ovation, the audience (raises, rises) up and applauds.
2. You have to (sit, set) still to fish.
3. (Set, Sit) the balance beam along this side of the gym.
4. The cardinal was (teaching, learning) its baby bird to fly.
5. Louise didn't even (rise, raise) her voice.
6. (Learn, Teach) the beginners how to hold their rackets.
7. The barometer is (raising, rising).
8. Uncle Frank (set, sat) up waiting for me.
9. (Raise, Rise) the hood and let's look at the engine.
10. Please (teach, learn) me how to ski.

Part 7   Using Negatives Correctly

Negatives are words that say "no." *Not, none, nobody, nowhere, nothing,* and *never* are negatives. Contractions such as *can't, don't, doesn't, wouldn't, won't, isn't,* and *aren't* are negatives. Each contains a shortened form of the word *not.*

Two "no" words used in the same sentence, when only one is needed, make what is called a **double negative**. Avoid double negatives in your talking and writing. Using double negatives can make you appear to be a careless user of the language.

178

Wrong: He doesn't have no paper.
Right: He doesn't have *any* paper.

Wrong: He doesn't have none.
Right: He doesn't have *any*.

Wrong: Can't nobody work this puzzle?
Right: Can't *anybody* work this puzzle?

Exercises **Using One Negative**

A. Write the following conversation, or take turns reading it aloud. Choose the right word from the parentheses.

RUTH: Thank you, I can't eat (no, any) more pie.

JACK: Didn't you have (none, any)?

RUTH: Oh, yes. I couldn't eat (any, no) more.

PETER: Isn't it (no, any) good?

RUTH: Yes, it's good, but I don't (ever, never) eat more than one piece.

PAUL: I don't know (nothing, anything) I like better than pie. I have never heard (nobody, anybody) refuse pie before.

JANE: Can't (anybody, nobody) eat Ruth's pie?

PAUL: I wouldn't (never, ever) want to see any pie wasted. I'll eat it.

B. Number your paper from 1 to 10. Choose the correct word from the parentheses. Write it on your paper.

1. Gary can't think of (nobody, anybody) else.
2. Don't you want (any, no) pop?
3. Sue wouldn't have taken the album (nowhere, anywhere).
4. Albert won't climb (any, no) ladder more than three feet tall.
5. We aren't going (nowhere, anywhere) this summer.
6. I don't (never, ever) want to eat doughnuts again.
7. Sara doesn't go (anywhere, nowhere) without her bike.
8. I haven't heard (nothing, anything).
9. We haven't (no more, any more) string.
10. Nina wouldn't like (no, any) cake.

179

Sentence Patterns   The N V N Pattern

The **N V N pattern** describes a sentence with three parts. The first N stands for the subject noun. The V stands for the verb. The second N stands for the direct object noun. Each of the sentences in the following chart is in the N V N pattern.

N	V	N
Rosa	ordered	waffles.
Henry	plays	chess.
The carpenter	pounded	the nails.
Birds	build	nests.
The class	presented	a play.

Exercises   The N V N Pattern

A. Make a chart like the one above. Label the three columns *N, V,* and *N*. Write these sentences on the chart.

1. Diana collects seashells.
2. Plants need sunlight.
3. My brother loves chocolate.
4. Yuri climbed that peak.
5. The judges awarded prizes.
6. Eric bakes tasty bread.
7. NASA launched a rocket.
8. Our team won the game.

B. Copy this chart. Complete each sentence in the N V N pattern.

N	V	N
1. _____	shook	the house.
2. King Kong	grabbed	_____.
3. _____	saw	_____.
4. Tony	_____	two hamburgers.
5. _____	called	Lou Ann.
6. The goat	rammed	_____.

C. Make a chart of your own for the N V N pattern. Write five sentences in the N V N pattern.

Reinforcement Exercises—Review

Using Verbs

A. Finding Action Verbs and State-of-Being Verbs

Make two columns on your paper. Head one column "Action Verbs" and the other "State-of-Being Verbs." Find the verb in each sentence and write it in the correct column.

1. The pens were in my desk after all.
2. My dad considered the question carefully.
3. Were you at the bicycle shop this morning?
4. Twenty years ago, my mother was a high school student.
5. Big Ben struck eight o'clock.
6. Anita knows a lot about the battle of Saratoga.
7. Are you Doctor Cleveland?
8. The village slept under the stars.
9. Were the coyotes around last night?
10. The old man cupped his ear.

B. Finding Main Verbs and Helping Verbs

Number your paper from 1 to 10. Make two columns. Head the first column "Helping Verbs." Head the second "Main Verb." Write the verbs for each of these sentences in the correct column.

1. Were you watching TV last night?
2. A candy thermometer will be needed.
3. The boys had been home for hours.
4. I may have pushed the wrong button.
5. What else could we say?
6. Barbara Walters may have attended that news conference.

7. The children were just pretending.
8. The fire could have destroyed the entire block.
9. Notebook prices have risen by fifteen cents this year.
10. Carol and Diane were often taken for sisters.

C. Finding Direct Objects

Number your paper from 1 to 10. Find and write the direct objects in these sentences.

1. Carrie delivers newspapers.
2. The baby sucked his fingers.
3. A snake can shed its skin.
4. The Oak Ridge Boys have released a new album.
5. Spelunkers explore caves.
6. My aunt and uncle own a farm in Iowa.
7. I have been taking piano lessons for three years.
8. Have you ever played soccer?
9. The sixth graders were avidly studying Spanish.
10. Pony Express riders changed horses every ten miles.

D. Finding Linking Verbs

Some of the verbs in the following sentences are linking verbs and the others are verbs with direct objects. Copy each of the sentences. Draw a circle around the linking verbs. Draw two lines under the verbs with direct objects.

1. A fire destroyed two houses.
2. The math test didn't seem very hard.
3. Is your sister an eighth-grader?
4. Lindsay smelled the lilacs.
5. Ocean breezes always smell delightful.
6. The workers are building a new library.
7. Yolanda collects shells of all kinds.
8. Hinduism is the common religion of India.

182

9. That noise in the attic sounds eerie.
10. Someone sounded the buzzer for a fire drill.

E. Recognizing and Using Verb Tenses

Number your paper from 1 to 10. Write the form of the verb asked for in each of the following sentences.

1. The baby (past of *cry*) all night.
2. Charlie Brown always (present of *lose*) the game.
3. Amy (future of *laugh*) at even the dullest joke.
4. The choir (future of *sing*) popular folksongs.
5. That pitcher (present of *throw*) curve balls.
6. The fog certainly (future of *clear*) before dawn.
7. Charlayne (present of *go*) to the dentist twice a year.
8. Jenina (past of *catch*) a large salmon.
9. Balboa (past of *discover*) the Pacific Ocean.
10. Sitting Bull (past of *fight*) in the Battle of Little Bighorn.

F. Using the Right Verb

Number your paper from 1 to 12. Choose the right verb from the parentheses and write it on your paper.

1. (Raise, Rise) the lid and insert the tape.
2. (Lie, Lay) the baby in its crib, Stephen.
3. (Can, May) I come in?
4. Don't (sit, set) that brush on the wet paint.
5. I'll (leave, let) the can full of birdseed.
6. Who (taught, learned) you to throw a knuckleball?
7. The spray (raised, rose) high above the falls.
8. Rachel and the others are (laying, lying) out on the patio.
9. (Leave, Let) the huckleberries that aren't ripe yet.
10. My father (learned, taught) us how to cook spaghetti.
11. Mark can (lie, lay) tile as fast as his father.
12. (May, Can) Roosevelt sew well enough to make a shirt?

183

Chapter 12

Using Pronouns

Part 1 What Are Pronouns?

Read the two paragraphs below. Which paragraph sounds better?

1

Maria gets up at seven-thirty each morning. Maria eats breakfast. Maria goes to school. Maria opens Maria's English book and reads from Maria's book.

2

Maria gets up at seven-thirty each morning. She eats breakfast. She goes to school. She opens her English book and reads from it.

You probably decided that the second paragraph sounded better. Why did you think so? Perhaps you felt that using the name Maria over and over again became boring, or irritating. Perhaps you felt that the repetition made the first paragraph choppy.

How did the second paragraph avoid that repetition? Did you notice how it used the pronouns *she* and *her* in place of the name *Maria?* Use of the pronouns didn't change the meaning of the paragraph, but it improved the sound.

A **pronoun** is a word used in place of a noun.

You learned to use pronouns as soon as you learned to talk. You learned to use certain pronouns to do three things.

1. To refer to yourself:
   I invited *my* cousin to visit *me.*

2. To refer to the person you are talking to:
   You forgot *your* umbrella.

3. To refer to other persons, places, or things:
   Jack climbed *his* beanstalk.
   The cat blinked *its* eyes.

Singular Pronouns

Person Speaking:	I	my, mine	me
Person Spoken To:	you	your, yours	you
Other Persons, Places, and Things:	he	his	him
	she	her, hers	her
	it	its	it

Plural Pronouns

Persons Speaking:	we	our, ours	us
Persons Spoken To:	you	your, yours	you
Other Persons, Places, and Things:	they	their, theirs	them

Exercises Using Pronouns

A. Copy the following sentences. Underline the pronouns.

1. The bottle popped its cork.
2. Donna promised she would give me her old bike.
3. Take us to the car show, please.
4. Your tomatoes are much riper than ours.
5. We told them all about the walkathon.
6. You should find Ramon's marbles and return them to him.
7. He coaxed the chickens out of their coop.
8. I saw the birds as they flew over my yard.
9. A swan preened its snowy feathers.
10. We walked past her house.

B. In the following story, the pronouns are underlined in red. Read the story. Write all the pronouns in a list. After each pronoun, write the word it stands for.

Since Ted is eleven years old this year, he (1) can enter the Soap Box Derby. Mr. Williams gave him (2) a copy of the rules for the race. Ted is building the racer in the garage. Ted's father and mother are interested in it (3). They (4) often give him (5) advice. Ted paid $29.95 for the wheel and axle set, but the steering gear cost him (6) only $5.75. Ted hopes to win the race. He (7) thinks he (8) can win it (9) easily.

187

Part 2 Pronouns in Subjects

Which of these sentences sounds right to you?

Her went to the party.
She went to the party.

You probably had no trouble in choosing the second sentence. Now let's add the name of someone else who went to the party.

Her and David went to the party.
She and David went to the party.

The second sentence is right. *She and David* is a compound subject. To figure out what pronoun to use in a compound subject, try each part separately.

David went to the party.
She went to the party.

Then put the two subjects together, *using the same pronoun.* Follow the same plan when there are two pronouns in the subject.

(He, Him) and (I, me) built a radio.
He built a radio. I built a radio.
He and I built a radio.

Here is another simple problem with pronouns. Which would you say: *We had a picnic* or *Us had a picnic?* As you probably know, the first sentence is right.

Now, which of these sentences is correct?

We girls organized a field trip. (Right. *We* is the subject.)
Us girls organized a field trip. (*Us* is not a subject pronoun.
    It should never be used as the subject.)

188

The subject pronouns are *I, we, you, he, she, it,* and *they.*
Use only these pronouns in the subject of the verb.

Exercises Using Pronouns in the Subject

A. Choose the correct pronoun from the parentheses. Write it.

1. (We, Us) boys planted a four-foot pine tree.
2. Ms. Tandy and (we, us) came on the bus.
3. The third graders and (me, I) were drenched.
4. Did you find two blue mittens? (Them, They) are mine.
5. (They, Them) and the other cans are behind the garage.
6. The raft and (us, we) girls got stuck under Daw's Bridge.
7. My dog and (me, I) went out to take a look.
8. (He, Him) and (us, we) clocked the runners.
9. Bryan and (she, her) found the Little Dipper.
10. (We, Us) are in a hurry.

B. Follow the directions for Exercise A.

1. Susie and (I, me) ran the cold drink counter.
2. The fifth graders and (us, we) use the pool together.
3. (Us, We) girls and our big Angora rabbit won.
4. (Him, He) and (her, she) both come from Louisville.
5. Those boots can't be the ones I lost. (They, Them) don't look like mine.
6. (We, Us) three got all the blame.
7. In the picture, Carla and (he, him) had no heads.
8. (He, Him) and (me, I) were talking to the prison guard.
9. Randy and (me, I) finished the cornflakes.
10. Kitty and (they, them) went up in the ski lift.

C. There are several subject pronouns in the picture below. Write five sentences using these pronouns.

He

She

We

189

Part 3 Pronouns After the State-of-Being Verbs

Look at these two sentences.

The captain is he.   He is the captain.

They mean the same thing. As you see, the pronoun following *is* can be made the subject without changing the meaning of the sentence. The same is true with pronouns that follow the state-of-being verbs such as *are, was, were,* and *will be.*

Change these sentences without changing their meaning.

The co-captains are Janet and he.
The tallest players are Andy and she.
The fastest runners were we Blues.

Use subject pronouns after state-of-being verbs, such as *is, are, was, were,* and *will be.*

Exercises   Choosing the Right Pronoun

A. Choose the right pronoun from the parentheses. Write it.

1. The leaders are Valerie and (he, him).
2. It was (he, him) at the counter.
3. The guests of honor will be (we, us) girls.
4. Our club sponsors are Miss Martin and (he, him).
5. The runners-up were (we, us) boys.
6. The traffic managers for the talent show were Maria and (her, she).
7. The only people in that whole pool were Wayne and (me, I).
8. The earliest arrivals were (him, he) and Ron.
9. Was it (her, she) at the door?
10. The stage managers for our play are Paul and (them, they).

B. Follow the directions for Exercise A.

1. There were several adults and (we, us) girls waiting at the bus stop.
2. Our dinner guests were John and (she, her).
3. That's (he, him) on the pier by the submarine.
4. The fastest outfielders are George and (her, she).
5. The soloists are Wendy and (I, me).
6. My teammates were Isabella and (they, them).
7. The speakers at the assembly will be you and (he, him).
8. The funniest actress in our room is (her, she).
9. Faith's backup singers were Jenny and (they, them).
10. The only person with new skates was (he, him).

Part 4 Pronouns as Objects

A noun does not change its form when it is used as an object in a sentence. Pronouns, however, have special forms to be used when they are objects. These forms are called the **object pronouns.** The object pronouns are *me*, *us*, *you*, *him*, *her*, *it*, and *them*.

Pronouns After Action Verbs

These sentences will sound natural to you.

Dad drove *us* to the party. We met *him* later.

> Use the object pronouns *me, us, you, him, her, it,* and *them* as objects of verbs.

Be on guard when one or more pronouns are parts of a compound object.

Dad drove Jane and *us* to the party. We met *him* and *her* later.

If you are not sure which pronoun to use, try each part separately.

Kay stopped (he, him) and (I, me).

Kay stopped him.
Kay stopped me.
Kay stopped him and me.

Pronouns After Prepositions

One kind of word always has a noun or pronoun after it, and shows a relationship between that noun or pronoun and the rest of the sentence. This kind of word is called a **preposition**. The noun or pronoun that follows a preposition is called the **object of the preposition**. Object pronouns are used as objects of prepositions.

	Preposition	Object
He called to Melina.	to	Melina
We waited for them.	for	them
I awoke at dawn.	at	dawn
Here is a letter from her.	from	her

In learning to talk, you learned to say *for me* rather than *for I*. You never say *to I*; you say *to me*.

Don't be fooled when there are a noun and a pronoun after a preposition. Don't be fooled when there are two pronouns after a preposition.

The presents are for Laura and *me*.
The presents are for *me*.

The driver called to *him* and *me*.
The driver called to *me*.

192

Use only object pronouns as objects of prepositions.

Here is a list of common prepositions:

of	with	under	over	along	below
in	at	about	across	around	beside
by	down	between	against	before	past
to	from	on	above	toward	behind
up	into	near	after	for	beneath

Exercises **Choosing the Right Pronoun**

A. Number your paper from 1 to 8. Write the verb. Choose the right pronoun to be used as the object of the verb. Write the pronoun.

Example: Help (we, us) and Nancy again, please. *help us*

1. Call (I, me) in the morning.
2. The sultan ruled (them, they) long and wisely.
3. Mom dropped Matt and (me, I) off at the City Hall.
4. The Kiwanis Club sponsored (he, him).
5. Judy's dog led (them, they) to the lost child.
6. Ms. Lee complimented the class and (he, him) on the photos.
7. That owl scared Doug and (I, me) out of our wits.
8. Don't you believe (she, her)?

B. Number your paper from 1 to 8. Write the preposition. Then write the pronoun to be used as the object of the preposition.

Example: The flashlights are for Tina and (we, us). *for us*

1. You play against Lou and (he, him).
2. The choice is between (she, her) and Dorothy.
3. The dialogue was written by Kim and (I, me).
4. In the class picture, Pat's cousin Don is just above (she, her).
5. Dripping stalactites were all around (us, we).
6. The relay race depends on Francine and (he, him).
7. The skunk didn't even glance at Ross and (me, I).
8. The box for those envelopes is under (they, them).

193

Part 5 Possessive Pronouns

To make the possessive form of a noun, you add an apostrophe or an apostrophe and an *s* to the noun. Pronouns have special possessive forms. These do not use apostrophes at all.

The possessive forms of pronouns are these:

my, mine   **our, ours**   **your, yours**

his, her, hers, its   **their, theirs**

The only problem most people have with possessive pronouns is confusing the possessive *its* with the contraction *it's*. *Its* (without an apostrophe) is the possessive form of *it*. *It's* (with an apostrophe) means *it is* or *it has*.

The horse broke *its* leg. (The leg belongs to the horse.) *It's* having an operation tomorrow. (*It is* having an operation tomorrow.)

Exercise **Using *Its* and *It's* Correctly**

Copy the following sentences. Insert apostrophes where they are needed.

1. The rat lost its way in the maze.
2. Its snowing throughout the Northwest.
3. Change the thermostat if its set too low.
4. That stuffed dog lost a lot of its stuffing.
5. Scoop up that groundball while its fair.
6. The store ends its sale next week.
7. Leave the puzzle in its box.
8. I hate gum when its stuck in my hair.
9. The school started its basketball season last weekend.
10. Its too late to go swimming now.

Sentence Patterns The N LV N Pattern

The **N LV N pattern** describes a sentence with three parts. The first N stands for the subject noun. LV stands for a linking verb. The second N stands for the noun that follows the linking verb.

N	LV	N
Chimpanzees	are	mammals.
Allen	is	my friend.
My favorite dessert	is	pudding.
The blizzard	was	a disaster.
Jade	is	a hard stone.

Exercises The N LV N Pattern

A. Make a chart like the one above. Label the three columns N, LV, and N. Write these sentences on the chart.

1. Dee is my sister.
2. Pumpkins are vegetables.
3. This chair is an antique.
4. The Tortugas are islands.
5. Pete is an artist.
6. Mushrooms are parasites.
7. The sun is a star.
8. My aunt is a jogger.

B. Make a chart like the one below. Complete each sentence in the N LV N pattern.

N	LV	N
1. _____	is	a useful tool.
2. My best friend	was	_____ .
3. _____	are	reptiles.
4. The Riveras	_____	my neighbors.
5. _____	are	_____ .

C. Make a chart of your own. Label the columns N, LV, and N. Write five sentences in the N LV N pattern.

195

Reinforcement Exercises—Review

Using Pronouns

A. Using Pronouns

Copy the following sentences. Underline the pronouns.

1. My aunt called them long distance in Alaska.
2. If your car won't start, take ours instead.
3. Tell Kevin to invite Mary when he sees her.
4. Mercury's winged sandals made his feet fly.
5. The Jacksons didn't take the trip. It was too expensive.
6. I saved my allowance but she spent hers.
7. Jonathan took his books with him.
8. Throw your best slider and watch me hit it.
9. The Plains Indians pitched their teepees near the waterhole.
10. You sound to me like an optimist.

B. Using Pronouns in the Subject

Number your paper from 1 to 10. Choose the correct pronoun from the parentheses. Write it on your paper.

1. The boys and (them, they) made their skateboards.
2. (We, Us) kids vote for a picnic in Lion's Park.
3. (Them, They) and the rest of the parade lined up at 8:30.
4. (She, Her) and three boys from the science club organized the display.
5. Davy, (her, she), and (I, me) rode in the helicopter.
6. On Saturday, (they, them) and (me, I) cleaned out the Martins' garage.
7. (Her, She) and (he, him) were standing next to the door.
8. For our art project, (we, us) girls used yarn and cloth scraps.

196

9. (They, Them) and about twenty others hiked up Coconino Trail.

10. (Him, He) and his collie are always together.

C. Choosing the Right Pronoun

Choose the right pronoun from the parentheses. Write it.

1. The volunteers were the boys and (they, them).
2. Your opponent will be Henry or (she, her).
3. The top students in math are Sally and (he, him).
4. The next contestants are you and (they, them).
5. The best storyteller in the school is (her, she).
6. The actors in the next scene are you and (he, him).
7. The caller at the square dance was (she, her).
8. Was it (he, him) who took the picture?
9. The only students absent today were Bonita and (him, he).
10. Is the next person (she, her) or (me, I)?

D. Choosing the Right Pronoun

Number your paper from 1 to 10. Choose the right pronoun from the two in parentheses. Write it.

1. Lord Gascon ordered Mordleigh and (he, him) into a cold, dark dungeon.
2. Is the puzzle from (they, them) or Aunt Jill?
3. A beaver swam very close to Karen and (he, him).
4. The judges chose (she, her) and two other finalists.
5. Were you talking about (us, we) or (they, them)?
6. The ball didn't get past (her, she).
7. Here are some more strawberries for you and (they, them).
8. Did you count Delores and (I, me)?
9. Bayview isn't near (we, us).
10. The decision is up to (he, him) and (I, me).

Chapter 13

Using the Dictionary

What can you do when you come across a word you don't know? You can turn to a dictionary. The dictionary will tell you a lot about the word. It will explain its meaning, of course, but it will tell you much more. It will tell what other words have meanings like the word. It will also tell you the history of the word.

How can the history of a word help you? How can knowing other words with similar meanings help you? They will help you become familiar with the word. This means you can add another word to your growing vocabulary. You will be able to choose the best word to say what you want to say.

To make a dictionary help you, you must learn to use it. This chapter will show you how.

Part 1 Using Alphabetical Order To Find a Word

The words in a dictionary are listed in alphabetical order. The first words in a dictionary begin with *a*. The last ones begin with *z*. The words in between are also in alphabetical order. Words beginning with *p* come before words beginning with *q*, and so on.

Suppose two words begin with the same letter. Then they are alphabetized by the second letter. Suppose the second letters are the same. Then the words are alphabetized by the third letter, and so on.

The following groups of words are arranged in alphabetical order:

animal	man	chair
doll	mess	cherry
pocket	mit	chill
rag	mop	chip

Exercise **Using Alphabetical Order**

Following are four groups of words. Arrange each group of words in alphabetical order.

1	2	3	4
lemon	glue	players	Miami
grape	hammer	bat	Boston
lime	level	uniform	San Francisco
prune	saw	glove	New York
banana	chisel	helmet	Chicago
raspberry	lathe	ball	Montreal
apple	clamp	umpire	Los Angeles
peach	screwdriver	fans	Tulsa
nectarine	nails	base	Houston
cherry	wood	field	Toronto

Part 2   Using Guide Words

To find words quickly, learn to open the dictionary to the right spot. Open your dictionary at a spot that seems close to the middle. You should be in the *l*'s or *m*'s. If you are looking for a word that begins with a letter from *a* through *l*, look in the first half of the dictionary. If the word begins with a letter from *m* through *z*, look in the second half.

A-L

M-Z

If you practice opening your dictionary to a specific letter, you will be able to find words more quickly.

Once you have opened to the right letter, look at the **guide words.** The guide words are found at the top of each page. The guide word on the left tells you the first word on the page. The guide word on the right tells you the last word on the page. Flip through the pages quickly. Look for guide words that come before and after the word you want.

On page 203 you will find the reproduction of a dictionary page. The guide words are *pliers* and *plumate*. Notice that all the other words fall between these two in alphabetical order.

Exercises   Using Alphabetical Order and Guide Words

A. Working with a classmate, practice opening the dictionary as close as you can to a particular letter. Have your classmate say a letter. Try to open your dictionary to that letter. Then switch roles and say a letter for your classmate. Continue until you can open the dictionary close to a specific letter most of the time.

201

B. Do the same thing you did in Exercise A, but use words instead of letters. Use the guide words to help you find the word your partner names. Continue until you can find a word quickly.

C. Remember that the purpose of guide words is to help you find words more quickly. See how quickly you can find the following words in your dictionary. Copy the guide words from the page where you find each word.

ladybug	goat	falcon	gazelle	snake
kiwi	iguana	sailfish	narwhal	bat
pheasant	millipede	trawler	lamprey	cricket

Part 3 Getting Information About a Word

The information a dictionary gives about a word is called the **entry.** There is much information given in each entry. Let's take a dictionary entry apart and look at its different parts. We'll use the entry for the word *plot* on the dictionary page reproduced on page 203.

Entry Word

plot

The first part of an entry is the word. In most dictionaries it is divided into syllables. This is done with a space or a centered dot.

Pronunciation

(plät)

The next part of an entry is the pronunciation. In most dictionaries the pronunciation is printed in parentheses. When you pronounce a two-syllable word, one syllable gets a stronger emphasis than the other. You say PLIers and PLUMage. You put a heavier emphasis on the first syllable of each of these words. The emphasis is shown in a dictionary by using accent marks (′).

pli·ers (plī′ərz)

plum·age (ploo′mij)

pli·ers (plī'ərz) *n.pl.* [< PLY[1]] small pincers for gripping small objects, bending wire, etc.

plight[1] (plīt) *n.* [< Anglo-Fr. *plit*, for OFr. *pleit*, a fold] a condition or state of affairs; esp., an awkward, sad, or dangerous situation [the *plight* of the men trapped in the mine]

plight[2] (plīt) *vt.* [OE. *plihtan*, to pledge < *pliht*, danger] to pledge or promise, or bind by a pledge —**plight one's troth** to make a promise of marriage

Plim·soll mark (or **line**) (plim'səl, -säl, -sôl) [after S. *Plimsoll* (1824–98), Eng. statesman] a line or set of lines on the outside of merchant ships, showing the water level to which they may legally be loaded

PLIERS
(A, slip joint; B, needle nose; C, arc joint)

☆**plink** (pliŋk) *n.* [echoic] a light, sharp, ringing or clinking sound —*vt., vi.* **1.** to make such sounds on (a piano, banjo, etc.) **2.** to shoot at (tin cans, etc.)

plinth (plinth) *n.* [< L. < Gr. *plinthos*, a brick, tile] **1.** the square block at the base of a column, pedestal, etc. **2.** the base on which a statue rests

Plin·y (plin'ē) **1.** (L. name *Gaius Plinius Secundus*) 23–79 A.D.; Rom. naturalist & writer: called *the Elder* **2.** (L. name *Gaius Plinius Caecilius Secundus*) 62?–113? A.D.; Rom. writer & statesman: called *the Younger*: nephew of *Pliny the Elder*

Pli·o·cene (plī'ə sēn') *adj.* [< Gr. *pleōn*, more + *kainos*, new] designating or of the last epoch of the Tertiary Period in the Cenozoic Era —**the Pliocene** the Pliocene Epoch or its rocks: see GEOLOGIC TIME CHART

☆**Pli·o·film** (plī'ə film') [< PLIABLE + FILM] *a trademark for* a sheeting of rubber hydrochloride used for raincoats, as a covering for packages, etc.

plis·sé, plis·se (pli sā') *n.* [< Fr. < pp. of *plisser*, to pleat] **1.** a crinkled finish given to cotton, nylon, etc. with a caustic soda solution **2.** a fabric with this finish

plod (pläd) *vi.* **plod'ded, plod'ding** [prob. echoic] **1.** to walk or move heavily and with effort; trudge [the old horse *plodded* along the street] **2.** to work steadily and monotonously; drudge [to *plod* away at one's work] —*n.* **1.** the act of plodding **2.** the sound of a heavy step —**plod'der** *n.* —**plod'ding·ly** *adv.*

-ploid (ploid) [< Gr. *-ploos*, -fold + -OID] *a combining form* meaning of or being a (specified) multiple of the basic (haploid) number of chromosomes characteristic of a group of related organisms [diploid]

plonk (pläŋk, pluŋk) *vt., vi., n. same as* PLUNK

plop (pläp) *vt., vi.* **plopped, plop'ping** [echoic] **1.** to drop with a sound like that of something flat falling into water **2.** to drop heavily —*n.* the act of plopping or the sound made by this —*adv.* with a plop

plo·sive (plō'siv) *adj.* [< (EX)PLOSIVE] *Phonet.* produced by stopping and then suddenly releasing the breath, as the sounds of *k*, *p*, and *t* when used at the beginning of words —*n.* a plosive sound

plot (plät) *n.* [OE., a piece of land] **1.** a small area of ground [a garden *plot*] **2.** a chart or diagram, as of a building or estate **3.** a secret, usually evil, scheme **4.** the plan of action of a play, novel, etc. —*v.* **plot'ted, plot'ting 1.** *a)* to draw a plan of (a ship's course, etc.) *b)* to mark the position or course of on a map **2.** to make secret plans for [to *plot* a robbery] **3.** to plan the action of (a story, etc.) **4.** *a)* to determine the location of (a point) on a graph by means of coordinates *b)* to represent (an equation) by joining points on a graph to form a curve **5.** to plan together secretly; scheme [to *plot* against the king] —**plot'less** *adj.* —**plot'less·ness** *n.* —**plot'ter** *n.*

SYN.—plot is used of a secret, usually evil, project or scheme the details of which have been carefully worked out [a *plot* to keep him from getting his inheritance]; **intrigue**, implying more complicated scheming, suggests hidden, underhanded dealing often of an illegal nature [the *intrigues* of the royal court]; **machination** emphasizes trickery and slyness in forming plots intended to harm someone [the *machinations* of the villain]; **conspiracy** suggests a plot in which a number of people plan and act together secretly for an unlawful or harmful purpose [a *conspiracy* to seize the throne]; **cabal** suggests a small group of persons involved in a political intrigue

plough (plou) *n., vt., vi. chiefly Brit. sp. of* PLOW

plov·er (pluv'ər, plō'vər) *n., pl.* **plov'ers, plov'er:** see PLURAL, II, D, 1 [< OFr., ult. < L. *pluvia*, rain] a shore bird with a short tail, long, pointed wings, and a short beak

PLOVER
(to 11 in. high)

plow (plou) *n.* [ME. *ploh* < Late OE.] **1.** a farm implement used to cut and turn up the soil ☆**2.** anything like this; specif., a SNOW-PLOW —*vt.* **1.** to cut and turn up (soil) with a plow **2.** to make furrows in with or as with a plow **3.** to make as if by plowing [he *plowed* his way through the crowd] **4.** to cut a way through (water) —*vi.* **1.** to use a plow in tilling the soil **2.** to cut a way (*through* water, etc.) **3.** to go forward with effort; plod **4.** to begin work vigorously (with *into*) **5.** to strike against forcefully (with *into*) —**plow back** to reinvest (profits) in the same business enterprise —**plow up 1.** to remove with a plow **2.** to till (soil) thoroughly —**plow'a·ble** *adj.* —**plow'er** *n.*

plow·boy (plou'boi') *n.* **1.** formerly, a boy who led a team of horses drawing a plow **2.** a country boy

plow·man (plou'mən) *n., pl.* **-men 1.** a man who guides a plow **2.** a farm worker

plow·share (-sher') *n.* the share, or cutting blade, of a moldboard plow

ploy (ploi) *n.* [? < (EM)PLOY] an action or maneuver intended to outwit or confuse another person in order to get the better of him

pluck (pluk) *vt.* [OE. *pluccian:* for IE. base see PILE[2]] **1.** to pull off or out; pick [to *pluck* an apple from a tree] **2.** to drag or snatch; grab [he *plucked* a burning stick from the fire] **3.** to pull feathers or hair from [to *pluck* a chicken, *pluck* eyebrows] **4.** to pull at (the strings of a musical instrument) and release quickly to sound tones **5.** [Slang] to rob or swindle —*vi.* **1.** to pull; tug; snatch (often with *at*) [he *plucked* at his long mustache] **2.** to pluck a musical instrument —*n.* **1.** a pulling; tug **2.** courage to meet danger or difficulty; fortitude —**pluck up** to stir up one's (courage); take heart —**pluck'er** *n.*

pluck·y (pluk'ē) *adj.* **pluck'i·er, pluck'i·est** brave; spirited; determined —see SYN. at BRAVE —**pluck'i·ly** *adv.* —**pluck'i·ness** *n.*

plug (plug) *n.* [MDu. *plugge*] **1.** an object used to stop up a hole, drain, etc. **2.** *a)* a cake of pressed tobacco *b)* a piece of chewing tobacco **3.** a device, as with prongs that stick out, for fitting into an electric outlet, etc. to make electrical contact **4.** *same as: a)* SPARK PLUG *b)* FIREPLUG **5.** [Colloq.] a defective or shopworn article ☆**6.** [Slang] an old, worn-out horse ☆**7.** [Colloq.] a boost, advertisement, etc., esp. one slipped into the entertainment part of a radio or TV program, a magazine article, etc. —*vt.* **plugged, plug'ging 1.** to stop up (a hole, etc.) with a plug (often with *up*) **2.** to insert (something) as a plug [he *plugged* the putty in the hole] **3.** [Colloq.] *a)* to promote (a song) by frequent performance ☆*b)* to promote with a plug (*n.* 7) **4.** [Slang] to shoot a bullet into —*vi.* [Colloq.] to work or study hard and steadily; plod —**plug in** to connect (an electrical device) with an outlet, etc. by inserting a plug in a socket or jack —**plug'ger** *n.*

☆**plug hat** [Old Slang] a man's high silk hat

☆**plug·o·la** (plug'ō lə) *n.* [PLUG, *n.* 7 + (PAY)OLA] [Slang] the paying of a bribe, or a bribe paid, for the dishonest promotion of something or someone on radio or TV

☆**plug-ug·ly** (-ug'lē) *n., pl.* **-lies** [Old Slang] a ruffian or gangster

plum (plum) *n.* [OE. *plume*] **1.** *a)* any of various small trees bearing a smooth-skinned fruit with a flattened stone *b)* the fruit eaten as food **2.** a raisin, when used in pudding or cake [plum pudding] **3.** the dark bluish-red or reddish-purple color of some plums **4.** something excellent or desirable [the new contract is a rich *plum* for the company]

plum·age (plōō'mij) *n.* [MFr. < L. *pluma*, a feather] a bird's feathers

plu·mate (-māt, -mit) *adj.* [< L. *pluma*, a feather] *Zool.* resembling a feather, esp. in structure

Notice that in the pronunciations the words have been respelled. These respellings are slightly different from the normal spellings. This kind of spelling is a way of showing the sounds in the word. In the word *plot*, the letter *o* stands for the short *o* sound. The dictionary shows this sound as *ä*. At the bottom of the right-hand pages of most dictionaries there is a pronunciation key. This explains the respellings and tells you how to pronounce the words.

Part of Speech

After the pronunciation, the dictionary tells what part of speech the word is. Most dictionaries use abbreviations for this. Here is a list of the abbreviations and their meanings.

n. = noun	**pro.** = pronoun	**conj.** = conjunction
v. = verb	**adv.** = adverb	**interj.** = interjection
adj. = adjective	**prep.** = preposition	

Some words may be used as more than one part of speech. These words have more than one abbreviation. Each abbreviation for a part of speech is followed by the definition. For example, the word *plot* is first defined as a noun (**n.**). Then it is defined as a verb (**v.**).

Word Origin

[OE., a piece of land]

Next comes the origin of the word. This tells what language first used the word.

Definition

plot (plät) **n.** [OE., a piece of land] **1.** a small area of ground *[a garden plot]* **2.** a chart or diagram, as of a building or estate. **3.** a secret, usually evil, scheme **4.** the plan of action of a play, novel, etc. —**v. plot'ted, plot'ting 1.** *a*) to draw a plan of (a ship's course, etc.) *b*) to mark the position or course of on a map **2.** to make secret plans for *[to plot a robbery]* **3.** to plan the action of (a story, etc.) **4.** *a*) to determine the location of (a point) on a graph by means of coordinates *b*) to represent (an equation) by joining points on a graph to form a curve **5.** to plan together secretly; scheme *[to plot against the king]* —**plot'less adj.** —**plot'less·ness n.** —**plot'ter n.**

The largest part of a dictionary entry is the definition. The definition is an explanation of the meaning of a word.

Synonyms

> **SYN. —plot** is used of a secret, usually evil, project or scheme the details of which have been carefully worked out [a *plot* to keep him from getting his inheritance]; **intrigue,** implying more complicated scheming, suggests hidden, underhanded dealing often of an illegal nature [the *intrigues* of the royal court]; **machination** emphasizes trickery and slyness in forming plots intended to harm someone [the *machinations* of the villain]; **conspiracy** suggests a plot in which a number of people plan and act together secretly for an unlawful or harmful purpose [a *conspiracy* to seize the throne]; **cabal** suggests a small group of persons involved in a political intrigue

One last part is found in some entries. It is a list of synonyms. This is useful for choosing the best word to say what you want to say. In Chapter 2 you were using synonyms when you chose specific words to say exactly what you meant.

Part 4   The Multiple Meanings of a Word

Many English words have more than one meaning. When you look up a word, you will have to choose the meaning that fits what you are reading.

Look up the word *go* in your dictionary. How many definitions are given for it? The Student Edition of *Webster's New World Dictionary of the American Language* gives forty definitions for this one word!

Look at the definitions for the word *pluck* on page 203. Notice that for most of the definitions there is a sentence or phrase given as an example. These examples show how the word is used for a particular definition. Sometimes these examples are as much help to you as the definitions themselves. Also notice that each definition is numbered.

205

In each of the following sentences the word *pluck* is used with a different meaning.

John plucked at his long mustache.

I felt a pluck at my sleeve.

Sandy plucked an apple from the tree.

It is easy to pluck the strings of a guitar.

It took pluck to rescue the drowning girl.

Exercise **The Multiple Meanings of a Word**

Number a sheet of paper from 1 to 10. Use the following dictionary entry for *front*. Write the number of the definition that fits each sentence on page 207. Choose from the first fifteen definitions in the entry.

Dictionary Entry for *front*

front (frunt) **n.** [< OFr. < L. *frontis*, genitive of *frons*, forehead] **1.** outward behavior or appearance, esp. when merely pretended [to put on a bold *front]* **2.** the part of something that faces forward; most important side **3.** the first part; beginning [toward the *front* of the book*]* **4.** the place or position directly before a person or thing **5.** a forward or leading position or situation ☆**6.** the first available bellhop, as in a hotel **7.** the land bordering a lake, ocean, street, etc. **8.** the most forward area, where actual fighting is going on in a war **9.** a specified area of activity [the home *front]* **10.** a broad movement in which different groups are united in order to achieve certain political or social aims ☆**11.** a person who serves as a public representative of a business, group, etc., as because of his prestige ☆**12.** a person, group, etc. used to cover up some activity, esp. an illegal one [the barber shop was a *front* for the numbers racket*]* **13.** a stiff shirt bosom, worn with formal clothes **14.** a face of a building; esp., the face with the principal entrance **15.** *Meteorol.* the boundary between two masses of air that are different, as in density —***adj.*** **1.** at, to, in, on, or of the front **2.** *Phonet.* sounded toward the front of the mouth [*i* in *bid* and *e* in *met* are *front* vowels*]* —***vt.*** **1.** to face; be opposite to [our cottage *fronts* the ocean*]* **2.** to be before in place **3.** to meet; confront **4.** to defy; oppose **5.** to supply or be a front to [white stone *fronts* the building*]* —***vi.*** **1.** to face in a certain direction ☆**2.** to be a front (senses 11 & 12) (with *for*) —**in front of** before; ahead of

206

1. The directions were in the front of the pamphlet.
2. She is at the front of all class activities.
3. He built his house on the ocean front.
4. The weather report said that a warm front is on the way.
5. When Martha was in the war, she was stationed at the front.
6. People on the home front joined Civil Defense.
7. The front of the church, including the steps, had caved in.
8. The Senator is a front for the big oil companies.
9. When she saw my luggage, the desk clerk called, "Front!"
10. He puts up a front to hide his nervousness.

Part 5 Synonyms

Synonyms are words that have similar meanings. The words *small* and *tiny* are synonyms. The words *tall* and *high* are also synonyms. However, synonyms do not have exactly the same meanings. They usually cannot be substituted for each other.

Look at the dictionary entry for *plot* on page 203. After the definition there is an abbreviation **SYN.** This abbreviation stands for *synonyms*. The list of synonyms for a word is called a **synonymy.**

Notice that the synonymy for *plot* does more than just list its synonyms. It also explains the special meaning and use of each of these words. Sometimes a synonymy will give sample phrases or sentences to help explain how each is used.

Often, a synonymy will help you choose the best word for what you want to say. Did Flight 766 *go, depart, leave,* or *withdraw* at midnight? A synonymy will explain the differences between each of these words. Then you can choose the best one.

Exercises Synonyms   **207**

A. Use your dictionary to find two synonyms for six of the following words. Use each synonym in a sentence to show its meaning.

explain	fault	last	group
give	perform	use	large
strike	bait	anger	regard

B. Number your paper from 1 to 5. Use the following dictionary entry for *firm*. In each of the following sentences replace the word *firm* with one of its synonyms. Use the entry to choose the synonym that fits best.

Dictionary Entry for *firm*

firm[1] (furm) **adj.** [< OFr. < L. *firmus*] **1.** not giving way easily under pressure; solid *[firm* muscles*]* **2.** not moved or shaken easily; fixed; stable *[*he stood as *firm* as a rock*]* **3.** remaining the same; steady *[*a *firm* friendship*]* **4.** unchanging; constant *[*a *firm* faith*]* **5.** showing determination, strength, etc. *[*a *firm* command*]* **6.** formally settled; definite; final *[*a *firm* contract*]* **—vt., vi.** to make or become firm; often with *up* *[*exercise will *firm* up flabby muscles*]* **—firm′ly adv. —firm′ness n.**
SYN.—firm refers to something whose parts hold together so tightly that it does not give way easily under pressure or springs back into shape after being pressed *[firm* flesh*]*; **hard** is applied to that which is so firm that it is not easily cut into or crushed *[hard* as rock*]*; **solid** refers to something which is firm or hard and suggests that it is heavy or has its parts packed close together *[solid* muscle*]*; **stiff** is used of that which is not easily bent or stretched *[*a *stiff* collar*]*

---

1. Allyn's legs are very firm after running yesterday.
2. I assure you that the bank's vault door is quite firm.
3. Maple is the firmest wood sold at the lumber yard.
4. Brand new clothes are sometimes so firm that they have to be washed before they can be worn.
5. "This mattress is as firm as a rock!" complained Bill.

Reinforcement Exercises—Review

Using the Dictionary

A. Using Alphabetical Order

Arrange the following words in alphabetical order.

Fiat	Ford	Datsun	Buick	Toyota
Dodge	Mercedes	Saab	Triumph	Volvo
Subaru	Pontiac	Porsche	Cadillac	Jaguar

B. Using Guide Words

Below are the guide words for ten dictionary pages. Copy the guide words on your paper. Beside each pair, write a word that you would find on that page.

anther	antidote	one	ooze
drill	drop	prize	procession
fisher	fix	rondo	rose
immune	impel	stir	stock
matted	maximum	vanilla	various

C. The Multiple Meanings of a Word

Read the sentences below. Each of the italicized words has an unusual meaning. Use your dictionary to find the meanings.

1. My mother allowed me to get a *hunch* of fudge.
2. People haven't worn *ruffs* since the seventeenth century.
3. Aaron is Lauren's *spark*.
4. He tried to *cow* us by telling a scary story.
5. The magician did several good *wrinkles*.
6. Because the ship was always *listing,* many of the passengers became sick.
7. In the attic was an old bear *fell* rug.
8. We all agreed that John *jigged* well.

209

Chapter 14

Using the Library

Libraries offer helpful and interesting information on thousands of topics. They offer books for enjoyment, reference books for facts and information, magazines and records, and many other useful materials.

This chapter will help you understand how books are arranged in a library. It will describe the kinds of books usually found there. It will also tell you how to write a book report. This information will help you become a more efficient library user.

Part 1 The Classification and Arrangement of Books

211

Since a library has so many books, finding one book among the hundreds or thousands may appear at first to be impossible. However, the job is not really difficult when you know what you are doing. Books in the library are arranged in a certain way. Learning about the arrangement of books will help you locate any book quickly.

The Classification of Books

Books in the library are divided into two groups: *fiction* and *nonfiction*. Each group is arranged according to a different system.

Fiction

Fiction books are stories that were made up by a writer, or *author*. Since fiction comes from the author's imagination, it is not necessarily true. The writer of a fiction book may base a story on some real events or experiences, but then invent certain elements to make a good story. All fiction books are grouped together in the library.

Fiction books are arranged on shelves alphabetically according to the author's last name.

For example, books by an author whose last name is *Adams* are placed before books by an author named *Byars*. Books by *Byars* are placed before those by *Cleary*.

If someone has written more than one book, all of those books are placed together on the shelf. They are then arranged alphabetically by the first word in the title. Words like *a, an,* or *the* are not considered in arranging titles alphabetically. If a title begins with *a, an,* or *the,* it should be alphabetized by the *second* word in the title. For example, *The Good Master,* by Kate Seredy, would be alphabetized under *G,* rather than *T.*

212

Exercises   Arranging Fiction Books

A. On a separate sheet of paper, arrange these fiction titles and authors in the order in which they should appear on the shelves.

1.	George, Jean	*My Side of the Mountain*
2.	Burnford, Sheila	*The Incredible Journey*
3.	Speare, Elizabeth	*The Witch of Blackbird Pond*
4.	Neufeld, John	*Edgar Allan*
5.	Sherburne, Zoa	*Jennifer*
6.	Klein, Norma	*Mom, the Wolf Man, and Me*
7.	Kjelgaard, Jim	*Outlaw Red*
8.	Gault, William	*The Last Lap*
9.	Kjelgaard, Jim	*Big Red*
10.	Bonham, Frank	*Durango Street*
11.	Pease, Howard	*The Jinx Ship*
12.	Gilson, Jamie	*Harvey, the Beer Can King*

B. On a separate sheet of paper, alphabetize these titles of fiction books, all of which were written by Marguerite Henry.

1. *King of the Wind*
2. *Misty of Chincoteague*
3. *Justin Morgan Had a Horse*
4. *Brighty of the Grand Canyon*
5. *Benjamin West and His Cat Grimalkin*

Nonfiction

Nonfiction books are books reporting facts or ideas. They contain information on every subject you can think of. The books are classified and arranged according to their subjects. The classification system used most often is the **Dewey Decimal System**.

The Dewey Decimal System classifies all nonfiction books into one of ten major categories. The chart on the next page lists the ten Dewey categories.

The Dewey Decimal System

000-099	**General Works**	(encyclopedias, almanacs, handbooks)
100-199	**Philosophy**	(conduct, ethics, psychology)
200-299	**Religion**	(the Bible, mythology, theology)
300-399	**Social Science**	(economics, law, education, commerce, government, folklore, legend)
400-499	**Language**	(languages, grammar, dictionaries)
500-599	**Science**	(mathematics, chemistry, physics)
600-699	**Useful Arts**	(farming, cooking, sewing, radio, nursing, engineering, television, business, gardening, cars)
700-799	**Fine Arts**	(music, painting, drawing, acting, photography, games, sports)
800-899	**Literature**	(poetry, plays, essays)
900-999	**History**	(biography, travel, geography)

In this way, the books in each smaller section are closely related.

Exercises **The Dewey Decimal System**

A. Assign the correct category number to each of these books.

1. *The Rainbow Book of Nature* by Donald Peattie
2. *The Legends of Hawaii* by Padraic Colum
3. *Ecology* by Peter Farb
4. *Illustrated Motor Cars of the World* by Piet Olyslager
5. *Making Mosaics* by Edmond Arvois
6. *Compton's Encyclopedia*
7. *The World of Ballet* by Anne Geraghty
8. *Ancient China* by John Hay
9. *Poetry Handbook* by Babette Deutsch
10. *The Story of Language* by Mario Pei

B. Draw a floor plan of your school library. Mark carefully each section that represents a classification of the Dewey Decimal System. Also, include the section where fiction books are shelved.

Call Numbers

In the Dewey Decimal System, a specific identification number is assigned to every nonfiction book. This identification number, known as the **call number** of the book, is like the address of the book. It tells exactly where each book in the library belongs on the shelves. The call number helps you locate books on the shelves.

Every nonfiction book has its call number on its spine.

Look at the call number of the following book. Notice how each part of the call number helps to identify the book:

Book: *Outdoor Survival*
Author: Charles Platt
Call Number: **796.5**
                         P422o

Dewey Decimal classification number —— **796.5** First letter of book title

First letter of author's last name —— **P422o** Author's assigned number

The top line of the call number identifies the subject of the book. The lower line identifies the author.

Among books classified by the Dewey system are three sections that deserve special attention.

Biography. A **biography** is the true story of a person's life written by another individual. An **autobiography** is the true story of a person's life written by the person himself or herself. Because biographies and autobiographies are true life stories, they are kept together among the nonfiction books. The Dewey class numbers for biography are 920 and 921.

920 This class number is reserved for collective biographies. These books contain the life story of more than one person. Collective biographies are arranged according to the author's last name. The call number of a collective biography is made up of 920 plus the first initial of the author's last name. For example, this is the call number of *Famous Underwater Adventurers* by Frederick Wagner:

920 Collective biography
W First initial of Wagner

921 This class number is used for individual biographies and autobiographies. Such books contain the life story of a single person. These books are arranged on the shelf by the last name of the person about whom the book is written. For this reason, the call number of biographies and autobiographies is made of 921 and the initial of the person the book is written about. For example, this is the call number of *Laugh Clown, Cry: The Story of Charlie Chaplin* by Walter Oleksy:

921 Individual biography
C First initial of Chaplin

Short Story Collections. Most libraries keep fiction books that contain several short stories in a special section. They are usually marked SC, for "Story Collection."

Such a book may be a collection of stories by one author. It may also be a collection of stories by several different authors. These stories were chosen and put into book form by an *editor*.

Books of short stories are usually arranged by the author's or the editor's last name. This is the call number of *Just So Stories*, all written by Rudyard Kipling:

SC
K

Reference Books. Reference books are special nonfiction books that are kept together in a certain section of the library. They are usually marked with an R above the classification number.

R
423.1
D56

Exercises **Call Numbers**

A. Each book below belongs in one of the special categories of biography, collective biography, or short story collections. Read the title carefully. Decide on the right category. Copy each title and author. Then assign the correct category number to each book.

Jules Verne: The Man Who Invented the Future by Franz Born
O. Henry's Best Stories edited by Lou P. Bunce
People in History by R. J. Unstead
The Story of My Life by Helen Keller
Martin Luther King: The Peaceful Warrior by Ed Clayton
Stories Boys Like compiled by Franklin M. Reck
My Animals and Me by Nan Hayden Agle
Baseball's Greatest Pitchers by Milton J. Shapiro
Helen Keller by Margaret Davidson
Evel Knievel and Other Daredevils by Joe Scalzo

217

B. Arrange the following call numbers for nonfiction books in correct order, the way they would appear on the library shelf.

770	796.3	929	770	551.7
J15i	G34p	J36e	N76p	W49s
623.8	133.8	301	551.4	551.4
B18s	O26p	K45f	P78e	B46s

Part 2   Using the Card Catalog

The **card catalog** is a cabinet of small drawers filled with cards printed with information about every book in the library. The cards are arranged alphabetically according to the top line of each card. In the upper left hand corner of each card in the catalog is the call number of the book listed on the card. This call number makes it easier to find the book on the shelves after you have found its card in the card catalog.

On the outside of each drawer there is a label that tells what letters of the alphabet are contained in that drawer. Inside each drawer there are **guide cards** that have tabs extending above the regular books cards. The tabs may have letters of the alphabet, complete words, or general subject headings printed on them. The guide cards separate the drawerful of cards into smaller groups. This makes it easier to find the exact card you are looking for.

There are usually three cards for the same book in the card catalog: the **author card**, the **title card**, and the **subject card**. All three cards give you the same information about the book, but in slightly different order. An author card has the name of the author of the book on the top line. A title card has the title of the book on the top line. A subject card has the general subject or topic of the book on the top line. All three cards for one book have the same call number in the corner.

Look carefully at the following examples of card catalog cards for the book *Wildlife in Danger* by Alan C. Jenkins.

218

The Author Card

When you know the author of a book you want to read, use the card catalog to look up the author's name. There will be an author card for each book in the library written by that author. All the cards for one author will be together, filed alphabetically under the author's last name (on the top line of each card). In the group of cards of one author, each card is also filed alphabetically by the first word in the title (on the second line of each card).

Here is an author card for the book *Wildlife in Danger.*

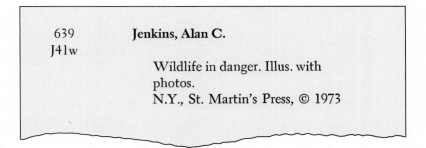

```
639          Jenkins, Alan C.
J41w
                 Wildlife in danger. Illus. with
                 photos.
                 N.Y., St. Martin's Press, © 1973
```

The Title Card

When you know the title of a book, but not its author, look for the title card of the book in the card catalog. Title cards are filed alphabetically by the first word in the title, which is on the top line of each title card. A, *An,* and *The* do not count as first words. Here is an example of a title card for the same wildlife book.

```
639          Wildlife in danger.
J41w
             Jenkins, Alan C.
                 Wildlife in danger. Illus. with photos.
                 N.Y., St. Martin's Press, © 1973
```

The Subject Card

If you were writing a report on wildlife, you would want to know the names and authors of several books on that subject in the library. The best way to find books on your topic would be to look in the card catalog under the subject heading WILDLIFE. The subject card for the book *Wildlife in Danger* would look like this.

```
639        WILDLIFE—CONSERVATION
J41w
           Jenkins, Alan C.
               Wildlife in danger. Illus. with photos.
           N.Y., St. Martin's Press, © 1973
```

The subject on every subject card is frequently printed in capital letters, which helps you tell the difference between it and an author or title card. Notice, also, on the subject card for *Wildlife in Danger*, that the author's name is given next. The title of the book immediately follows the author's name. Only the first word and proper names in the title are capitalized on the card. When you copy the title, underline it and follow the rules for capitalization. The title of the book would be written <u>Wildlife in Danger</u>.

Exercises   Using the Card Catalog

A. Each of the five words or phrases below is the first line of a card in a card catalog. Copy words or phrases in the order you would find them in the card catalog.

1. PHOTOGRAPHY
   The Pigman
   Parlin, John
   People Who Made America
   Phoebe

2. Wilder, Laura Ingalls
   The Wizard Islands
   Workshops in Space
   White, Robb
   The White Mountains

220

3. CAREERS

Careers in the Health Field

CAMERAS

Careers in Consumer Protection

Cameron, Eleanor

B. What subject cards would give you information about the following topics? Try to think of several subjects for each topic.

Example: Development of the railroads
Railroads
American history
Transportation

1. How to study for a test
2. Famous women athletes
3. Rules of tennis
4. History of the National Football League
5. How to grow a vegetable garden

C. Use the card catalog to find the title, author, and call number of a book on one of the following subjects:

1. A book about skiing
2. A book of detective stories
3. A book about dinosaurs
4. A book of poems by Robert Louis Stevenson
5. A book about Pablo Picasso
6. A book about Harriet Tubman
7. A book about the Alamo
8. A book about U.S. presidents
9. A book about UFO's
10. A book of math games and puzzles

Part 3 Finding What You Want in Books

You have learned how to locate books in the library. There are different reasons for which you may want to find certain books.

You often read both fiction and nonfiction books just for the enjoyment they give you. When you find a good book, you can share your discovery with your friends. You can tell them about it or you can write a book report. Then, if your report interests them, your friends can find the book.

Once in a while, you will read a book you don't enjoy. Then in your book report, you should tell what parts of the book you didn't like and give your reasons. Then people who read your book report can decide for themselves whether they might like the book anyway.

A book report must include the following information.

1. The title of the book
2. The author of the book
3. What the book is about and whether it is fiction or nonfiction
4. Reasons why you like or dislike the book

When you report on a fiction book, tell when and where the story takes place. Then tell a little about the people or animals in the story and at least one problem they face. Don't tell the whole story.

Give good reasons why you like or dislike the book. Whoever reads this report will be interested in your opinion.

Book reports can be long or short. They may include many details or very few. All book reports, however, must include the information listed above.

Exercise **Writing Your Own Book Report**

222 Read a fiction or nonfiction book. Write a book report about it. Be sure to include the information every book report needs. Follow the guides concerning revising and proofreading on pages 84 and 85. Correct your mistakes and make a clean copy.

Reading for Information

Nonfiction books are useful when you are gathering information on a special topic. You can find out if a certain book will help you by checking its **table of contents** and its **index.**

You will find a **table of contents** at the front of most nonfiction books. It lists the title of each chapter in the book and the page on which it begins. It may also list the main topics that each chapter discusses. Check to see whether the topic you are looking for is listed. Locate and study the table of contents in this book.

At the back of most nonfiction books, you will find an **index.** Every important topic that is discussed in the book is listed in alphabetical order in the index. Each topic is followed by the numbers of the pages on which it is discussed. Locate and study the index in this book.

The index is a good place to look for specific terms. Look for broader topics in the table of contents.

Another useful part of some nonfiction books is a **glossary**. A glossary lists difficult words in alphabetical order, and defines them according to the way they are used in the field discussed in that book. A glossary is especially handy in books that use unfamiliar terms or familiar terms in specialized ways.

Exercise   Using Parts of the Book

Look for each of these terms in the table of contents and the index of this book. Tell the part of the book that lists each term. Some terms can be found in both places. Some can be found in only one place.

1. suffixes
2. pronouns
3. card catalog
4. topic sentences
5. verbs
6. conjunctions
7. reference books
8. ZIP codes

Part 4 Using the Encyclopedia

Every library has a special section of reference books. These special books offer you facts and information on every topic you can think of. They are called **reference books** because you *refer* to them to find some specific information you need. When you look up something in a reference book, you often read only one page, or even less. In this way reference books are different from regular fiction and nonfiction books, which you may read from cover to cover.

Another way in which reference books are different from regular library books is that reference books are usually not allowed to be checked out. They are to be used only in the library. In this way, they are always available for library users to look up information.

The reference works you are most likely to use are the encyclopedias. An **encyclopedia** is a reference book that contains general articles on many subjects. Most encyclopedias consist of several volumes, covering a wide variety of subjects. Sometimes, a whole set of encyclopedias is about one subject, such as art or biography. There are some encyclopedias that consist of one volume on a single subject, such as baseball or careers.

The following encyclopedias are used frequently by young people:

Britannica Junior Encyclopaedia
Collier's Encyclopedia
Compton's Encyclopedia
Encyclopaedia Britannica
Encyclopedia Americana
World Book Encyclopedia

224 The Arrangement of Articles

Encyclopedias are easy to use. Information is arranged in the volumes alphabetically by subject. Volumes are usually numbered to keep them in order. On the back, or spine, of each volume are letters or words to tell you what part of the alphabet is included in that volume. For example, in the *World Book Encyclopedia,* volumes are numbered in this way:

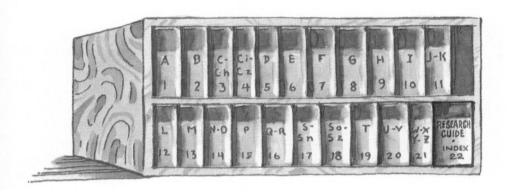

If you examine Volume 3 of *World Book Encyclopedia,* you will see that it begins with an article on "C," the alphabet letter, and concludes with an article on "churn"—the container in which cream or milk is stirred or beaten. Articles about people are usually alphabetized by the person's last name. Volume 4 begins with an article on John Ciardi, the American poet. The guides on the spines help you choose the volume that will have information on your topic.

At the top of each page of the encyclopedia are guide words. Like guide words in a dictionary, they help you locate the page that will have the article you seek. Most encyclopedias place guide words in both the upper left-hand and upper right-hand column of each two-page spread. For example, in Volume 2 of *Britannica Junior Encyclopaedia* (1982 edition), pages 252-253 cover "Angelico" to "Angola." Articles on those two pages deal with these topics:

Fra Angelico

Angkor, Cambodia

Anglo-Saxon

Angola, Africa

225

The Encyclopedia Index

Every set of encyclopedias has an **index**. The index may be a separate volume, or it may be part of the last volume. Always consult the index of an encyclopedia to help you find all articles on your topic. The index will direct you to every volume and page that contains information on your topic.

For example, if you were doing a report on the medication *terramycin*, you might look in the *World Book* Index and see this entry.

Teresa *See* Theresa, Saint *in this index*
Tereshkova, Valentina Vladimirova
   [Russian cosmonaut] **T :135** *with portrait*
   Astronaut (Achievements in Space) **A :792**;
      (table) **A :976**. (The Cosmonauts) **A :797**
   with picture
Terhune, Albert Payson [American author]
   T :136
Terias hecabe [insect]
   Butterfly *picture on* **B :624**
Terkel, Studs [American author]
   Great Depression (Economic Breakdown)
      G :340b-340c
Term [mathematics]
   Algebra (Other Definitions) **A :339**
   Fraction (table) **F :382**
   Progression **P :716**
Term policy
   Insurance (Three Basic Kinds of Life
      Insurance) **I :234**
Terman, Lewis Madison [American
   psychologist] **T :136**
   Intelligence Quotient (History) **I :243**

   Irrigation (Preparation of the Land) **I :368**
Terrain map
   Map (What Maps Tell Us) **M :136**; *picture*
      on **M :138**
Terral, Thomas J. [American political leader]
   Arkansas (table) **A :674b**
Terramycin [medication] **T :138**
   Antibiotic (Chloromycetin) **A :514**
   Drug (Creating a New Drug) **D :288c**
   Food Preservation (Antibiotics) **F :307**
Terrapin [animal] **T :138** *with picture*
Terrarium [biology] **T :138** *with diagram*
   Gardening (Terrariums) **G :38**
Terrazzo
   Flooring **F :211**
Terre Haute [Indiana] **T :139**
Terre Haute Prison [Indiana]
   Terre Haute **T :139**
Terrell, Joseph M. [American political leader]
   Georgia (table **G :134**
Terrell, Mary Church [American social
   reformer] **T :139**

It directs you to four articles, appearing in volumes, *T, A, D,* and *F*. The index also tells you what page to look at in each of the four named volumes.

The Encyclopedia Article

An article in an encyclopedia gives you brief, reliable information on any subject. Included in most encyclopedia articles are several aids to help you understand your topic. Find the article from *World Book Encyclopedia* on the subject of Hibernation. Notice these features as you read the article:

226

1. The subject title is in boldface type, using all capital letters.

2. Subheadings are in boldface type as well. They help you see at a glance what ideas or facts are discussed in the article.

3. Illustrations that accompany the article help you to see the main ideas presented. There may be photos, drawings, charts, maps, or graphs to help you visualize main ideas.

4. "See also" cross references are listed at the end of the article. They direct you to other articles in the encyclopedia that include information on your topic.

Exercises **Using Encyclopedias**

A. If you were looking for answers to the following questions, what key word in each question would you look for in the encyclopedia?

1. Who invented air brakes for trains?
2. What battle ended the Civil War?
3. How does an instant camera work?
4. When did Richard Nixon resign from the presidency?

B. Refer to the *World Book Encyclopedia* volumes shown on page 225. In what volume would you find articles on each of these topics?

1. Aaron Burr
2. University of Chicago
3. Elizabeth II, Queen of Great Britain
4. Solar energy
5. The game of football

C. Choose one of the following topics and look it up in an encyclopedia index. List all articles on that topic. Give the titles of the articles, their volumes, and their pages.

1. Mummies
2. Hercules
3. Dentistry
4. Soccer
5. Fashion

D. Look up one of the following topics in an encyclopedia. List the cross references appearing at the end of the article.

1. The United States Post Office
2. Motion pictures
3. Ulcers

227

Chapter 15

Writing Compositions

You have learned how to develop an idea in a paragraph. You have also learned to write different kinds of paragraphs to suit your subject. Sometimes, however, you may need several paragraphs to explain an idea completely. These paragraphs together form a **composition**.

This chapter will provide you with several model compositions. It will also teach you the skills of planning, organizing, writing, and revising as you write a composition of your own.

Part 1   What Is a Composition?

A composition is a group of paragraphs that work together to develop an idea. Does this information sound familiar? It should. It's almost like the definition of a paragraph. Both a paragraph and a composition are written to explain one idea. However, a composition is much longer than a paragraph. It gives more information about a topic.

A good composition is divided into three parts. Each part has its own special role.

The Three Parts of a Composition

1. The **introductory paragraph** tells what the composition is about.

2. The **body paragraphs** develop the main idea given in the introductory paragraph.

3. The **ending paragraph** summarizes what has been said and ends the composition.

These paragraphs all work together to explain the main idea of the composition.

A Model Composition

The following is a five-paragraph composition about a special kind of fair. Each paragraph contains a topic sentence. To help you, the topic sentences are underlined.

A TRIP TO THE PAST

I have always wanted to live in the age of Robin Hood. Without a time machine, though, my dream seemed impossible. Then last week my family went to a place where my dreams came true. At King Richard's Faire, a visitor can live in a completely different world.

As soon as we arrived at the fair, we saw people who seemed to be from another time. There were knights in armor, women in long gowns, and jesters in bright outfits. These costumed characters strolled among the visitors, speaking to them with perfect English accents. Soon my family was speaking with an accent, too.

As we walked through the fairgrounds, we saw that several of the costumed people were demonstrating some kind of craft or skill. One group of musicians played old melodies on instruments called recorders. A woman showed us how to make pottery by hand. Four men staged a swordfight. There were also jugglers, clowns, artists, and storytellers. No matter where we looked, something exciting was happening. Several of the knights even competed in a joust!

Visitors were able to take part in the activities, too. In one area, we learned different kinds of folk dances. After that, a magician showed us how to do some tricks. Then we got more daring and entered some contests. First, my sister Janet and I stood on a raised log and batted each other with burlap sacks until one of us fell off into a pile of hay. I was the one who fell. Then I challenged Janet to an archery match. We were shown how to use a bow and arrow, and we shot at straw targets. This time I won. Robin Hood would have been proud of me.

Finally, it was time to leave. As we walked to our car, I felt a little sad. I was leaving the world of knights and magic behind. But I knew that next year it would all be back, and so would I.

Introductory Paragraph

Body Paragraphs

Ending Paragraph

Notice how each paragraph contains details that support the idea stated in the topic sentence. In turn, each topic sentence develops the main idea of the introductory paragraph.

Exercise Studying the Parts of a Composition

Here is a five-paragraph composition about going to camp. First read the introductory paragraph. Explain the main idea presented in that paragraph. Then read the rest of the composition and find the topic sentence of each paragraph. Finally, identify which paragraphs belong to each of the three main parts of the composition.

DAY CAMP

Yesterday brought back a vivid memory. My mild-mannered younger brother stamped his foot and yelled. "I refuse to go to that dumb old day camp." Three years ago, I, too, was dead-set against going to camp. I'll never forget how much I hated it or how, little by little, I came to love it.

The first day at camp was awful. I didn't know one person on the entire bus. I decided I would probably hate everyone anyway. That went double for Miss Priss, who sat next to me. After the bus arrived at camp, we had relay races. Miss Priss was great! I finally learned her real name—Maggie.

The next day wasn't quite so bad. Maggie sat next to me again. This time we had something to talk about. She asked me to call her Mag. She told me she had five brothers. I told her about my little brother, my gerbils, and my cat Samantha. Later that day we made terrariums out of pieces of glass and tape.

The third day I decided that camp just might turn out to be kind of fun. For lunch we roasted hot dogs on sticks. We toasted marshmallows and spread the marshmallow goo on graham crackers. We put Hershey bars on top. No one felt much like running around after eating, so we learned camp songs.

I guess the day of the marshmallow treats was the turning point. After that I stopped complaining about camp. I started to dread the day when it would be over. It finally was over, but never in my mind. I still can bring back the special sounds, sights, and smells if I close my eyes and think hard enough.

Part 2 Pre-Writing: Finding a Subject

When you are asked to write a composition, do you say, "I don't have anything to write about"? It would be more accurate to say, "I could write about anything." Anything that you have done, seen, or even thought about could be the subject for a composition.

You have had experiences that are different from anybody else's. Therefore, you have writing ideas that are different, too. To find those ideas, begin by doing some thinking about yourself. What do you like? What don't you like? What do you feel? You will probably be surprised at how many ideas begin to pop into your head. Write them down. Soon you will have a whole list of possible subjects. Here are some questions to start your thinking:

Who is the person in your family you most admire?
What happened during your nicest summer?
What will be different in your life twenty years from now?
What's your favorite TV program?
If you could choose any time to live in all of history,
    when would you choose?
Do you like animals? Why? Why not? Which ones?
What's your favorite way to spend Saturday morning?
What's your favorite color?
What's your idea of a perfect day?
What place have you most enjoyed visiting?
Who is the most unusual person you've ever met?
What has been your most embarrassing moment?
What's the most important quality in a friend?
Have you ever sent a fan letter?

Exercise **Choosing a Subject**

233

By now you should have several ideas. Write your list of possible subjects. Then think about each one and choose five subjects that interest you the most. Write them on a separate piece of paper.

Part 3 Pre-Writing: Planning the Composition

Choosing a subject is not all there is to planning a composition. There are also several other steps you should take before you begin to write. Take time with these steps. The more carefully you plan, the easier it will be to write the composition.

Narrowing the Subject

You have already chosen a subject. Now you must be sure that the subject is narrow enough to be covered in a five-paragraph composition. For example, let's say you have chosen the subject "Favorite times of the year." This subject is much too broad to be covered in a few paragraphs. You probably enjoy many different times and seasons, including vacations and holidays. Any one of these would take several paragraphs to describe.

To narrow this subject, you must focus on one particular time of year. Try to find a special way of looking at it. One writer narrowed the subject this way:

1. Favorite times of the year
2. Summer
3. Favorite summer activities

Narrow your subject in a similar manner. As you continue to plan your composition, you may change your subject even more. At this point, though, your narrowed subject will provide a good starting point for gathering supporting ideas and details.

Exercises **Narrowing a Subject**

234

A. The following subjects are too broad for short compositions. Narrow each one until you feel you can cover the subject comfortably in a five-paragraph composition.

1. Sports	4. Games	7. Houses
2. Family	5. Friends	8. Dreams
3. Books	6. Pets	9. Movies

B. Take a look at the list of subjects you made in Part 2. Choose one you'd like to write about. Be sure that the subject can be covered in a five-paragraph composition. If not, narrow it.

Thinking of Details

After you have narrowed your topic, put your memory and imagination to work. Think through your subject thoroughly. Write down as many ideas and details about your topic as you can.

The writer who wanted to describe her favorite summer activities began by jotting down these notes. This list was just a beginning. The writer knew that ideas could be added or taken out later.

Climbing my favorite tree	Taking bicycle rides
Playing basketball	Baby sitting
Watching cartoons	Swinging on the swing set
Swimming	

As the writer prepared these notes, she realized that not all of the activities on the list interested her equally. There were several she had outgrown, and some that were new and enjoyable. This gave her an idea for making her subject even more specific. She decided that she would write about the summer she outgrew her favorite pastimes. When you make your own notes, you may get similar ideas. Don't be afraid to use them to improve your composition.

Exercise   Writing Down Details   **235**

Think about the subject you have chosen for your composition. Write down all the details you can about your subject. Carry this list around with you. Add to it whenever you have a new idea.

Part 4 Pre-Writing: Organizing Ideas

Once you have made notes about your topic, you are ready to plan the body of your composition. Follow these three steps:

1. List your main ideas.
2. Arrange your ideas into a logical order.
3. Add details to your list.

Listing and Organizing Main Ideas

Reread your notes. You will find that most of your details fit under a few main ideas. Decide what these ideas are. List them.

Look again at the list of details on page 235. The writer of this composition decided on the following main ideas.

1. New activities I enjoy
2. Outgrown activities at home
3. Outgrown activities away from home

You now have a list of main ideas. The next step is to organize them to make the composition easy to write and to read.

The order you choose for your composition will depend on your subject. For example, if you are describing something, you would arrange your details in the order a viewer would notice them. If you are telling a story, you would arrange details into a time sequence, the order in which they happened.

Sometimes, one idea leads logically to the next. The writer of the composition on summer activities decided to begin by telling about her old pastimes. She could then tell about the new activities that replaced them. The writer organized her main ideas this way.

First Main Idea: Outgrown activities at home
Second Main Idea: Outgrown activities away from home
Third Main Idea: New activities I enjoy

After you have listed and organized your main ideas, you may be able to decide on a title for your composition. The writer of this story decided on "The Summer Everything Shrank."

Adding Details

Once you have organized the main ideas, add the details that belong with each one. If a detail doesn't fit with a main heading, don't use it. You may, however, add new details that you think of. Look at this sample. Notice that the writer has added to her original list. She has also reworked her first ideas to fit the new subject.

Introduction—Last summer everything became too small for me.
First Main Idea—I outgrew my activities at home.
   I was too heavy for the swing set.
   I was too heavy for my climbing tree.
   I was too long to stretch out and read under the picnic table.
Second Main Idea—I outgrew my activities away from home.
   It was too easy to swim the length of the city pool.
   I no longer sat on the curb to watch the parade.
   It took too short a time to walk to the library.
Third Main Idea—I realized I needed to find new things to do.
   I began to play basketball.
   I took long bike rides.
   I babysat.
Conclusion—I had moved into a bigger world.

This list will become the writing plan for the composition. You may wish to rework your own list several times. Don't be afraid to add details, or to change the order of your ideas.

Exercise **Organizing Ideas and Details**

Reread your notes. List your main ideas. Arrange the ideas in logical order. Then put each detail from your list under the related main idea. Rework your notes as many times as necessary.

Part 5   Writing the First Draft

You are now ready to begin a rough draft of your composition. At this stage, just try to get your ideas down on paper. Try to make each sentence flow smoothly and naturally into the next one. You can fine-tune your writing later when you revise.

Writing the Introduction

The **introductory paragraph** is an important part of a composition. First of all, it tells the readers what the composition is about. Even more important, this paragraph must catch the readers' interest.

Read this introductory paragraph:

> Last summer everything became too small for me. I was too big to do the things I like to do. This was a sad situation.

This paragraph does tell readers the main idea of the composition. However, it is too dull to make anyone want to go on reading. Now read this paragraph, which the writer revised several times.

> When I was younger, every summer brought the same problem. On the first warm day I always found that my comfortable old shorts and T-shirts had become to small for me. I was used to that. Last summer though I decided that I was too big for something much more important than last year's clothes. I had also outgrown my comfortable old activities.

This introduction does not simply give readers an idea of what the composition is going to be about. It also tempts the readers to keep going.

Exercises Working with Introductory Paragraphs

A. Read these four paragraphs. Decide which paragraphs are good and which are poor. Check to see whether you can find the topic sentence in each. Also decide whether these paragraphs are thought-provoking or interesting.

1

Last Saturday Mortimer Shortimer puzzled the entire neighborhood. He got out a shovel and started to dig a hole. He just dug and dug and dug. After an hour we began to wonder if he ever planned to stop.

2

If you think aquariums are interesting, keep reading. My topic for this composition is how to set up an aquarium.

3

If you think it's time to clean your room, think again. Cleaning a room can be a long, long job. It requires patience, energy, and courage. I know. I had to do it once.

4

I used to be very shy. When I was in first grade, I was the only one in the class who never brought anything to show-and-tell. I had many toys I would have liked to show and tell about. My best toy was probably my musical robot, but it would've been too expensive to take to show-and-tell. The teacher didn't want us to bring in expensive toys. Come to think of it, noisy toys were not allowed, either.

B. Write the introductory paragraph to your composition. Like every good paragraph, it should have a topic sentence that tells the main idea, and other sentences that develop that main idea. Make sure your paragraph also does the following:

1. It tells what the composition is going to be about.
2. It catches the reader's interest.

Writing the Body

The main part of the composition is the **body**. It develops the idea introduced in the first paragraph. The body is made up of several paragraphs arranged in a logical order. Each paragraph has a topic sentence. All the details in that paragraph develop one of the main ideas of the composition.

Look at the three body paragraphs below. They are written from the notes for "The Summer Everything Shrank" on page 244. Remember that this is a rough draft. It will be revised later.

> Everything at home that used to make vacation fun had somehow shrunk. The swing set had gotten flimsy. The tree I loved to climb had become too weak to hold me. I could no longer stretch out under the picnic table and read on a hot day.
>
> I had outgrown my activities away from home, too. It was no longer a challenge to swim the length of the city pool. Walking to the library took only a few minutes. It used to be a long, daydreamy stroll. The curb I always sat on to watch the Fourth of July parade had become too low.
>
> I found new summer pastimes. My new height made it more fun to play basketball. I could ride a long way on my bicycle. I also realized that I might be old enough to get a job. Soon I was taking care of the toddler next door.

Each paragraph helps develop the idea presented in the introduction. The main ideas in the pre-writing plan have become the topic sentences of the paragraphs. The writer has also added some new details and colorful phrases. The body still needs improvement, but this rough draft is a good beginning.

Exercise   Writing the Body Paragraphs

240   Write the three body paragraphs of your composition. Make sure each paragraph contains a topic sentence. Follow the writing plan you made for Part 4. Do not be afraid to add new ideas if they fit your subject.

Writing the Ending

The third main part of a composition is the **ending**. Some endings, like this one, are very short:

We never went near that empty house again.

Others are longer. They end a composition by telling what happened later. The next paragraph is an example of this type. It concludes a true story about a cat named Tom. Tom wandered onto a stage during a performance and became a part of the cast.

Tom was glad when the play ended. Now he just sleeps in his box in the back of the theater. At night when no one is in the theater, Tom catches mice. —MARGUERITE P. DOLCH

A third type of ending summarizes the composition.

For almost nine days we lived in the wilderness, under the skies, next to lakes and streams, in sight of the deer and raccoons, with only the things we could carry. On our backs we had everything we needed—food, shelter, and clothing. We had Debbie, Chuck, and Kenny to guide us. Best of all, we had a great time! We made it to the top of the mountain, and we have a patch to prove it. It says, "I CLIMBED MOUNT WHITNEY." How many people can say that? —JEAN KEELAN

These three sample endings are very different. However, they do have one thing in common. They all signal the reader that the composition is over.

The conclusion of the composition "The Summer Everything Shrank" briefly describes a result.

By August, I was happy in my bigger world. There was more room to move around in.

Exercise **Writing the Conclusion**

Write the final paragraph of your composition.

Part 6 Revising Your Composition

Remember that a first draft is seldom perfect. Read your composition. Check to see that the order of your ideas is logical. Delete unrelated information. Add necessary details. Replace dull words with lively ones.

When you are satisfied that your composition says everything you want it to say, read it once more. This time, check for errors in grammar, capitalization, punctuation, and spelling. See the Guidelines on pages 84 and 85 for further help.

The writer of "The Summer Everything Shrank" knew that the composition could be improved. Look at this version of the rough draft. What changes have been made during the revision process?

THE SUMMER EVERYTHING SHRANK

When I was younger, every summer brought the same

problem. On the first warm day I always found that my

cut-offs
comfortable old ~~shorts~~ and T-shirts had become to*o* small

for me. I was used to that. Last summer,*though,* I

discovered that I was too big for something much more

important than last year's clothes. I had also outgrown my
summer *that its concrete base*
comfortable old activities. *pulled away from the*
ground when I swung.

Everything at home that used to make vacation fun had
so
somehow shrunk. The swing set had gotten flimsy. The tree
scrawny *apple*

I loved to climb had become too weak to hold me. ~~I could~~
When I *ed* *to*
no longer stretch out under the picnic table and read on
my head stuck out one end and
a hot day. *my feet stuck out the other.*

242

I had outgrown my activities away from home, too. It was

no longer a challenge to swim the length of the city pool.

~~Walking to the library~~ took only a few minutes. It used to
Now it *The walk to the library*

be a long, daydreamy stroll. The curb I always sat on to

watch the Fourth of July parade had become too low.
even

Gradually I moved into a new, bigger world.
~~I found new summer pastimes.~~ My new height made it more

fun to play basketball. I could ride ~~a long way~~ on my
further

bicycle I also realized that I might be old enough to get a
than I ever had before.

job. Soon I was taking care of the toddler next door,
one afternoon a week.

By August, I was happy in my bigger world. There was

more room to move around in.
It was different from my old one, but

Exercise   **Revising the Rough Draft**

Read your rough draft carefully. Revise it to make ideas clearer and more interesting. Use the guidelines on pages 84 and 85 to guide you. Finally, proofread your composition for mistakes in grammar, capitalization, punctuation, and spelling. Use the proofreading symbols on page 82 to help make your corrections clear.

Making a Final Copy

When you are satisfied with your composition, make a neat, final copy. Make sure you leave wide margins at the top, bottom, and sides of your paper.

Proofread your final copy. Check for errors in grammar, capitalization, punctuation, and spelling. Correct them neatly.

Read this final copy of "The Summer Everything Shrank." Notice how the corrections written on the rough draft have improved the composition.

THE SUMMER EVERYTHING SHRANK

When I was younger, every summer brought the same problem. On the first warm day, I always found that my comfortable old cut-offs and T-shirts had become too small for me. I was used to that. Last summer, though, I discovered that I was too big for something much more important than last year's clothes. I had also outgrown my comfortable old summer activities.

Everything at home that used to make vacation fun had somehow shrunk. The swing set had gotten so flimsy that its concrete base pulled away from the ground when I swang. The apple tree I loved to climb had become too scrawny to hold me. When I stretched out under the picnic table to read on a hot day, my head stuck out one end and my feet stuck out the other.

I had outgrown my activities away from home, too. It was no longer a challenge to swim the length of the city pool. The walk to the library used to be a long, day-dreamy stroll. Now it took only a few minutes. Even the curb I always sat on to watch the Fourth-of-July parade had become too low.

Gradually I moved into a new, bigger world. My new height made it more fun to play basketball. I could ride further on my bicycle than I ever had before. I also realized that I might be old enough to get a job. Soon I was taking care of the toddler next door one afternoon a week.

By August I was happier in my bigger world. It was different from my old one, but there was more room to move around in.

244 **Exercise** **Making the Final Copy**

Make a clean final copy of your composition. Include all of the changes you marked in your revision. Proofread the final copy. Correct any errors neatly.

Guidelines for Writing and Revising Compositions

As you write a composition, follow the steps in the Guidelines for the Process of Writing on page 84. Also use the guidelines on this page as you write and revise your first draft.

1. Is the subject narrow enough to be covered in a few paragraphs?
2. Does the composition have an introduction, a body, and a conclusion?
3. Does the introduction tell the main idea? Does it catch the reader's interest?
4. Does each paragraph in the body explain the main idea? Do the paragraphs work together to develop that idea?
5. Does each paragraph contain a clear topic sentence? Do the details in each paragraph develop the topic sentence?
6. Are the ideas in each paragraph arranged in logical order? Are the paragraphs arranged in logical order?
7. Does the conclusion clearly signal that the composition is over?

Chapter 16

Different Kinds of Compositions

In Chapter 5 you learned the important steps in developing any writing. In Chapter 15 you learned how to apply these steps in developing a composition. You saw how your plan for a composition must include these three parts:

1. **An introduction**. The introductory paragraph should tell what the entire composition is about. It should catch the reader's interest.
2. **A body**. The body paragraphs must work together to develop the main idea of the composition.
3. **An ending**. The ending paragraph should signal the reader that the composition is over.

You can follow these steps in developing many different kinds of compositions. Three kinds are described in this chapter.

1. The narrative composition, or story
2. The descriptive composition
3. The explanatory composition

Part 1 The Narrative Composition or Story

You have studied narrative paragraphs. They relate something that happened either to the writer or to someone else. A narrative composition does the same thing. It is made up of several paragraphs that tell what happened. Like a narrative paragraph, a narrative composition relates events in the order in which they happened. It follows a time sequence. It tells what happened first, what happened next, and so on.

Writing About a Personal Experience

Here is an example of a narrative composition. It relates something that happened to the writer. You can tell that the composition is about a personal experience because the writer uses the word *I*.

RASCAL LEARNS A LESSON

I decided one day that Rascal the raccoon was clean enough and bright enough to eat with us at the table. I went to the attic and brought down the family highchair. I had used it when I was a baby.

Next morning while my father was fixing eggs, toast, and coffee, I went to get Rascal. I placed him in the highchair beside me at the table. On his tray I put a heavy stoneware bowl of warm milk. Rascal could reach the milk easily by standing in the chair and placing his hands on the edge of the tray. He seemed to like the new arrangement and chirred and trilled his satisfaction. Except for dribbling a little milk, easily wiped from the tray of the highchair, his table manners were excellent. They were much better than those of most children. My father was amused as usual. He even petted the raccoon as we finished our meal.

Breakfast for three became part of the daily plan, and we had no trouble until I offered Rascal a lump of sugar. Rascal felt it, sniffed it, and then began his usual washing ceremony. He swished it back and forth through his bowl of milk. In a few moments, of course, it melted entirely away. A more surprised little raccoon you have never seen in your life. He felt all over the bottom of the bowl to see if he had dropped it. He turned over his right hand to assure himself it was empty. He examined his left hand in the same way. Finally he looked at me and trilled a shrill question. Who had stolen his sugar lump?

Recovering from my laughter, I gave him a second sugar lump. Rascal examined it carefully. He started to wash it, but stopped. A shrewd look came into his bright black eyes. Instead of washing away a second treat, he took it directly to his mouth. He began to munch it with complete satisfaction.

When Rascal had learned a lesson, he had learned it for life. Never again did he wash a lump of sugar.   —STERLING NORTH

Following a Time Sequence

In the introductory paragraph, the writer tells you that the composition is about Rascal the raccoon, eating with the family. In the body paragraphs, the writer tells what happened. You could list the events he has described. Your list might look like this.

1. Rascal was placed in a highchair.

2. A bowl of milk was put in front of him.

3. Rascal reached the milk.

4. Rascal showed excellent manners.

5. The writer's father was amused and petted the raccoon.

249

6. Rascal began eating with the writer and his father every day.

7. The writer offered Rascal a lump of sugar.

8. Rascal "washed" the sugar and it melted away.

9. Rascal looked for the sugar and couldn't figure out what had happened to it.

10. The writer gave Rascal a second sugar lump.

11. Rascal put the lump right into his mouth.

The writer ends the composition by stating the lesson that Rascal has learned. Notice how the writer relates all the events in the composition in a time sequence. He tells about what happens first, what happens next, and so on.

Exercise   **Writing a Narrative or Story**

Go back to Chapter 15, Part 2. Use the way described there for finding a subject based on personal experience. Then write a five-paragraph narrative composition. Follow the Guidelines for the Process of Writing, on pages 84 and 85, and include the three parts listed at the beginning of this chapter. In case you have trouble finding a subject, here are a few suggestions.

1. The day my dog almost lost his happy home
2. Trapped in a _____
3. Learning how to _____
4. Moving day
5. The most memorable birthday I've ever had
6. Stung!
7. Nobody's perfect
8. The time I felt totally alone
9. Opening day at the _____
10. The hardest thing I've ever done

Part 2   The Descriptive Composition

A descriptive composition, like a descriptive paragraph, paints a picture with words. It is made up of several paragraphs. They work together to create a vivid picture in the mind of the reader.

A descriptive composition includes many details. They appeal to one or more of the senses. These details help the reader to see what the writer sees, smell what the writer smells, hear what the writer hears, taste what the writer tastes, and feel what the writer feels. In this lesson we will work only on descriptive compositions that appeal to the sense of sight.

Using Details

Let's look at a composition that paints a word picture of the monster Ubir. The details used are so specific that you could probably draw a good picture of the monster.

UBIR

In the forests of eastern Asia there once lived a monster named Ubir. She was one of the greediest monsters around. Day and night she prowled the forests, gobbling up the unfortunate men and cattle that crossed her path. Ubir was also very, very ugly.

Ubir wasn't especially tall for a monster, but what she lacked in height she made up in width. Her great stomach measured fifteen feet around. Like most of her body, it was covered with flat, fish-like scales. They changed from blue to green with the shifting light.

Only Ubir's head and face were without scales. They were both shiny and hairless and were colored with mud-brown spots. On the sides of Ubir's head were large pointed ears covered with black hair. These ears were certainly large enough to hear anything. The truth of the matter is that Ubir was just a little bit deaf. However, there was nothing wrong with her sight. Her bulging yellow eyes, overhung with fierce black brows, never blinked. They swept from side to side searching for tasty morsels. She would often lower her horny beak to sniff the ground for the scent of food. Whatever food she found went immediately into a huge mouth lined with rows of pointed teeth.

Ubir's body was equipped with several weapons. One was her magnificent but deadly tail. It was long and covered with blue-green body scales. Near its end were a dozen razor-sharp points. One flick of that tail meant death to whatever was in its path. Ubir's fingers, too, were tipped with sharp points. No one ever knew what her toes looked like. Ubir always wore heavy, spiked mountain-climbing boots.

The sight of Ubir was enough to make knees shake and stomachs do flip flops. She was the stuff of nightmares, from the top of her head to the tip of her tail.

The writer begins her composition by giving a few facts about Ubir. She lived in eastern Asia. She was greedy. She ate men and cattle. The writer ends her introductory paragraph by stating that Ubir was very ugly. This makes the reader want to know more about Ubir's appearance. The next three paragraphs supply this information. The second paragraph gives details about Ubir's size, shape, and body covering. The third describes Ubir's head and face. The fourth describes her natural weapons. A topic sentence at the beginning of each paragraph lets the reader know what that paragraph is going to be about.

Following a Logical Order

The writer has arranged the details about Ubir's appearance in a logical order. She has started with the monster's overall size and shape. This a natural place to begin. It's what you usually notice first. She then goes on to Ubir's head and moves down. She describes the monster's ears, eyes, nose, mouth, tail, fingers, and feet. She has arranged the entire composition in top-to-bottom order.

The writer of the next composition has followed a different order. He describes a stage set. He focuses first on the left-hand side of the stage, next on the background, and finally on the right-hand side. This is a natural order. An audience would be likely to examine a set from left to right.

LIFE STAR 101

The set for *Space Dog Saves Life Star 101* was finally finished. The carpenters had pounded the last nail. The painters had finished the last bit of scenery. The furniture movers had shoved everything into place. The curtain hangers had hung the side drapes in perfect pleats. The stage of the J. B. Norton Middle School had been changed into the spaceport and meeting area on Life Star 101.

On the left-hand side of the stage was a large, round space ship. From its shiny silver surface projected six movable observation tubes. A large *D* with an *S* inside it was painted on the top third of the ship.

The backdrop of the set showed the stars and planets surrounding Life Star. Against a background of pale blue were twelve stars —bright silver disks of different sizes. Among the stars floated three planets and their moons. The first planet had a purple-and-white striped surface and seven pale yellow moons. The second planet was bright yellow and had three black moons. The third was different shades of green, blue-green, grass green, and a green so dark it was almost black. It was circled by a large orange moon and by swirls of wispy pink clouds.

The right-hand side of the stage was the meeting area. It was the site of the Life Star peace conference. A white plastic table with six low stools stood ready. At each place was a dish of water. Space Dog's dish was marked with the same *D* and *S* design that was painted on the space ship.

The setting was ready and waiting for the action to begin. **253**

The writer starts this composition by catching your interest. As you read the opening sentences, you probably began to wonder just what the set looks like. In the next three paragraphs the writer tells you.

As he describes the main parts of the set, the writer uses many color words. He uses "shiny silver," "purple-and-white striped," "bright yellow," "blue-green," "grass-green," "green so dark it was almost black," and "wispy pink clouds." These help you, the reader, to form a vivid mental picture of the set.

It's now time for you, the reader, to become you, the writer. In developing a descriptive composition, you'll follow the usual prewriting, writing, and revising steps listed in the Guidelines for the Process of Writing on pages 84 and 85. When you make a list of the ideas and details that you plan to use, be sure to have a clear mental picture of what you want to describe. This will help you remember that you want your readers to see in their minds the same thing that you see in yours. Give special attention to arranging the details according to a logical and natural order.

Exercise Writing a Descriptive Composition

Here are some possible subjects for descriptive compositions. Choose one of the subjects or make up one of your own. Then develop a five-paragraph composition. Follow the Guidelines for the Process of Writing, pages 84 and 85.

1. A veterinarian's office on a busy afternoon
2. A perfect island
3. A recreation room after a party
4. A classroom
5. A shopping center
6. A park after a rainstorm
7. A tree house
8. A junk yard
9. An imaginary character in a story
10. An interesting looking person you have seen

Part 3 The Explanatory Composition

The explanatory composition, like the explanatory paragraph, explains something. There are many different types of explanatory compositions. This lesson focuses on two:

1. Those that explain how something is done

2. Those that state an opinion, with reasons to support that opinion.

The "How" Composition

The "how" composition is a group of paragraphs that explain how to do something. A "how" composition gives step-by-step directions in a time sequence. It tells what to do first, what to do second, and so on.

Here is an example of a "how" composition. It tells how to make candles from old crayons. The directions are clear and specific. You would have no trouble following them if you decided to use your old crayons in this way.

CANDLES FROM CRAYONS

Have you ever wondered what to do with old, half-used crayons? Have you ever needed an inexpensive gift for someone? Here's a solution to both of these problems. You can make candles out of crayons.

Begin by getting your supplies together. To make one candle, you'll need a pound of paraffin, which you can buy at a supermarket; cotton twine or candlewick, which you can get at a hobby store; and crayons. You'll need a one-pint cardboard juice can with a peel top. If the can has a metal rim, you'll have to cut it off. You'll also need a double boiler or a coffee can in a pan of water, a wooden spoon, a pencil or stick, a small metal weight such as a washer, scissors, and potholder mitts.

Next get your paraffin and wick ready. Break the pound of paraffin into chunks. Melt the chunks in the top of a double boiler, over water, or in a coffee can set in water. Do not melt paraffin directly over heat. It may catch fire. After the paraffin has melted, color it by breaking up a crayon and putting the pieces into the hot wax. For a medium shade, use half a crayon to a pound of paraffin. Stir the melting crayon into the paraffin with a wooden spoon. Then cut a piece of cotton twine or candlewick two inches longer than your juice-can mold. Dip the string into the melted paraffin. Set the wick aside to dry. After it dries, tie one end to the center of a pencil or stick. Tie a weight to the other end to keep the wick straight. Place the stick across the top of the mold. Make sure that the wick hangs down into the container.

You're now ready to pour the candle. Using potholder mitts to protect your hands, pour the paraffin mixture into the mold. The wax may splash, so keep your face away. If you want to make a striped candle, fill only part of the mold. Prepare another paraffin mixture using a different color of crayon. Let each layer harden before adding another color. Let the candle cool overnight. Then untie the stick and cut the wick about half an inch above the top of the candle. Peel off the mold.

Step back and admire your creation. You have made an original gift out of something you'd ordinarily have thrown away.

—National Geographic World

The introductory paragraph immediately catches the reader's interest by suggesting a good use for old crayons. The body paragraphs then explain the steps for making a candle in a time sequence. Words like *begin, next, then, now,* and *after* help to move the reader along through the paragraphs. The ending reminds the reader that making candles from crayons is a useful skill.

Exercise **Writing a "How" Composition**

256

Make a list of things that you know how to do well. Choose a subject. Then write a five-paragraph "how" composition. Follow the Guidelines for the Process of Writing on pages 84 and 85.

The "Why" Composition

The introductory paragraph for a "why" composition states an opinion or idea that the writer believes to be true. The writer of the following opening paragraph, for example, believes that students should take part in making the rules for their school.

STUDENTS MAKING RULES

Every school has rules and regulations. In most schools students have to be in their rooms at a set time. Students have to follow lunch room, learning center, and playground rules. Most of the time these rules are made by the school board, the principal, the teachers, and sometimes by a group of parents. I think it would be better for everyone if the students helped to make the rules.

The topic sentence of the paragraph lets you know that the paragraph is about school rules and regulations. The entire paragraph tells you that the composition is about why students should help to make the rules.

Giving Reasons

The body paragraphs give the reasons why the writer believes as she does. Each paragraph develops a different reason. All the sentences in each paragraph help to explain that reason.

Working with the principal and teachers would help the students to see problems from a different point of view. Most students have a hard time understanding the reasons for some rules. They often think that rules are made to keep them from having fun. They forget about reasons like the safety of younger children or getting along better as a group. If students helped to make the rules, they could explain the reasons behind them to their friends and classmates.

257

Students would be more likely to follow rules that they understand and that they had a part in making. The rules would be their rules, not just the teachers' rules or the principal's rules. Therefore, the students would be more likely to see that the rules were followed by everyone.

Most important, by helping to make the school rules, students would learn to accept responsibility for their actions. They would have to think about how the rules they suggested would affect everyone in the school. They would have to decide whether to be for or against suggested rules and to have good reasons for their choices. They would have to answer to all of the students for the success or the failure of the rules they helped to make.

Arranging the Reasons

The writer has given three main reasons to support her opinion:

1. Students would see problems from a different point of view.
2. Students would be more likely to follow rules they helped to make.
3. Students would learn to accept responsibility.

She has arranged these reasons from the least important to the most important. She has then developed each of them into a paragraph.

Summarizing the Reasons

The writer ends the composition by explaining how, if her suggestion were carried out, school would be improved for everyone.

Including students in making rules would be good for the entire school. The students who worked on the rules would be better able to see problems from different points of view. They would be more likely to follow the rules. They would learn to accept responsibility for their actions. This would free up the teachers and the principal to spend time in planning interesting projects or in helping students.

Exercise **Writing a "Why" Composition**

Following are ten opinion statements. Each one could be developed into a "why" composition. Choose one or write an opinion statement of your own. Then write a five-paragraph composition giving reasons to support the opinion. Be sure to follow the Guidelines for the Process of Writing listed on pages 84 and 85.

1. Decisions affecting everyone in a family should be made at a family conference.
2. No one should be allowed to have an exotic pet.
3. Apartment buildings are interesting places to live.
4. Students should help make up school cafeteria menus.
5. Everyone in a family should share in the chores.
6. Everyone should have a private place.
7. Every town should have a curfew.
8. Every child should have to work for an allowance.
9. Every child should have a fixed allowance.
10. Students should have to take part in an after-school activity.

Chapter 17

Using Adjectives

Part 1 What Are Adjectives?

Look at the horse in the picture. Does the sentence below tell you what kind of horse it is?

Brian owns a horse.

Can you tell what kind of horse Brian owns when you read the following sentence?

Brian owns a brown horse with a white blaze on its nose and forehead.

What words are added in the second sentence to tell you which kind of horse Brian owns? *Brown* and *white* make the meaning more exact. They are **adjectives**. Adjectives are words that are used with nouns and pronouns. They are called **modifiers** because they change, or modify, the meaning of the word they go with.

261

Only the adjectives differ in the following sentences. How does the adjective change, or modify, the picture you have in your mind as you read each sentence?

1. Kathy drove along the *crowded* highway.
2. Kathy drove along the *deserted* highway.
3. Kathy drove along the *narrow* highway.
4. Kathy drove along the *bumpy* highway.

> An **adjective** is a word that modifies a noun or pronoun.

One or more adjectives may be used before the noun or pronoun being modified. Very often, when we use two or more adjectives together, we separate them with commas.

The *hot, thick, sticky* topping smothered the ice cream.

Adjectives may also follow the noun or pronoun being modified.

I met Al, *tired* and *hungry*, at the top of the canyon trail.

Some Adjectives Tell What Kind

We use adjectives to describe what we are talking about. They can tell *what kind* of thing we have in mind.

1. Henry wore *furry* gloves and a *colorful* scarf.
2. The alligator's *sharp* teeth are *dangerous* weapons.
3. Lately we have had *warm, rainy* weather.
4. Goldilocks found a *comfortable* bed.

Many adjectives that tell *what kind* are formed by adding an adjective ending to a noun. Here are some examples:

Noun		Adjective Ending		Adjective
rain	+	y	=	rainy
color	+	ful	=	colorful
danger	+	ous	=	dangerous
comfort	+	able	=	comfortable

262

Some other adjective endings are *-less*, *-ible*, and *-al*.

careless driving   *terrible* storms
experimental model

Some Adjectives Tell How Many

We use adjectives to tell *how many* we are talking about.

1. Mr. and Mrs. Ellsworth own *twenty* trucks.
2. Their trucks travel across *several* states.
3. Some trucks have *many* license plates.
4. They have *frequent* repairs but *few* accidents.

Some Adjectives Tell Which Ones

Some adjectives tell *which one* or *which ones* we are talking about.

1. *These* trucks hold nine rooms of furniture.
2. *Those* trucks transport new automobiles.
3. *This* truck is used for hauling coal or dirt.
4. *That* truck is used to tow away wrecks.

Exercises   Using Adjectives

A. Copy these sentences. Draw a line under each adjective that tells *what kind.*

Example: Karen has long, curly hair.

1. Tina complained of stiff knees.
2. Bonnie scraped sticky gum from her shoe.
3. Do you know how to do artificial respiration?
4. An unearthly howl made Rich tremble.
5. These green darts are for Tim.
6. Peculiar rhythmic noises came from the closet.
7. The sky was filled with white, puffy clouds.
8. The boys looked for small starfish.

263

B. Number your paper from 1 to 8. Make two columns. Head one column *Which Ones*. Head the other *How Many*. Find the adjectives in these sentences and write them in the correct column.

Example: Those trees have grown two feet this year.

Which Ones	How Many
those, this	two

1. That light flashed a signal to some men on the shore.
2. Many people prefer this brand of frozen dinners.
3. Look at this odometer now.
4. Mr. Harvey had several boxes of cartridges.
5. Is this saddle for Sara?
6. These cards belong to that game.
7. Janet has used this saw many times.
8. We have ordered several cakes from that bakery.

Part 2   The Articles

The words *a*, *an*, and *the* are called articles. Since they always modify nouns, they are also adjectives.

Use *a* before words beginning with consonant sounds.

a box   *a* hat   *a* horse   *a* moth

Use *an* before words beginning with vowel sounds:

an apple	*an* engineer	*an* island	*an* ostrich	*an* umbrella
an ape	*an* eagle	*an* icicle	*an* overcoat	*an* uncle

Some words begin with a silent *h*. In these words, you do not say the *h* sound. Instead, you begin the word with the vowel sound after the *h*. Therefore, you follow the rule given above, and use *an*:

an honor   *an* hour   *an* honest person

Exercises Using Articles

A. Copy the following sentences. Fill in the blanks with *a* or *an*.

1. I just peeled _____ onion.
2. _____ acrobat could do that.
3. Carlos was riding _____ bicycle.
4. Is that _____ iceberg near the horizon?
5. Can you ride _____ horse?
6. Dennis is known as _____ honest person.
7. Mom's gone to _____ important meeting.
8. Does the car have _____ undercoating to prevent rust?
9. Our national bird is _____ eagle.
10. The boat drifted in _____ aimless pattern.

B. There are twelve nouns below. Write six sentences, using two of the nouns in each sentence. Place an article and another adjective before each noun.

1. man   4. rocks   7. brook   10. stream
2. trees   5. leaves   8. bushes   11. flowers
3. valleys   6. dog   9. mountains 12. path

Part 3 Predicate Adjectives

When an adjective follows a state-of-being verb like *is* or *seemed*, it is part of the predicate. However, it often modifies a noun or pronoun in the subject. Look at these examples.

He is right.   The patient seemed dazed.

When an adjective following a state-of-being verb modifies the subject, it is called a **predicate adjective.**

Exercises **Using Predicate Adjectives**

A. Copy these sentences, putting an adjective in the blank. Draw an arrow from the adjective to the word it modifies.

1. Lemons are _____.
2. Before a test, we are very _____.
3. The boys were _____ after their victory.
4. Every day at noon, I am _____.
5. The sky was _____ this morning.
6. With the new addition, the house will be _____.
7. You are _____ than any other student here.
8. This rose is _____.
9. Ann will be _____ when she sees your present.
10. From far away, the bell sounded _____.

B. Follow directions for Exercise A.

1. The plane to Omaha will be _____.
2. The early settlers were very _____.
3. Your new suit looks _____.
4. That book was _____.
5. The week-old milk smells _____.
6. Without water, the plants will become _____.
7. Vincent's violin sounds _____.
8. This apple tastes _____.

Part 4 Proper Adjectives

266

In this chapter, you have already used many adjectives formed from common nouns, for example, *rainy, dangerous, comfortable.* **Proper adjectives** are adjectives formed from proper nouns.

You know that a proper noun names a particular person, place, or thing. By adding adjective endings to some proper nouns, we change them into proper adjectives. Here are some examples:

Proper Noun	Proper Adjective + Noun Modified
Arthur	Arthurian legend
Britain	British royalty
Japan	Japanese yen
Mexico	Mexican jewelry

Very often a proper name is used as an adjective without the addition of an adjective ending. Here are some examples of the second kind of proper adjective:

Hitchcock thriller   Cinderella story   Ford engine

1. A **proper adjective** is an adjective that has been made from a proper noun.

2. A proper adjective begins with a capital letter.

Exercises   Using Proper Adjectives

A. Number your paper from 1 to 10. Write each proper adjective in these sentences. Capitalize correctly.

1. Is that an irish setter?
2. The austrian ski team won the downhill competition.
3. My sister bought a japanese stereo set.
4. This delicatessen sells polish sausages.
5. When was the alaskan pipeline started?
6. The jewish community is celebrating Rosh Hoshana.
7. We had kentucky fried chicken.
8. The canadian Rockies are higher than the american Rockies.
9. Napoleon's army was defeated by the russian winter.
10. The museum just purchased a picasso painting.

267

B. Follow the directions for Exercise A.

1. When was the gregorian calendar developed?
2. Valerie had a siamese kitten and a persian cat.
3. Cleopatra ruled the egyptian people.
4. I like italian dressing better than french dressing.
5. Lawrence is taking german lessons.
6. My aunt bought some real indian turquoise.
7. Mrs. Haas was a dutch immigrant.
8. It is hard to add roman numerals.
9. The bantu chief greeted the travelers with dignity.
10. Eduardo drove an italian car across the canadian border.

Part 5 Demonstrative Adjectives

Four adjectives that tell which one, or which ones, are *this*, *that*, *these*, and *those*. When they modify nouns or pronouns, they point out specific things.

> *This* cake tastes sweeter than *that* one.
> *These* notebooks cost a quarter each. *Those* notebooks cost a dollar.

This, *that*, *these* and *those* are called the **demonstrative adjectives.** We use *this* and *that* with singular nouns. We use *these* and *those* with plural nouns.

this Frisbee	these Frisbees
that field	those fields

The nouns *kind* and *sort* are singular. Therefore, we say *this kind* and *this sort*. We use *these* and *those* only with the plurals: *these kinds* or *those sorts*.

Using *Those* and *Them*

Those is a word with many uses. It may be used as an adjective:

> Where did you find *those* skates?

Those may also be used as a pronoun. As a pronoun it can be the subject of a verb or it can be an object.

Those are my books. (subject)

We'll clean these shelves today. Leave *those* for tomorrow.
(object of verb)

Them is always an object pronoun. It is never used as an adjective. As a pronoun, it is never used in the subject.

Right: My uncle gave me *those* stamps.

Right: *Those* are my stamps. He gave *them* to me.

Exercises   Using Demonstrative Adjectives and *Them*

A. Number your paper from 1 to 10. Write the correct pronoun.

1. Bill needs (that, those) kind of car to finish his train set.
2. (Them, Those) flowers across the street are snapdragons.
3. Do you like (this, these) kind of coat?
4. (These, Them) girls with me are my cousins.
5. (Those, These) swimming lessons last summer were fun.
6. Lois often buys (them, these) sorts of rings.
7. Can you see (those, them) geese flying south?
8. I think (those, them) kinds of cookies are the best.
9. These cookies have chopped walnuts in (those, them).
10. (Them, These) illustrations are by Wanda Gag.

B. Copy these sentences. Use *them* or *those* in the blanks.

1. You can't ask _____ for all _____ labels.
2. Are _____ posters dry yet?
3. Tell _____ to come back tomorrow.
4. _____ slacks fit me better than these.
5. Joan took the boxes and painted _____.
6. Where did you get all _____ old magazines?
7. _____ missions were built by the Spaniards.
8. I want those posters. How much do you charge for _____?

269

Part 6 Making Comparisons with Adjectives

A bear is big. An elephant is big. A dinosaur was big.

Are all three animals the same size? Certainly, the answer is no. If we want to say the animals are of different sizes, will the word *big* do the job? Again, the answer is no. However, we can change the word *big* so that it will show the differences in the group.

We use the word *bigger* to compare two persons or things.

An elephant is *bigger* than a bear.
A dinosaur was *bigger* than a bear.

We call *bigger* the **comparative form** of *big*.

We use *biggest* to compare three or more persons or things.

A dinosaur was the *biggest* of the three.
A dinosaur was the *biggest* of all animals.

We call *biggest* the **superlative form** of *big*.

> Use the **comparative form** of an adjective to compare *two* things.
>
> Between the history and spelling tests, the history test was harder.
>
> Use the **superlative form** of an adjective when you are concerned with *three or more* things.
>
> The math exam was the hardest test of all.

Usually, we form the comparative form of a short adjective by adding *-er*, and the superlative form by adding *-est*.

270

Adjective	Comparative Form	Superlative Form
long	longer	longest
old	older	oldest
funny	funnier	funniest

For longer adjectives, we form the comparative by using the word *more*, and the superlative by using the word *most*.

Adjective	Comparative Form	Superlative Form
difficult	more difficult	most difficult
noticeable	more noticeable	most noticeable
careful	more careful	most careful

Use only one form of comparison at a time. Do not use *more* and *-er* with the same word, or *most* and *-est* with the same word.

Wrong: This pillow is *more softer* than that one.
Right: This pillow is *softer* than that one.

Wrong: That painting is the *most prettiest* of all.
Right: That painting is the *prettiest* of all.

The Forms of *Good* and *Bad*

A few adjectives do not change their forms by adding *-er* or *-est*. The comparative and superlative forms of the adjectives are completely new words. Here are two important ones to remember:

good   better   best   bad   worse   worst

Exercise   Making Comparisons with Adjectives

Choose the correct form of the adjective from the parentheses.

1. Claire is the (carefulest, most careful) bike rider I know.
2. Tomorrow will be (colder, more colder) than today.
3. Bill scored the (more, most) goals of all.
4. I was wearing my (bestest, best) jeans.
5. The Sky Harbor weather is (badder, worse) than ours.
6. Have you heard the (latest, most late) news?
7. In our class, Todd sold the (more, most) tickets.
8. Cindy has the (most, mostest) beautiful guitar.
9. The snow was (worse, worser) in the parking lot.
10. That is the (best, better) picture in the whole book.

271

Sentence Patterns   The N LV Adj Pattern

There are three parts to sentences that have the **N LV Adj pattern**. The N stands for the subject noun. *LV* stands for a linking verb. *Adj.* stands for the predicate adjective. Each of the sentences in the following chart is in the N LV Adj pattern.

N	LV	Adj
Peter	is	friendly.
The water	looks	murky.
Evonne	was	sunburned.
Your voice	sounds	hoarse.
This melon	tastes	sweet.

Exercises   The N LV Adj Pattern

A. Make a chart like the one above. Label the three columns *N, LV,* and *Adj.* Write these sentences on the chart.

1. Lottie seems cautious.
2. This ice is slippery.
3. Cherry pie is delicious.
4. Skydivers are adventurous.
5. Jeff seemed lucky.
6. The Cubs were victorious.
7. The sky looked gloomy.
8. My father will be late.

B. Make a chart like the one below. Complete each sentence in the N LV Adj pattern.

N	LV	Adj
1. _____	is	cheerful.
2. The snow	became	_____.
3. Clowns	look	_____.
4. The Soos	_____	busy.
5. _____	was	_____.

C. Make a chart of your own. Label the columns *N, LV,* and *Adj.* Write five sentences in the N LV Adj pattern.

272

Reinforcement Exercises—Review

Using Adjectives

A. Using Adjectives

Number your paper from 1 to 10. Make three columns. Head them *What Kind, How Many,* and *Which Ones.* Find the adjectives in these sentences and write each in the correct column.

1. That lake has a sandy beach.
2. There are nine planets in the solar system.
3. Those coins fell out of my back pocket.
4. For several miles, we drove in dense, soupy fog.
5. That heavy rain saved many farmers.
6. Babe Zaharias won several important tournaments.
7. These four months are named for ancient gods.
8. Strong west winds bent those trees.
9. During the evening, Kim killed twenty mosquitoes.
10. That experimental model made many trial flights.

B. Using Articles

Copy the following sentences. Fill in the blanks with *a* or *an.*

1. Mary Poppins always carried _____ umbrella.
2. I feel a draft from _____ open window.
3. _____ huge crowd turned out for the fireworks.
4. A figure with eight sides is _____ octagon.
5. The governor's visit is _____ honor for our school.
6. The lab did _____ analysis of the patient's blood sample.
7. This fairy tale is about _____ enchanted princess.
8. Evelyn saw _____ cardinal in her back yard.

273

9. That terrible shipwreck was caused by _____ iceberg.

10. You will never find _____ mastodon in the zoo.

C. Using Predicate Adjectives

Copy these sentences, putting an adjective in the blank. Draw an arrow from the adjective to the word it modifies.

1. That pie was _____.
2. The water under the ice is _____.
3. Most of your answers are _____.
4. The ambulance siren sounded _____.
5. That radio station is not _____.
6. After the parade, the streets were _____.
7. Some toothpicks are _____.
8. Courtney will look very _____ on those stilts.
9. This candy is too _____.
10. The toaster is _____, but it still works.

D. Using Proper Adjectives

Number your paper from 1 to 10. Write each proper adjective in these sentences. Capitalize correctly.

1. Tomorrow is the japanese firefly festival.
2. Those long loaves are french bread.
3. Vanya has a strong russian accent.
4. My favorite paintings are rembrandt portraits.
5. We had chinese chop suey at the restaurant.
6. Some african countries are very small.
7. The spanish language is spoken in latin american countries.
8. "The Entertainer" is a scott joplin rag.
9. Those gloves are italian imports.
10. They were weighing california oranges.

274

E. Using Demonstrative Adjectives

Number your paper from 1 to 10. Choose the correct pronoun from the parentheses. Write the correct pronoun.

1. Mr. Redlin gave the students' papers back to (those, them).
2. Did Alice find (them, those) missing keys?
3. Many people like (that, those) kind of music.
4. (Those, Them) melons are almost ripe.
5. Dan grew (this, these) sort of peppers in his garden.
6. Joanne listened to (those, them) records all afternoon.
7. These windows look streaked. I'll wash (those, them) again.
8. (That, Those) kinds of shoes are not good for hiking.
9. Barbara will buy (those, them) skates with her savings.
10. I can eat all (them, those) pieces of pizza.

F. Making Comparisons with Adjectives

Number your paper from 1 to 10. Choose the correct form of the adjective from the parentheses. Write it.

1. Of the two sisters, Jean sings the (better, best).
2. Elena is the (goodest, best) swimmer on the team.
3. Is Bill (stronger, strongest) than you?
4. Mr. Jensen is the (most honest, most honestest) man I know.
5. This is the (better, best) of the three shows.
6. My alarm clock has a (more loud, louder) buzzer than yours.
7. You should use a (lighter, more light) bowling ball than that one.
8. Teresa's ice skates are (newer, more new) than mine.
9. Sean has the (baddest, worst) temper in the family.
10. Mother bought the (softer, softest) pillows she could find.

275

Chapter 18

Using Adverbs

Part 1 What Are Adverbs?

Adjectives modify nouns and pronouns. **Adverbs** modify verbs, adjectives, and other adverbs.

Adverbs Modify Verbs

Jo kneeled.

How? Jo kneeled *carefully*.

Where? Jo kneeled *outside*.

When? Jo kneeled *immediately*.

Adverbs Modify Adjectives

That is a bright light.

How bright? That is a *very* bright light.

This stunt is dangerous.

How dangerous? This stunt is *too* dangerous.

277

Adverbs Modify Other Adverbs

John dances well.

How well?　John dances *extremely* well.

The horse ran away.

To what extent?　The horse ran *far* away.

As the above examples show, adverbs usually tell *how, when, where*, or *how much* about the words they modify. If you are not sure whether a word is an adverb, ask yourself if it answers one of these questions. Generally, an adverb that modifies an adjective or another adverb comes before the word it modifies, as in *very bright* or *extremely well.* An adverb that modifies a verb may often be placed in more than one position in the sentence: *He watched TV often. Often he watched TV. He often watched TV.*

Many adverbs are formed by adding -ly to an adjective:

bad — badly　　slow — slowly　　careful — carefully
quick — quickly　happy — happily　suspicious — suspiciously

> An **adverb** is a word that modifies a verb, an adjective or another adverb.

Exercises　Finding and Using Adverbs

A. Number from 1 to 20. Copy each adverb below. Write *how, where, when,* or *to what extent* to show what each adverb tells.

1. angrily	6. quite	11. well	16. soon
2. meekly	7. now	12. almost	17. often
3. slowly	8. too	13. always	18. afterward
4. quickly	9. never	14. very	19. sometimes
5. outside	10. ever	15. there	20. early

B. Number your paper from 1 to 10. Write every adverb used in each sentence.

1. Roberto was there yesterday.
2. Suddenly Jill looked up.
3. Soon the sun came out.
4. Because of his cold, Dennis can hardly talk.
5. When the fire alarm rang, the class filed outside quickly.
6. Fortunately I didn't slide on the ice too often.
7. Those two boys are never sleepy.
8. The explosion happened so quickly.
9. Did you ever hear Louisa play?
10. Soon afterward the mist cleared.

Part 2 Making Comparisons with Adverbs

Since adverbs, like adjectives, are words that describe, they can be changed to comparative and superlative forms. You use the **comparative form** when you consider two persons or things:

Jack ran *faster* than the giant.

You use the **superlative form** when you consider three or more persons or things:

The cheetah runs the *fastest* of all animals.

The comparative and superlative forms of adverbs are formed in three different ways.

1. Some short adverbs add -*er* for the comparative and -*est* for the superlative.

Adverb	Comparative Form	Superlative Form
fast	faster	fastest
hard	harder	hardest

2. Most adverbs that end in *-ly* form the comparative with the word *more*. They form the superlative with the word *most*.

Adverb	Comparative Form	Superlative Form
easily	more easily	most easily
carefully	more carefully	most carefully

3. Some adverbs make their comparative and superlative forms by complete word changes.

Adverb	Comparative Form	Superlative Form
well	better	best
much	more	most
little	less	least
badly	worse	worst

Exercises **Making Comparisons with Adverbs**

A. Number your paper from 1 to 12. Make three columns. Copy the words below in the first column. Write the comparative form in the second column and the superlative in the third.

1. often
2. heavily
3. peacefully
4. carefully
5. quickly
6. well
7. easily
8. slowly
9. badly
10. early
11. strongly
12. soon

B. Number from 1 to 10. Choose the right word from the parentheses. Write it on your paper.

1. Sheila pitches (most fast, fastest) when the pressure is greatest.

280

2. Gayle skates (more carefully, most carefully) than Kenneth.
3. Of these two kinds of cookies, I like this kind (better, best).
4. The swift flies (more rapidly, most rapidly) of all the birds.

5. That stunt driver is driving (more recklessly, most recklessly) than ever before.

6. This lid came off (more easily, most easily) of all.

7. Push the car (more hard, harder) if you want to get it out of the snowbank.

8. I did (worse, more badly) than you in the test.

9. Power brakes will stop a car (more quickly, quicklier) than standard brakes.

10. Nora is the (less, least) noisy person in the room.

Part 3 Adjective or Adverb?

Some adverbs are made by adding -ly to an adjective:

Adjective	Adverb
careful	carefully
happy	happily

Because these words are so much alike, it is sometimes hard to know whether to use the adjective or adverb form. Which would you say?

Anita worked very *careful*.
Anita worked very *carefully*.

In this example, *carefully* is right. It tells *how* Anita worked. It goes with, or modifies, *worked*, which is a verb. *Carefully* is the adverb.

Which of these two sentences would you use?

Snow Treasure is a *real* good book.
Snow Treasure is a *really* good book.

You want the word you choose to modify *good*, an adjective. Therefore you need an adverb. *Really* is the adverb.

Remember:

Adjectives tell *which one, how many,* or *what kind* about nouns and pronouns.

Adverbs tell *how, when, where,* or *to what extent* about verbs, adjectives, and other adverbs.

Exercise **Choosing the Right Word**

Number from 1 to 10. Choose the right modifier, and write it on your paper. Next write the word it modifies. Then write *Adjective* or *Adverb* to show how the modifier is used.

Example: The choir sang (good, well).

Well, sang, adverb.

1. Karen didn't look (really, real) sure.
2. Dan pitched (wild, wildly).
3. The team felt (bad, badly) about losing the game.
4. The actor sang too (poor, poorly) to get the role.
5. The barn looked (dim, dimly) in the moonlight.
6. The edge of the paper was (real, really) crooked.
7. I go to the library (regularly, regular) on Friday.
8. Melissa appeared (proud, proudly).
9. The teams were matched fairly (even, evenly).
10. Our telephone rang (promptly, prompt) at ten.

Using *Good* and *Well*

The words *good* and *well* are often confused. They form their comparative and superlative forms in exactly the same way:

good   better   best
well   better   best

Good is always an adjective that describes a noun or pronoun. It is never used as an adverb.

You are a good student. (*Good* modifies *student*.)

That cake looks good.
(*Looks* is used as a linking verb here, so *good* modifies *cake*.)

Well is an adjective when it describes a noun or pronoun and means healthy.

If you take your medicine, you will be well. (*Well* modifies *you*.)

I feel well. (*Feel* is a linking verb here, so *well* modifies *I*.)

Well is an adverb when it modifies a verb, adverb, or adjective, and tells *how* something is done.

You cook well. (*Well* modifies *cook*).

Exercise **Using *Good* and *Well* Correctly**

Number your paper from 1 to 10. Write *Adjective* or *Adverb* to tell how each word in italics is used. Then write the word or words that the word in italics modifies.

Example: Carey is the *best* jumper in our room.

Adjective, modifies *jumper*

1. The witness had a *good* look at the robber.
2. In training camp, the football players eat *well*.
3. Ted takes *good* care of his kitten.
4. Can you see *better* without sunglasses?
5. Dana gave the *best* answer.
6. These shoes fit me *best*.
7. Kelly is *good* at tennis.
8. You are *better* at soccer than I am.
9. Andy writes *good* reports.
10. Sue speaks Spanish quite *well*.

Reinforcement Exercises—Review

Using Adverbs

A. Finding and Using Adverbs

Number your paper from 1 to 10. Write all the adverbs used in these sentences.

1. The mail has already arrived.
2. Lately the creek has been very low.
3. The bowl of onion dip was almost empty.
4. The toast popped up quickly.
5. We are almost sure to win.
6. The rain came down hard.
7. Then the tall man turned around.
8. The letter was obviously addressed incorrectly.
9. The solution was perfectly simple.
10. The terribly loud claps of thunder frightened the baby.

B. Making Comparisons with Adverbs

Number from 1 to 10. Choose the right word from the parentheses. Write it on your paper.

1. Tip performs (worse, worst) than the other dog in the act.
2. Sarah runs (faster, more faster) than any other girl here.
3. The wind blew more and more (fiercely, fiercer).
4. The pigeon pecked at the bell more (cautiously, cautious).
5. Do you feel (weller, better) than yesterday?
6. Of the two players, Chico works (harder, the hardest) to improve.
7. A smart detective could solve that mystery (easier, easily).
8. Tina is the (less, least) selfish person I know.

9. On this path you have to go (more slowly, slowlier) to avoid chuckholes.

10. Among all the songbirds, which one sings (more sweetly, most sweetly)?

C. Choosing the Right Word

Number from 1 to 10. Choose the right modifier, and write it on your paper. Next write the word it modifies. Then write *Adjective* or *Adverb* to show how the modifier is used.

Example: The soloist sang very (soft, softly).

softly, sang, adverb

1. The actors and actresses knew their parts (perfect, perfectly).
2. The goal line was drawn (uneven, unevenly) across the field.
3. That hailstorm started very (sudden, suddenly).
4. Was the baby sleeping (sound, soundly)?
5. Betsy can spell (well, good).
6. The mountains are (real, really) gigantic.
7. Red Hawk and his brothers work (good, well) as a team.
8. After eating five hot dogs, Dale didn't feel too (good, well).
9. Lillian copied the instructions (careful, carefully).
10. Mr. Steven's lesson was very (good, well).

Chapter 19

Using Prepositions and Conjunctions

Earlier chapters of this book have discussed **nouns, verbs, pronouns, adjectives,** and **adverbs**. A word may be placed in one of these groups according to its use in a sentence.

Besides the five groups listed above, there are three other classifications of words. They are **prepositions, conjunctions,** and **interjections**. All together, these eight groups are called the **parts of speech**. Grouping our words in this way makes it easier to study them and the rules for using them.

This chapter discusses prepositions and conjunctions. These are words that do not have meaning in themselves. They are used only to connect other words in a sentence. They relate other words in a sentence to each other.

287

Part 1　What Are Prepositions?

Read these sentences and notice what is changed:

I took a photo of the boys.
I took a photo of the class.
I took a photo of the evening sky.

In these sentences, the subject, verb, and object remain the same: *I took a photo.* However, your understanding of the photo changes as the words following *photo* change: photo *of the boys*; photo *of the class*; photo *of the evening sky*.

Each of these phrases begins with the word *of*. *Of* relates the words following it (*boys, class, sky*) to the word before it, *photo*. The phrase beginning with *of* modifies *photo*, telling you *what kind* of photo.

The word *of* is a preposition. The noun or pronoun following a preposition is called the **object of the preposition**. A preposition is a word that stands before its object and shows a relationship between that object and another word in the sentence.

The pencil is near the notebook.
The pencil is on the notebook.
The pencil is inside the notebook.
The pencil is under the notebook.

The prepositions *near, on, inside,* and *under* give four different ways of relating the notebook to the pencil.

288

A **preposition** is a word that relates its object to some other word in the sentence.

Here is a list of words we often use as prepositions:

about	before	down	of	to
above	behind	during	off	toward
across	below	for	on	under
after	beneath	from	onto	underneath
against	beside	in	out	until
along	between	inside	outside	up
among	beyond	into	over	upon
around	but (except)	like	past	with
at	by	near	through	without

Exercises — Finding Prepositions

A. Number your paper from 1 to 10. Write the preposition in each of the following sentences.

1. Jeff opened his book to the index.
2. There is gum stuck on my shoe.
3. Under the new rules, our team can't compete.
4. This portrait of George Washington is two hundred years old.
5. Louisa May Alcott wrote about her own times.
6. All the cans under that sign are dented.
7. Mom's tire was sliced by some broken glass.
8. The Plains Indians depended primarily upon the buffalo.
9. The pinch hitter drove the ball deep into left field.
10. Everybody in my family has blue eyes.

B. Complete the sentences that follow. How many different prepositions can you find for each blank space? You may refer to the list above. Write all the prepositions that will make sense.

Example: Pick up the ball _____ the table.
on, under, beside, behind

1. B.J.'s dog was playing _____ the house.
2. Cornelia heard a strange noise _____ the hall.

3. A flock of birds flew _____ the river.
4. Who put the butter _____ the oven?
5. An American flag flew _____ the house.
6. We found these coins _____ the bookcase.

Part 2 Objects of Prepositions

Using Nouns as Objects of Prepositions

You have seen that nouns may be used as subjects or objects of verbs. You will now study nouns used as objects of prepositions. Here are some examples of nouns used as objects of prepositions:

The Indians pitched their tents near the *river*.
Micky left his gym shoes in his *locker*.
The winning run was scored by *Bonita*.
The movie was about the *arrival* of *aliens* on *earth*.

Exercise **Finding Nouns Used as Objects of Prepositions**

Number from 1 to 10. Head one column *Preposition* and another *Object.* For each sentence write the preposition and its object.

1. Kathy cleared the dishes from the table.
2. These Civil War photographs are by Matthew Brady.
3. Nobody in that movie is well known.
4. Elizabeth Blackwell began the study of medicine here.
5. The new couch will be delivered before Friday.
6. The temperature went below the freezing point last night.
7. Around the Christmas tree were piled numerous presents.
8. Later that year, gold was discovered in California.
9. The lid on this jar won't budge.
10. The football sailed over the goal posts.

Using Pronouns as Objects of Prepositions

When a pronoun is used as the object of a preposition, its object form must be used. The object forms are these:

me   us   you   him   her   it   them

Examples: The prize was awarded *to us.*
            Was there a message *for me?*
            Laura's mother was looking *for her.*

Using Pronouns in Compound Objects

You will probably make few mistakes in using the object form of a pronoun as the object of a preposition. But you may become confused when the object of a preposition is compound.

Simple Object	Compound Object
Play with *her.*	Play with *Darren* and *her.*
We stood near *him.*	We stood near *Jackie* and *him.*
Give that to *me.*	Give that to *her* and *me.*

If you are not sure which form to use, say the sentence with the pronoun alone following the preposition. Then say the complete sentence.

Example: We're waiting for James and (she, her).
           We're waiting for *her.*
           We're waiting for James and *her.*

Using *Between* and *Among*

We use *between* when we speak of two persons or things. We use *among* when we speak of three or more. Here are examples:

Choose *between* these two programs.
The next game is *between* the Jefferson High team and us.
We will divide the jobs *among* Nancy, you, and me.

291

Exercises   Using Pronouns as Objects of Prepositions

A. Choose the correct pronoun from the two given in parentheses. Write it with the preposition.

> Example: The villain shot at Marshall Dillon and (he, him).
>
> at him

1. The coach called on Leo and (I, me).
2. The roof over Marcia and (them, they) started to leak.
3. Vote for one person among Loretta, Jorge, and (she, her).
4. Will you sit beside your mother and (me, I)?
5. The car traveling behind Beverly and (us, we) broke down.
6. A firecracker exploded near Timothy and (we, us).
7. My advice to Norita and (him, he) was ignored.
8. The howling of wolves came from all around Thompson and (they, them).
9. The album by James Taylor and (her, she) went on sale today.
10. The rivalry between Ohio State and (them, they) started years ago.

B. Follow the directions for Exercise A.

1. On your cue, turn toward Mr. Bennett and (she, her).
2. As Paula hurried past Brian and (him, he), she tripped.
3. Miss Washington was looking right at Jason and (I, me).
4. The softball championship will be between the Blues and (we, us).
5. Terrence's kite flew above the other boys and (he, him).
6. That car almost bumped into Gayle and (they, them).
7. I ordered a cheese and mushroom pizza to be split among Susan, me, and (her, she).
8. Everyone but Peter and (us, we) has already had a turn.
9. The paper carried an article about the marching band and (they, them).
10. My pet duck likes to waddle after my friends and (I, me).

Part 3 Using Prepositional Phrases

A prepositional phrase is a group of words that begins with a preposition and ends with its object. Words that modify the object are part of the phrase.

Mary Kay's house is *on the corner*.

We rode *in an old, broken-down bus*.

The prepositional phrases in these sentences are *on the corner* and *in an old, broken-down bus*.

If a preposition has a compound object, all the parts of the object are included in the prepositional phrase.

Weeds grew *in the lawn, the flower garden, and the vegetable garden*.

293

Exercises Finding the Prepositional Phrases

A. Number your paper from 1 to 10. Write all the prepositional phrases in each of the following sentences.

Example: The yarn was stuck to the paper with glue.

to the paper, with glue

1. The doll beside the lamp has a dress with red buttons.
2. Everybody in the classroom could hear the accident down the street.
3. Draw a line under the word that begins with a vowel.
4. Maria and her little brother played on the swings for hours.
5. Donald plays clarinet in the orchestra at school.
6. The acrobat fell from the tightrope stretched between two buildings.
7. Mary Ann waited near the school door until four o'clock.
8. Alone in the room, Shawn listened to his stereo.
9. The apartment across the hall has been empty for a month.
10. Mother hung a clock with a flower design above the door.

B. Follow the directions for Exercise A.

1. During its journey, the space probe will travel past Mars, Jupiter, and Saturn.
2. Rosa tied a ribbon around the present for her cousin.
3. The team from El Paso plays against us before Thanksgiving.
4. Janet finished her painting of the willow trees along the river.
5. Tell me about the characters in the soap opera.
6. After the hurricane, the river spilled over its banks and the nearby streets.
7. The squirrel ran up the maple tree outside my window.
8. You may choose among the last three dinners on the menu.
9. Dave shopped at the drugstore beside the restaurant.
10. The child climbed onto the table and knocked a plate to the floor.

Part 4 Preposition or Adverb?

Several words that are used as prepositions are also used as adverbs. Some examples are *up*, *down*, *around*, *in*, and *out*.

We looked *up*. (adverb)
We looked *up* the chimney. (preposition)

The children ran *around*. (adverb)
The children ran *around* the track. (preposition)

If you aren't sure whether a word is an adverb or a preposition, look at how it is used. If it begins a phrase, it is probably a preposition. If it is used alone, it is probably an adverb.

Exercise Finding Prepositions and Adverbs

In each pair of sentences that follows, one word is used both as an adverb and as a preposition. Number your paper from 1 to 10. After each number, write *a*. and *b*. After each letter, write the word that is used two ways in the two sentences. Then write the way the word was used in that sentence.

Example: a. Look out!   b. Look out the window.

a. out, adverb   b. out, preposition

1. a. There was litter all around the store.   b. There was litter all around.
2. a. Don't come near!   b. Don't come near the cliff!
3. a. Can you get past the barrier?   b. Can that big Cadillac get past?
4. a. Those cans should be stored underneath the cabinet. b. Those cans should be stored underneath.
5. a. Miguel will soon be coming along.   b. Miguel is coming along the path.
6. a. Please stand by.   b. Please stand by the window.

7. a. Above the party room, the lights burned brightly.
b. Above, the lights burned brightly.

8. a. Two skaters fell through.   b. Two skaters fell through the ice.

9. a. We've met before today.   b. We've met before.

10. a. Puffs of white smoke drifted up.   b. White smoke drifted up the chimney.

Part 5   What Are Conjunctions?

How is the word *and* used in each of these sentences?

A. The bird *and* the butterfly flew over the fence.
B. Allen's puppy barked loudly *and* chased the squirrel.
C. Yastrzemski hit a double *and* two singles in the game.

Did you see that in each sentence, *and* connected words or groups of words? Did you notice that those words or groups of words were of the same type? In Example A, two subjects were joined. In B, two predicates were joined. In C, *and* connected two objects of the verb.

We call *and* a conjunction.

296

> A **conjunction** is a word that connects words or groups of words.

Two other conjunctions that are often used are *but* and *or*. Like *and*, they may be used to connect sentence parts.

Andrew *or* Ginny will bring the potato chips. (compound subject)
The forward shot for the basket *but* missed it. (compound predicate)
Buy some raisin bread *or* some sweet rolls. (compound direct object)
The package was bulky *but* light. (compound predicate adjective)
The orchestra performed for the faculty *and* parents.
(compound object of a preposition)

Exercises Using Conjunctions

A. Number your paper from 1 to 10. In each sentence there is a compound subject, a compound predicate, or a compound object. Write which of the three you find. Write the compound subject, predicate, or object with its conjunction. Underline the conjunction.

Example: The Mets survived that season and gradually improved.

compound predicate—survived that season <u>and</u> gradually improved

1. Tecumseh and his brother led their forces against the U.S. Army.
2. For breakfast, Lorraine likes poached eggs or oatmeal.
3. The wind shook the roof and whistled down the chimney.
4. Glue the string and the toothpicks to the cardboard.
5. Our neighbor's TV and our stereo were stolen last night.
6. Gerald takes piano lessons but doesn't practice.
7. The puppy yawned and shook himself.
8. Football and soccer are Lennie's favorite sports.
9. Trudy splashed Doug and me with her paint.
10. The snow and ice made the roads impassable.

297

B. Write sentences with compound subjects, predicates, or objects as the directions ask. Use *and, but,* or *or.*

Example: Compound direct object. Use a noun and a pronoun.

Please take Amy and me to the library.

1. Compound subject. Use two nouns.
2. Compound predicate.
3. Compound direct object. Use two nouns.
4. Compound subject. Use a noun and a pronoun.
5. Compound direct object. Use two pronouns.
6. Compound object of preposition. Use two nouns.

Part 6 Using Conjunctions To Combine Sentences

The conjunctions *and, but,* and *or* can do more than connect parts of sentences. Sometimes they can combine whole sentences.

Sentences combined by *and, but,* or *or* must express ideas that are closely related. Here are some examples that use conjunctions correctly to combine sentences:

The rain started, *and* everyone ran for cover.
We wanted another ride on the Double Loop, *but* the line was too long.
The princess had to guess the little man's name, *or* he would take her first-born child.

Notice that a comma is used at the end of the first sentence, before the conjunction. The comma alerts the reader to the end of one idea and prepares him or her for a second idea. This makes it easier to understand the long sentence. You may leave out the comma only when the two sentences that you join are very short.

Sit down and I'll help you.

Exercises   Combining Sentences

A. In six of the following sentences, conjunctions are used to combine sentences. Commas are needed. In the others, they combine parts of sentences. Commas are not needed. Number your paper from 1 to 10. If the conjunction in an example joins two sentences, copy that example and put in the comma. If the conjunction joins parts of sentences, write *Correct.*

1. The day was warm but the old woman wore a heavy sweater.
2. Margaret and Hal went to the park.
3. Gloria is on a diet and she won't eat candy.
4. Phil must put his dog on a leash or it will run away.
5. For my partner, I want Beverly or Wanda.
6. Dominic ordered a hamburger and a cola for lunch.
7. We might spend a few days at Niagara Falls or we might camp at the Finger Lakes.
8. The classroom window was open and a bee flew inside.
9. The grandfather clock in the hall and the alarm clock in my room stopped this morning.
10. This suit was expensive but I can use it for a long time.

B. Rewrite the following sentences, combining each pair with *and, but,* or *or.* Choose the conjunction you think is best. Use commas where needed.

1. The yard is covered with leaves. I have to rake them.
2. Jerry might play centerfield. He might pitch.
3. Deanna got up late. She missed the bus.
4. The window isn't open. I feel a draft.
5. Harriet would have come on time. She would have told us that she would be late.
6. The wind was high. The forest fire spread quickly.
7. Ramon worked hard all day. He didn't finish cleaning the basement.
8. Lena called the office. There was no answer.

Part 7 Avoiding Run-on Sentences

Often students combine sentences that do not belong together. When you combine sentences that are not related, you form a **run-on sentence.** Here is an example:

I visited my cousin he is sixteen years old.

There are two complete and separate ideas in this sentence. They should be in two separate sentences:

I visited my cousin. He is sixteen years old.

When you are writing, be careful to use only one complete idea in each sentence. Mark the end of each idea with a period, question mark, or exclamation point. Begin each new idea with a capital letter.

Exercises   Avoiding Run-On Sentences

A. Six of the following sentences are run-on sentences. Four are correct. Number your paper from 1 to 10. For each sentence write either *Run-on* or *Correct.*

1. We had art class today we worked with chalk.
2. All of the books in that part of the library are nonfiction.
3. Lou and Bruce went to the game there was a long line.
4. May I use your scissors I lost mine.
5. Scientists are developing ways to predict earthquakes.
6. Brazil is a large country people speak Portuguese there.
7. Terry has his own calculator he got it for his birthday.
8. During colonial times, children went to school for only a few years.
9. Valerie and Susan took lessons in ballet and tap dancing.
10. Anita got an A on the science test she had studied for it all weekend.

B. Four of the following sentences are correct. Six are run-on sentences. Number your paper from 1 to 10. If the sentence is correct as it is, write *Correct.* If it is a run-on, rewrite the sentence as two sentences, with correct capitalization and punctuation.

1. John bought a sandwich it had beef, pickles, and tomatoes in it.
2. Last summer I went swimming it's too cold now.
3. Balboa discovered the Pacific Ocean and claimed it for Spain.
4. Betsy has a garden she grows flowers.
5. The strong wind across the deck made my eyes water.
6. Have you ever read this book by Madeleine L'Engle I like it.
7. Tabitha kept careful records of all her experiments.
8. Two companies of firemen fought the fire it was on my street.
9. Edith and her family visited Idaho they went in a camper.
10. Bill "Bojangles" Robinson was a popular dancer and appeared in movies.

C. The following book report is one long run-on sentence. Break it into shorter sentences. Write them, using correct punctuation.

Carlo Collodi wrote a book about a wooden puppet named Pinocchio Pinocchio acts like a real boy he promises to be good but forgets his promise he runs away from home and gets into trouble there is an exciting ending to the story you will enjoy reading it.

Part 8   Using Words as Different Parts of Speech

In Part 4 of this chapter, you learned that the same word could be used as either an adverb or a preposition. For example, *up* is an adverb in *Come up* and a preposition in *Come up the ladder*.

Other words also may be used as several different parts of speech. For example, the word *book* may be used in these three ways:

Used as a noun

This is my English *book*.

Used as a verb

The officer will *book* the suspect.

Used as an adjective

Trudy gave a *book* report in class today.

When a word is used as a certain part of speech, it follows the rules for that part of speech. For example, when you use *book* as a noun, you form the plural by adding -*s*: *books*. When you use it as a verb, you form the past tense by adding -*ed*: *booked*.

There is only one sure way to decide what part of speech a word is. You must see how the word is used in the sentence. Here are several examples:

The farmer will *plant* the seedlings next spring.

In this sentence, *plant* means an action. Also, the helping verb *will* comes just before it. We can be sure it is used as a verb.

The *plant* grows best in light, sandy soil.

Here, *plant* is the name of a thing. It is used as a noun.

My father is a *plant* foreman.

In this sentence, *plant* tells *what kind* of foreman. It modifies a noun, so it is used as an adjective.

I feel very *well*.

Here, *well* modifies the pronoun *I*. It is used as an adjective.

You skate very *well*.

Now, *well* modifies the verb *skate*. It is used as an adverb.

Exercise Telling the Part of Speech

In each pair of sentences that follows, one word is used as two different parts of speech. Number your paper from 1 to 10. After each number, write *a.* and *b.* After each letter, write the word in italics and tell how it is used. It may be a *noun, verb, adjective, adverb,* or *preposition.*

Example: a. Open a *can* of beans. b. My mother *cans* tomatoes.

a. can, noun b. cans, verb

1. a. The class president *chaired* the meeting. b. This *chair* is too hard.

2. a. A lyric soprano sings *high* notes. b. The team's fortunes have reached a new *high.*

3. a. My family is moving to a new *house.* b. The university will *house* the visiting athletes in a dormitory.

4. a. Vince went *outside* for a walk. b. We saw several deer *outside* the cabin.

5. a. Ms. Taylor made a *pencil* sketch of the waterfall. b. I have to sharpen my *pencil.*

6. a. Carla built a roof *over* the patio. b. Those thunderclouds will soon blow *over.*

7. a. My brother usually *drives* to work. b. Nellie enjoys *drives* in the country.

8. a. The king had a *fool* to entertain him. b. A good magician *fools* the audience.

9. a. Turn off the *light,* please. b. The store has a wide variety of *light* bulbs.

10. a. Look *up!* b. Alice urged her horse *up* the steep hill.

Reinforcement Exercises—Review

Prepositions and Conjunctions

A. Finding Prepositions

Complete the sentences that follow. How many different prepositions can you find for each blank space? Write all the prepositions that will make sense in the sentence.

1. Martha put the notice _____ the door.
2. Christopher saw a snake _____ that rock.
3. The mug _____ that box is broken.
4. Please dust the table _____ the window.
5. Nels sat down and talked _____ Sara.
6. Juanita moved the chair _____ the wall.
7. A potted plant would look attractive _____ that ledge.
8. The ball flew _____ the shortstop.

B. Using Pronouns as Objects of Prepositions

Choose the correct pronoun from the words in parentheses. Write the sentence.

1. The sales department is under Ms. Hyman and (he, him).
2. There was a strong friendship between Helen Keller and (her, she).
3. Are you coming with Benjamin and (me, I)?
4. Radiation from space is constantly passing through our atmosphere and (we, us).
5. Give your new address to Alice and (I, me).
6. The novel tells of (they, them) and their families.
7. A blackbird swooped over Tim and (she, her).
8. The waves crashed against Gladys and then (him, he).

C. Finding Prepositions and Adverbs

In each pair of sentences that follows, one word is used both as an adverb and as a preposition. Number your paper from 1 to 10. After each number, write *a.* and *b.* After each letter, write the word that is used two ways in the two sentences. Then write the way the word was used in that sentence.

1. a. Sam likes to ramble on the beach. b. Sam likes to ramble on.
2. a. The parade has gone by. b. The parade has gone by the reviewing stand.
3. a. You can crawl under. b. You can crawl under the wire.
4. a. Cut the cake into two layers and spread the filling between. b. Spread the filling between the two layers.
5. Beyond, the sea stretched to the horizon. b. Beyond the rocky shore, the sea stretched to the horizon.
6. a. We must walk up the stairs. b. We must walk up.
7. a. We played outside. b. We played outside the fence.
8. a. When will this poster be taken down? b. Will this poster slide down the wall?
9. a. Several geese flew over us. b. Several geese flew over.
10. a. What lies beyond this galaxy? b. What lies beyond?

D. Using Conjunctions

Number your paper from 1 to 10. In each sentence, there is a compound subject, a compound predicate, or a compound object. Write which of the three you find. Write the compound subject, predicate, or object with its conjunction. Underline the conjunction.

1. At dinner, Spencer had ribs and sweet potato pie.
2. Unicorns and dragons are imaginary animals.
3. Lydia concentrated on her bowling form and rolled a strike.
4. You can check out books, magazines, and records from the library.

305

5. A contestant quits the game after one turn or goes on for a bigger prize.

6. Madeline and Hal played six games of checkers.

7. Bruce collected spiders and unusual insects.

8. I want a taco but don't have enough money.

9. Ms. Burke or Mrs. Mitchell will go on the field trip with us.

10. The choir sang two spirituals and several folk songs.

E. Combining Sentences

Rewrite the following sentences, combining each pair with *and, but,* or *or.* Choose the conjunction you think is best. Use commas where needed.

1. The letter on the eye chart may be an E. It may be an F.

2. I sprayed insect repellent on my arms. Mosquitoes bit me anyway.

3. Jarita has several assignments. They are all difficult.

4. You may have cookies for dessert. You may have an orange.

5. The car had engine trouble. We had to call a tow truck.

6. Rhea's arm is still in a cast. She played baseball today.

7. The pies from that bakery are delicious. The prices are high.

8. You can wait in the car. You can come into the store with me.

9. The weatherman predicted rain. The sun is shining.

10. The herd of buffalo moved north. The hunters followed.

F. Avoiding Run-on Sentences

Four of the following sentences are correct. Six are run-on sentences. Number your paper from 1 to 10. If the sentence is correct as it is, write *Correct.* If it is a run-on, rewrite the sentence as two sentences, with correct capitalization and punctuation.

306

1. My favorite holiday is Christmas the best part is the presents.

2. A forest fire destroys an important natural resource it takes many years for new trees to grow.

3. The sun rises later during the winter the temperature of the air drops.

4. Staple the blue sheets of paper and the art projects to the bulletin board.

5. In the story, Katherine wishes on a magic coin and gets into a tournament with Sir Lancelot.

6. Give me more cake, please I'm still hungry.

7. None of the apples in that basket is ripe yet.

8. Mother bought some hamburger, a dozen buns, and a watermelon at the supermarket.

9. Craig tried on six different jackets they were all too tight.

10. The producer held auditions he chose some schoolchildren for small parts in the movie.

G. Telling the Part of Speech

In each pair of sentences that follows, one word is used as two different parts of speech. Number your paper from 1 to 8. After each number, write *a.* and *b.* After each letter, write the word in italics and tell how it is used.

1. a. Ron bought *paper* cups for the party.   b. Dad will *paper* the dining room walls this weekend.

2. a. I'd like a push-button *phone* in my room.   b. The store accepts *phone* orders.

3. a. Cola *bubbles* up when you pour it.   b. Gloria blows huge *bubbles* with her gum.

4. a. The ducks swam in the *water*.   b. Cypress Gardens presents a famous *water* show.

5. a. The dogs *chased* the fox for several miles.   b. Almost every Keystone Cops film had a *chase* scene.

6. a. Please stand in the light *near* the window.   b. The end of the story is *near*.

7. a. Edith works very *hard*.   b. This bread has a *hard* crust.

8. a. Snow *covered* the city.   b. Put a *cover* on the baby.

307

Chapter 20

Writing Reports

In Chapter 15 you learned how to write a composition. When you chose your subject, you may have decided to write about something that happened to you, or about your ideas or feelings. The subject was personal. All of the details you needed came from within you.

Sometimes you will be asked to write a composition about a subject you know little about. For example, you may be asked to write about optical illusions in science class, or about your state resources in social studies. You would have to gather facts from books or magazines and organize them to tell about your subject. This type of composition is called a **report**. In this chapter, you will learn new skills that will help you organize and write this special kind of composition.

Part 1 Pre-Writing: Selecting a Subject

You have already learned to write compositions about your own experiences. A report, however, should be based on facts that you must study and learn about. For a report, look outside yourself for a subject.

The library is a good place to search for a subject for your report. Think of the things that you want to know more about. Flip through some books and magazines to get ideas. Would you like to know what it's like inside a space shuttle? Are you interested in computers or chimpanzees or the Loch Ness monster? The best subject for a report is the one that interests you most. Just make sure that the library has information on that subject.

Exercise   Finding a Subject

Make a list of five subjects you would be interested in learning more about. Then go to the library and find five more subjects. Keep this list. Add to it at any time.

Narrowing the Subject

As with any composition, you must be sure that you have narrowed your subject enough. Remember that you must be able to cover it thoroughly in five paragraphs.

When you narrow the subject of a report, you can get help from other sources. Begin the narrowing process by reading a general article about your subject in an encyclopedia or other reference book. The article will give you an idea of how broad your subject is. It may also help you find a more limited subject.

Let's say that you are interested in American pioneers moving west. After reading an encyclopedia article, you realize that this subject is very broad. To cover it all, you would have to describe the following subjects:

Why people moved West
The hardships of the Oregon Trail
Life on a wagon train
The role of scouts
The duties of a wagon master
What happened to the Native Americans

You must narrow the subject further. You might decide to focus on life on a wagon train. When you read more, though, you see that this subject is still too general. You will have to narrow it even more. The complete narrowing process might look like this:

The History of the United States
Pioneers Moving West
Life on a Wagon Train
Children on a Wagon Train

Exercises Narrowing the Subject

A. These subjects are too broad for short reports. Narrow each subject until it could be covered in a short report. If necessary, read about these subjects.

Example: General subject—Medicine
Narrowed subject—How Penicillin Was Discovered

1. Robots
2. Mummies
3. Jungle cats
4. Marsupials
5. Microchips
6. Pyramids
7. Prairie dogs
8. Dinosaurs
9. Laser beams
10. Swamps

311

B. Read the list of ten or more subjects that you made for the exercise on page 310. Choose one subject. Read about it. Narrow the subject so that it can be covered in a five-paragraph report.

Part 2 Pre-Writing: Gathering Information for a Report

It is time to look for specific information for your report.

Check the card catalog in the library and make a list of the books on your subject. Write down their titles, authors, and call numbers. To find magazine articles with information you can use, look up your subject in the *Readers' Guide to Periodical Literature*. You can also look at articles in encyclopedias and other reference books. Try to use several different sources as you gather information.

Taking Notes

As you read, write down information for your report on 3" by 5" note cards. Write only one piece of information on each card. Also, write down the source of the information for that note. You may need to use the source again. Later, you will list your sources.

When you write down the source, include the following:

For books—the title and author

For magazines—the name and date of the magazine, title of the article, author, and page numbers

For reference books—the name of the reference book, volume number, title of the entry or volume, and page number

312

Title

The First Book of the Oregon Trail

by Walter Havighurst Author

Information

To go from Missouri to Oregon on the Oregon Trail was a five-month, 2000 mile trip.

Magazine   **Date**

Cobblestone, December 1981,

Title

"Wagons on the Oregon Trail"

by Pauline Bartel **Author**   **Pages**   pages 17-18

Information

A wagon train began traveling before dawn and covered 12-15 miles each day.

A report must be written in your own words. Therefore, write all your notes in your own words. Do not use those of your source.

Study the note card written from this encyclopedia article. Notice how the writer reworded the material.

Encyclopedia Excerpt

As long as the pioneers of the 1840's kept moving westward, the Plains Indians allowed them to pass through their hunting grounds. Some tribes guided the early pioneers, or helped them at difficult river crossings. The Indians even supplied some wagon trains with vegetables and buffalo meat in exchange for tobacco or pieces of iron.

Student Note Card

Encyclopedia   **Volume**

World Book Encyclopedia,   Volume 15

Title   **Page**

"Pioneer Life in America,"   page 441

Information

Some Indians helped early pioneers by guiding them, assisting them at rough river crossings, or trading with them.

313

Exercises **Taking Notes on a Subject**

A. Read this article from *The World Book Encyclopedia,* Volume 14, page 478. Write three note cards based on the article. Put the notes in your own words.

OAKLEY, ANNIE (1860-1926), an American markswoman, starred in Buffalo Bill's Wild West Show for 17 years. She was popular throughout the United States and Europe. She was an expert shot with a pistol, rifle, or shotgun. Once, with a .22 rifle, she shot 4,772 glass balls out of 5,000 tossed in the air on a single day. At 90 feet (27 meters), she could hit a playing card with the thin edge toward her, and puncture a card five or six times while it fell to the ground. Since then, free tickets with holes punched in them have been called "Annie Oakleys."

Annie Oakley was born Phoebe Anne Oakley Mozee on Aug. 13, 1860, in a log cabin in Patterson Township, Ohio. She began shooting at the age of 9. After her father died, she supported the family by shooting small game. Only 5 feet (152 centimeters) tall, she was called "Little Sure Shot." Annie Oakley joined Buffalo Bill's Wild West Show in 1885 (see BUFFALO BILL). HOWARD R. LAMAR

B. Take notes for your report on 3" by 5" cards. Write the information in your own words. Save your notes to use later.

Part 3 Pre-Writing: Organizing a Report

You have done the reading for your report, and taken notes. Now you are ready to organize your information.

Read through your notes. You will probably see that most of your information falls under certain main ideas. List these ideas. Then organize your notes by dividing them into groups. Let each group contain only the note cards related to one of the main ideas. You can begin separating your cards this way while you are taking notes.

The writer with the topic "Children on a Wagon Train" divided her notes into these groups:

  I. The children spent most of each day walking.

  II. The children had work to do each day.

  III. At the end of the day the children were free to enjoy themselves.

The note cards within these three groups contain the details that are needed to support each main idea in the report.

When you sort through your notes, leave out any that are not related to one of the main ideas. If you find that you do not have enough notes on an idea, do more reading. Remember, you can add or take out information at any point in the writing process. You may even decide to change one of the main ideas.

The final step in organizing a report is to put the material in some sort of logical order. Begin by arranging the main ideas. Then organize the details that support each main idea. You may use any of the orders you learned about in Chapter 8. You might also find a different way of organizing that works just as well.

Making an Outline

Once you have organized your notes, you are ready to write an outline. An outline shows how the parts of a report fit together.

Each group of notes becomes a major division, or part, of the outline. The main idea of each group becomes the topic of the part. These topics are labeled with Roman numerals.

The important facts from the note cards become subtopics in each main division. Subtopics are labeled with capital letters.

> I. Topic
>   A. Subtopic
>   B. Subtopic
> II. Topic

Here is the outline for "Children on a Wagon Train."

I. Introductory paragraph

II. The children spent most of each day walking.

    A. Walked 12–15 miles a day

    B. Rode in the wagons on the hottest afternoons

    C. Rode on horseback when herding cow columns

III. The children had work to do each day.

    A. Milked cows

    B. Fetched water

    C. Searched for prairie dog holes

    D. Gathered "buffalo chips" for fuel

    E. Studied school lessons

    F. Learned how to hook rugs, make quilts, preserve meat in salt, start a fire from flint, and use an ax

IV. At the end of the day the children were free to enjoy themselves.

    A. Played games like tag and hide-and-seek

    B. Sang around campfire

    C. Listened to adults talking

V. Conclusion

An outline such as this will guide you as you write your own report.

Exercises **Making Outlines for Reports**

A. Here is part of an outline for a report. Copy the outline. Complete it by putting these headings or subheadings where they belong.

Lava caves   No natural light   Stalagmites
Green plants   Life in caves   Mammoth Cave

CAVES

I. Definition of cave
   A. Hollow chamber in earth
   B. Large enough for a person to enter
   C.

II. Types of caves
   A. Solution caves
   B.
   C. Sea caves

III. Formations in caves
   A. Stalactites
   B.
   C. Drapery
   D. Flowstone

IV.
   A. Animals that need light
   B. Animals that live without light (Troglobites)
   C.
   D. Fungi

V. Famous caves
   A. Carlsbad Caverns
   B.
   C. Jewel Cave
   D. Wind Cave

317

B. Put your own cards into three or four related groups. Arrange the groups and the cards within them in logical order. Make an outline for your report.

Part 4 Writing the First Draft: Working from an Outline

A report has the same three main parts that any composition has. They are the introduction, the body, and the ending. Refer to your outline as you write. It already lists the ideas you want to include. It also shows the best order for presenting them.

Writing the Introduction

As with any composition, the introduction of a report should tell the reader what the report is about. Just as important, the introduction should catch the reader's attention.

Look at this introduction for "Children on a Wagon Train." Notice how the writer used strong details and specific words to create interest.

> Thousands of children traveled west in the long wagon trains that lumbered over the grassy plains, burning deserts, and rugged mountains of the Oregon Trail. These children did their chores, studied their lessons, and played games, just as they would have done at home. This time, though, "home" was a wagon moving slowly across a 2,000-mile stretch of unknown and sometimes dangerous land.

Exercises **Working with Introductory Paragraphs**

A. Decide which of the following introductory paragraphs are good and which are poor. Explain why.

1

This report will be about the second war going on in the colonies during the American Revolution. The second war was the frontier war. It's amazing that the colonies won the Revolution. They were fighting what was back then a real super-power.

2

You can think of seeds as space capsules for infant plants. They contain an embryo plant, a food supply to feed the plant until it gets established, a tiny bit of water to keep it alive, and a tough outer coat or coats.

3

From the earliest times people have looked at the night sky and tried to understand what they saw there. Long before anyone knew that the stars were great burning globes of gas, men and women saw the sky as full of magical pictures.

4

Earthquakes under the ocean cause tidal waves. Tidal waves are gigantic and travel fast. They are very interesting.

5

Sherlock Holmes had one enemy who was an even greater threat to him than the worst vilain. Although Holmes is beloved by mystery fans, one person hated the detective and did his best to stop Holmes forever. That would-be killer was none other than Holme's creator, Sir Arthur Conan Doyle.

B. Write the introduction of your report. Make sure that the introduction is interesting and informative.

The Body

The body paragraphs of the report present most of the information. You did most of your work on these paragraphs when you wrote your outline. Each main division in the outline becomes a paragraph in the body of the report. Each main topic in the outline becomes the topic sentence of the paragraph. The subtopics are the supporting facts.

As you write, remember that in the process of writing you can constantly rework ideas. You may realize that the order you used

319

in your outline could be improved. You may find new information or think of better ways to present the ideas you already have. Include these changes in your rough draft. Just be sure that the report still flows smoothly and develops one main idea.

The complete report "Children on a Wagon Train" appears on pages 322 and 323. Read the introduction and body paragraphs. Compare the body paragraphs to the outline on page 316. How closely did the writer follow the outline? Were any details added?

Exercise   Writing the Body Paragraphs

Write the three body paragraphs of your report. Follow your outline, but make any improvements that occur to you. Make sure each paragraph has a topic sentence.

The Ending

The last paragraph of your report is very important. It ties together all of the ideas you have presented in the introduction and body paragraphs. The last paragraph also provides a clear, definite finish for the report.

The ending paragraph is often a summary of the main ideas. However, it should not just repeat an earlier part of the report. Such an ending would bore the reader. The final paragraph should be bright and fresh because it is your last chance to share your information with the reader.

Read the ending paragraph of "Children on a Wagon Train" on page 323. Does it provide a strong ending to the report? Does it hold the reader's interest?

Exercise   Writing the Ending for a Report

Write the last paragraph of your report. Make sure that it ties the ideas together and shows the reader that the report is over.

Naming Sources

Your final step in writing the first draft of a report is showing where you got your information. You must credit your sources.

Look at your note cards. List the books and articles that you used. Put the list in alphabetical order, using the author's last name or the title of the article. Look at the list at the end of "Children on a Wagon Train" on page 323.

Exercise **Naming Sources**

List the sources you used for your report. Underline the titles of books and magazines. Write out your sources at the end of your report or on a separate paper.

Part 5 Revising a Report

The report you have been reading was not the result of one draft. The writer worked and reworked ideas several times. Read the rough draft of your own report carefully. Use the Guidelines on pages 84 and 85 to help you improve it. Make sure that the report covers your topic thoroughly. The writing should be lively and clear. Rewrite parts that need work.

For a report, you must add one more step to the revision process: Check your facts. Make sure that all the information is correct. Check to see that you have listed your sources accurately.

When you are satisfied with the content of your report, proofread it for errors. Use proofreading symbols to indicate corrections on the rough draft.

After you have revised your report, make your final copy. Proofread this clean copy a final time.

Exercise **Revising a Report**

Read, revise, and proofread your report. Make a final copy.

Sample Report

Now read once more the report "Children on a Wagon Train" on pages 322 and 323. As you read, ask the following questions:

Introduction

Does the introduction present the subject of the report?

Does it capture the reader's interest?

Body Paragraphs

How closely does the body follow the outline on page 316?

Does each paragraph have a topic sentence?

Are the paragraphs and the details within them in logical order?

Ending paragraph

Does the ending summarize the report?

Are any new or interesting ideas presented?

CHILDREN ON A WAGON TRAIN

Thousands of children traveled west in the long wagon trains that lumbered over the grassy plains, burning deserts, and rugged mountains of the Oregon Trail. These children did their chores, studied their lessons, and played games, just as they would have done at home. This time, though, "home" was a wagon moving slowly across a 2,000 mile stretch of unknown and sometimes dangerous land.

The children spent most of the day walking alongside the wagons. Only on the hottest desert afternoons did many ride in the shelter of the backs of the jolting wagons. Every day except

Sunday the wagons covered—and the children walked—twelve to fifteen miles. The only ones who did not walk were groups of older children. They herded the "cow column," the milk cows and spare horses and oxen that followed the wagon train. These children spent most of the long journey on horseback.

The children had work to do each day. They milked the cows, fetched buckets of water from the creeks, and gathered wild fruits and berries. They searched for prairie dog holes and alerted the hunters in the train to their locations. One of their most important jobs was gathering "buffalo chips." They were the disks of dried buffalo dung that were burned for cooking and warmth. The children also studied their school lessons. They used books that had been packed into the wagons. In addition, they learned skills such as how to hook rugs, make quilts, preserve meat in salt, start a fire from flint, and use an ax.

When the wagons finally pulled up at the end of a long day and the supper dishes were done, the children were free to have some fun. They could then get together with the children from other wagons to play games like tag and hide-and-seek. They could join the singing around the campfires and listen to the adults share their dreams of a new life in Oregon. Recreation time ended early for those on a wagon train. Everyone had to be up before dawn to begin a new day.

The children on a wagon train did ordinary things. They worked, played, studied, ate, and slept. However, they also experienced out-of-the-ordinary things. They endured hard wagon seats, tired feet, merciless heat, and long stretches of boredom as they crossed the vast West. These children were true pioneers, just like their parents.

My information was taken from these sources:

Bartel, Pauline. "Wagons on the Oregon Trail," *Cobblestone*, December 1981, pages 16–17.

Havighurst, Walter. *The First Book of the Oregon Trail*.

"Pioneer Life in America," *The World Book Encyclopedia*. Volume 15, pp. 440–443.

Westward on the Oregon Trail. American Heritage Junior Library.

Chapter 21

Writing Letters

Did you visit an unusual place last summer? Maybe you went on a vacation or visited relatives. If so, you probably met some new people or renewed old friendships. The best way to continue these friendships is by writing letters. Writing letters can also help you order materials and request information.

This chapter will explain the correct form to use for various kinds of letters. It will also help you make your letters more interesting and easier to write.

Part 1 Writing Friendly Letters

When you have had an experience that you want to share with a friend, you first have to organize your ideas so the reader can follow them easily. The following guides will help you to organize your ideas:

Guides for Organizing Your Ideas

1. Write as naturally as if you were speaking to the person.

2. Begin by answering the other person's questions or by commenting on the information in his or her last letter.

3. Write about things that are interesting both to you and the person to whom you are writing.

4. Describe a new or interesting experience you have had. Add vivid details, strong verbs, and a variety of adjectives and adverbs to make your description come alive.

A Sample Letter

Read the following friendly letter. Notice that each part has a specific form and purpose.

Heading

1201 West Leonard Street
Pensacola, Florida 32501
October 5, 1985

Salutation

Dear Miguel,

Body

Today our class went to a wooded area for a science lesson. We had to find specimens of different leaves. When I found some poison ivy, I thought of you right away! Remember when we went on that hike at camp and the poison ivy found you! Boy, did you itch.

I've been pretty busy so far this fall. We formed a neighborhood skateboarding team. Every Saturday a different person is in charge of making a new obstacle course. It's my turn this week. I'm using cones and a small ramp that Dad helped me build. I'm sending you a copy of the design for the course. Does it look difficult to you? Have you been doing a lot of skateboarding? You have much better hills in Georgia, so I bet you're really good.

I would like to know what you've been doing. If you can, send me a picture of your dog doing one of his famous tricks. Also, have you added any new albums to your collection?

Closing   Your friend,

Signature   Jerry

Using Correct Letter Form

Each part of a letter has its own specific form and purpose. This organization makes it easier for you to write a letter. Review each of these parts in the following chart:

Part	Place	Purpose
Heading	The **heading** is written in the upper right-hand corner.	The **heading** tells where you are and when you are writing. It consists of three lines: house number and street name city, state ZIP code month, day, year
Salutation	The **salutation** is written on the line below the heading and begins at the left margin.	The **salutation,** or greeting, is the way you say "hello" to your friend. It can be casual, such as *Hi, Dear Mary,* or *Greetings.*
Body	The **body** begins on the line below the salutation. Each paragraph is indented.	The **body** of a letter is for talking to your friend. Arrange the body in paragraphs for each subject you discuss.
Closing	The **closing** should line up with the first line of the heading.	The **closing** is a simple way of saying "goodbye." Some common closings are *Love, Sincerely, Always,* or *Your friend.*
Signature	After the closing, skip a line. Your **signature** should line up with the first word in the closing.	In a friendly letter, only your first name is needed unless you don't know the person well.

Using Correct Capitalization and Punctuation

Using correct capitalization and punctuation will make your letter much easier for your friend to read. Review the following rules for letter writing:

Heading
1. Capitalize all proper names.
2. Place a comma between the name of the city and state.
3. Put the ZIP code after the state. No comma is necessary to separate the state and the ZIP code.
4. Place a comma between the day and the year.

Salutation
5. Capitalize the first word and any proper nouns in the salutation.
6. Use a comma after the salutation.

Closing
7. Capitalize only the first word of the closing.
8. Use a comma after the closing.

Exercises Writing Friendly Letters

A. Choose two of the following subjects. Write an interesting paragraph about each that could be used in a friendly letter. Include vivid details:

getting a new pet
winning an event or contest
moving to a new town
receiving a birthday present

going to a party
seeing a movie
going on a field trip
making something new

B. In your best handwriting, copy the following parts of a letter, using the correct capitalization and punctuation. Use separate lines where necessary. Label each section.

1. 336 old mill road phoenix arizona 85040 august 7 1985
2. dear mary anne
3. 852 busse avenue mount prospect illinois 60056 june 3 1985
4. missing you laura
5. dear aunt sarah and uncle ted

329

6. sincerely yours jeff parker

7. 71 south madison avenue mapleton iowa 51034 september 11 1985

8. your friend michelle

C. Write a friendly letter to a real or an imaginary friend. Follow the Guides for Organizing Your Ideas on page 286. Use the proper form for each part of your letter. Use correct capitalization and punctuation. Make the main subject of your letter about one of the following ideas. You may choose your own subject if you wish.

1. An interesting person you have met
2. An interesting place you have visited
3. Something unusual you have seen or done

Part 2   Writing Social Notes

Everyone enjoys receiving gifts, giving parties, and going to parties. These kinds of occasions require the writing of **social notes**. Writing social notes is a form of courtesy that people appreciate. These notes have the same forms as a friendly letter except that they are much shorter and generally use only the date in the heading.

You will use the following social notes most frequently:

1. Thank-you notes

2. Invitations

3. Notes of acceptance or regret

The Thank-You Note

After you have received a gift, or someone has done you a special favor, you should write a thank-you note as soon as possible. This will let the person know that you appreciate his or her thoughtfulness.

Another occasion for writing a thank-you note is when you have spent the night at someone's home. This kind of thank-you note is sometimes called a "bread-and-butter" note. It helps to show that you appreciate the person's hospitality.

The following are examples of the two types of thank-you notes. Notice that these notes are both courteous and friendly.

A Sample Thank-You Note

April 6, 1984

Dear Aunt Loretta,

It was nice of you to remember my birthday. I especially like the pillow you stitched for my bed, and so does my new kitten, Pepper. He curled up next to it and made himself right at home. The colors in the pillow match my bedroom perfectly.

I had a good time on my birthday and your gift made it even better. Thank you again.

Love,
Marsha

A Sample Bread-and-Butter Note

July 18, 1984

Dear Mr. and Mrs. Johnson,

Thank you for inviting me to your summer cottage last weekend. It was great to visit with Jack again.

Riding in your boat was exciting, and now I can say I know how to water-ski. I've been wanting to learn for a long time. The cookout on the beach was fun, and the food was delicious.

Thank you again for inviting me. I really enjoyed myself and hope that Jack can visit me soon.

Sincerely,
Todd Monroe

The Invitation

Everyone enjoys receiving invitations, so be sure that yours are written clearly and carefully. Invitations should include the following information:

1. Type o.
2. Purpose of activity
3. Where the activity will take place
4. The day, date, and time of the activity
5. How the person should reply

An invitation should include all the necessary details and should be written in a friendly tone. It is also a good idea to include your return address in the heading so people can easily respond. Use the following example as a model.

An Invitation

> 4402 Nancy Lane
> Phoenix, Arizona 85040
> October 17, 1985
>
> Dear Ellen,
>   You are invited to attend a Halloween party at my house on Saturday, October 31, at 7:30 P.M. This is going to be a costume party, so start thinking of something original.
>
>   Sincerely,
>   Bruce
>
> R.S.V.P.

Notes of Acceptance or Regret

Suppose you have been invited to attend an event such as the party in the sample invitation. You should reply as soon as you know if you can go. The R.S.V.P. at the end of an invitation is an abbreviation for a French phrase that means "please respond." Sometimes there will be a phone number included so you can just telephone your response. It is much better, however, to write a note of acceptance or regret.

Use the following examples as guides for responding to an invitation.

A Note of Acceptance

October 20, 1985

Dear Bruce,
    Your Halloween party sounds like great fun. I already have an idea for a surprise costume, so you can count on my being there.
    Thanks for inviting me.

Yours truly,
Ellen

A Note of Regret

October 20, 1985

Dear Bruce,

I would really like to come to your party but my family is going out of town that weekend to visit my sister. I hope that your party is a success and that you take some good pictures of the costumes.

Thanks for the invitation.

Sincerely,
Ellen

Exercises Writing Social Notes

Choose one situation from each of the following categories. Write the appropriate form of social note for each situation. Label each kind of note you write. Use your best handwriting.

335

A. 1. A note to your aunt and uncle for taking you skiing (or somewhere of your own interest).

2. A note to your grandmother for letting you spend the weekend.

3. A note to your best friend, who recently moved, for the birthday present he or she sent. You decide on the present.

B. 1. A note asking your friends to go on a camping trip.

2. A note asking the members of a club to come to a special meeting.

3. A note asking your cousin to watch you in a swimming meet or some type of performance.

C. 1. A note telling your friend you will attend a surprise birthday party for a mutual friend.

2. A note telling your aunt you can't spend the weekend at her house.

3. A note telling your cousin you will be attending the play she is in.

Part 3   Writing Business Letters

The most common types of business letters you will need to write are the following:

1. Letters requesting information

2. Letters ordering materials

3. Letters complaining about merchandise

A business letter is written for a specific purpose. The letter should be written clearly and to the point so that you achieve your purpose.

Business letters follow a specific form and include exact information. The following guidelines will help you write successful business letters.

Parts of a Business Letter

The parts of a business letter are similar to those of a friendly letter except that they are written more formally. A business letter also has one additional part, the **inside address**. Review the following parts of a business letter. Notice the exact information that is included in each part.

1. **Heading.** The heading of a business letter is the same as the heading for a friendly letter. Write your street address on the first line. Write your city, state, and ZIP code on the second line. Write the date on the third line. Use correct capitalization and punctuation, and try not to abbreviate.

2. **Inside Address.** In a business letter, the name and address of the organization to which you are writing appear in the letter itself. This address follows the same punctuation and capitalization rules as the heading. The inside address comes below the heading and begins at the left margin. The inside address should be exactly the same as the address on the envelope.

3. **Salutation.** The salutation of a business letter is more formal than that of a friendly letter. If the letter is being written to a specific person, use *Dear* followed by the person's name:

Dear Ms. Hopkins: Dear Mr. Steinberg:

Many times you don't know the name of the person to whom you are writing in a business letter. In this case, you use a general greeting such as the following: *Dear Sir or Madam:*
Dear Ladies and Gentlemen:

All salutations begin two lines after the inside address at the left margin and end with a colon (:).

4. **Body.** The body of a business letter is usually short. It should be courteous and state clearly the subject you are writing about.

Use the following checklist for the body of different types of business letters:

Letter of Request

1. Tell *what* specific information you need.
2. Tell *why* you need that information.
3. Tell *when* you need the information.

Order Letter

1. Tell the name of the product and how many you want.
2. Tell the name of the publication where you saw the ad.
3. Tell the catalog number, size, and color.
4. Tell the price. List postage and handling separately.
5. Compute the total price of the order.
6. Tell what you are enclosing with the letter, such as a check, subscription form, or coupon.

Letter of Complaint

1. Tell the name and model of the order.
2. Tell where and when the product was purchased.
3. Tell the nature of the problem.
4. Ask for instructions for having the problem corrected.

5. **Closing.** The closing appears on the first line below the body. The closing should line up with the heading. The most common closings for a business letter are these:

Sincerely,   *Respectfully yours,*

Very truly yours,   *Yours truly,*

6. **Signature.** Print or type your name four spaces below the closing. Write your signature in the space between. This way the reader will have no trouble reading your name so that he or she can reply to you. It is best to make a copy of your business letters so that you will have a record of what you wrote and when you wrote it. You can do this easily by using carbon paper. Mail the original and keep the copy.

Study the following business letter to see how all of the parts work together to form a well organized, clearly stated letter.

A Business Letter

Heading
51 Bank Street
Stamford, Connecticut 06901
September 22, 1985

Inside Address
Tropical Shell Institute
Dept. BH-8
Box 21490
Fort Lauderdale, Florida 33335

Salutation
Dear Sir or Madam:

Body
In the August issue of Better Homes and Gardens, I read your advertisement for your shell collection offer and catalog. I would like to order both of these items. Please send me the following order as soon as possible.

1 shell collection (150 shells) $12.95
1 catalog   1.00
postage   3.00
total $16.95

I am enclosing a money order for the amount of $16.95.

Closing
Sincerely,

Signature
Laurie Douvris
Laurie Douvris

Exercise **Writing Business Letters**

Choose one of the following items and write the letter described. Supply any names and facts needed to complete the letter. Use your own name and address and your best handwriting.

1. Your family will be vacationing in California this spring. Write to ABC Guest Relations, 41-51 Prospect Avenue, Hollywood, California 90027, and ask for tickets to your favorite TV show. Consider when you will be there and how many tickets you will need.

2. You need information about basketball for a report you are writing. Write to Basketball Hall of Fame, P.O. Box 175, Highland Station, 460 Alden Street, Springfield, Massachusetts 01109, for the free booklet *Basketball Was Born Here*. Include a self-addressed stamped envelope.

3. You finally received your address labels, but the ZIP code is wrong. The 1,000 labels cost $1 plus 25¢ for handling from Imprint Products, 482 Sunrise Highway, Rockville Centre, New York 11570.

4. Your string art kit arrived, but the instruction booklet is missing. Write to Kelly's String Art Division, Dept. BH-88, Box 36195, Cincinnati, Ohio 45236.

Part 4   Addressing Envelopes

Addressing the envelope correctly is an important part of writing letters. If you want your letter to reach its destination, you must be sure you have the correct address and ZIP code. If you're not sure of a ZIP code, call your local post office.

Use the following checklist when addressing envelopes:

1. Make sure the envelope is right-side up.

2. Put your return address on the envelope.

3. Make sure all numbers are in proper order.

4. Include the correct ZIP code.
5. Write as neatly as possible.

Look carefully at the following example.

Miss Faith Copeland
510 South Fulton
Mt. Vernon, New York 10550

Mr. Miles Kimball
2244 Bond Street
Oshkosh, Wisconsin 54901

Envelopes for social notes are often smaller in size. In this case, the return address may be put on the back of the envelope.

Exercise **Addressing Envelopes**

Write each of the following addresses in proper order as it should appear on an envelope. Capitalize and punctuate correctly and use your best handwriting.

1. hobbit house p o box 12684 dallas texas 75225
2. ms jan bleeker lincoln junior high school 700 west lincoln street mount prospect illinois 60056
3. national wildlife federation 1412 16th street washington d c 20036

Chapter 22

Making Subjects and Verbs Agree

Do these sentences sound correct to you?

The rides is exciting.
One cloud float in the sky.
Our friends is watching us.
We calls down to them.

If you have been speaking English all your life, the four sentences may sound unusual to you. Each one of them puts together words that don't normally fit together. Each one of them breaks a basic rule in our language: the subject and verb in a sentence must agree.

343

Part 1 Rules for Making the Subject and Verb Agree

When a noun stands for one thing, it is **singular.**

student   fox   penny

When a noun stands for more than one thing, it is **plural.**

students   foxes   pennies

Verbs, too, have singular and plural forms. In a sentence, the verb must always agree in number with its subject. The word *number* refers to singular and plural.

Notice these examples:

Singular	Plural
She *sings* in the next act.	Many girls *sing* soprano parts.
The baby *crawls* everywhere.	Babies *crawl* before they can walk.
That boy *speaks* in the program.	Those boys *speak* clearly.

When we talk about one girl, we say she *sings*. When we talk about more than one girl, we say the girls *sing*. One baby *crawls* but many babies *crawl*. One boy *speaks*, but many boys *speak*.

The *s* at the end of verbs like *sings, crawls,* and *speaks* shows that the verbs are used with singular nouns. In the examples, the singular nouns *girl, baby,* and *boy* were the subjects. When the subject is plural, the *s* is dropped. Look again at the sentences above.

344

1. If the subject is singular, use the singular form of the verb.
2. If the subject is plural, use the plural form of the verb.

Prepositional Phrases after the Subject

Be careful with prepositional phrases that come after the subject and before the verb. Do not let yourself confuse the subject of the verb with the object of the preposition.

Example:

The children on my block (rides, ride) a school bus.

Who rides? *The children.*

On my block is a prepositional phrase describing the *children*. The verb must agree with *children*, not *block*, so we use the plural form *ride*.

Exercises **Studying Singular and Plural Forms**

A. In each complete subject, find the subject of the verb. Write it and tell whether it will take the singular or the plural form of the verb.

1. the apples	7. the passengers in the car
2. a carnival	8. a box of pencils
3. Sheila	9. the men on the moon
4. the wristwatch	10. wild geese
5. autumn leaves	11. the Johnson twins
6. the mice	12. umbrellas in the rain

B. Number your paper from 1 to 6. Find the subject and the verb in each sentence below. Write the subject and verb.

Example: The dogs in the yard barked at us. *dogs, barked*

1. The men in the truck work with my father.
2. The three customers at the counter need service.
3. My friends on the next street visit me often.
4. Many new recruits for the Army are women.
5. The girl on stilts walks very quickly.
6. Those students in the hall will audition for the talent show.

Special Forms of Certain Verbs

A few verbs have special forms that you should keep in mind.

Is, Was, Are, Were. The verb forms *is* and *was* are singular. The forms *are* and *were* are plural.

Singular: Carlos *is* here. Carlos *was* here.
Plural: The boxes *are* here. The boxes *were* here.

Has, Have. The verb form *has* is singular. The form *have* is plural.

Singular: Pam *has* a plan.
Plural: They *have* a plan.

Does, Do. The verb form *does* is singular. The form *do* is plural.

Singular: Joe *does* the cooking.
Plural: They *do* the cooking.

Exercises **Using the Right Verb Form**

A. Choose the right form of the verb from the parentheses.

1. Two ski poles (was, were) standing in the drift.
2. Bob's teeth (has, have) never had a cavity.
3. The locker rooms (is, are) newly painted.
4. My cousin (has, have) been singing in the choir this year.
5. At high tide, those boats (is, are) floating on the water.
6. (Is, Are) the Boy Scouts coming?
7. The noises in this cave (has, have) weird echoes.
8. Toni's swollen knee (is, are) getting better.
9. Rico (doesn't, don't) waste time.
10. The two stores on Central Street (is, are) closed.

346

B. Follow the directions for Exercise A.

1. Our bus (has, have) a flat tire.
2. My feet (is, are) too big for these shoes.

3. The girls (was, were) diving for oysters.
4. How many people (is, are) in your family?
5. Some friends of my sister (is, are) coming for dinner.
6. (Isn't, Aren't) the cookies for dessert?
7. All along the street (was, were) Japanese lanterns.
8. (Does, Do) the canary ever sing?
9. The brakes on this bike (is, are) not working properly.
10. In *Peter Pan*, all of the children (is, are) lost.

Part 2   Tricky Subjects To Watch

Certain Pronouns

The words listed below are singular. Each is used with a singular verb form.

each	either	everyone	anyone
one	neither	everybody	nobody

Everybody is hungry.
Either of the answers *is* right.
Nobody leaves after eight o'clock.

Watch out for these words when they are used as subjects and followed by a prepositional phrase. If the object of the preposition is plural, you may make the mistake of using a plural verb form.

Is the verb correct in this sentence?

Neither of the dogs *was barking.*
What is the complete subject? *Neither of the dogs*
What is the prepositional phrase? *of the dogs*
What is left? *Neither*

Neither is the subject of the verb.
Neither is singular, so the singular form *was barking* is correct.

347

Exercise **Choosing the Right Verb Form**

Copy these sentences, leaving a space for the verb. Draw a circle around the prepositional phrase. Then, choose the right form of the verb and write it.

Example: Neither of the bolts (fits, fit).

Neither (of the bolts) fits.

1. Nobody in our class (swim, swims) a full length under water.
2. One of the propellers (was, were) bent.
3. Each of you girls (is, are) allowed five minutes for your act.
4. Neither of the cats (has, have) been fed.
5. One of the bathroom taps (are, is) leaking.
6. Each of the uniforms (has, have) the sponsor's name on it.
7. Either of the digital clocks (tell, tells) perfect time.
8. Everybody from both classes (was, were) invited.
9. Each of the displays (is, are) on a different country.
10. (Has, Have) either of you brought the hammock?

There Is, Where Is, Here Is

Many of our sentences begin with *There*, *Where*, or *Here*. These words are never subjects. In sentences beginning with these words, the subject usually comes after the verb.

Before you can choose the right verb form, you have to know what the subject is. You have to know whether it is singular or plural.

There are your books. (*Books* is the subject; the plural form *are* is correct.)

Here is the path. (*Path* is the subject; the singular form *is* is correct.)

Where do the pencils belong? (*Pencils* is the subject; the plural form *do belong* is correct.)

348

Exercise   Choosing the Right Verb Form

Choose the right form of the verb for each sentence.

1. Where (does, do) this road go?
2. Here (is, are) your paper and pencil.
3. There (was, were) no salt in the salt shaker.
4. (Was, Were) you waiting long?
5. Where (is, are) everybody?
6. Here (is, are) four more pieces for the puzzle.
7. Where (are, is) that cushion with the stripes?
8. There (was, were) many reasons for the president's action.
9. Here (is, are) one of the oars.
10. Where (does, do) the books on the table belong?

Compound Subjects

When two or more parts of a compound subject are joined by the conjunction *and*, use the plural form of the verb.

The mayor and the police chief *were* in the parade.

When the parts are joined by *or*, *either-or*, or *neither-nor*, use the form of the verb that agrees with the nearer subject.

Carol or Janet *is* singing.

Neither Mathew nor his brothers *are* coming.

Either six pencils or one pen *costs* a quarter.

Exercise   Choosing the Right Verb Form

Choose the right form of the verb for each sentence.

1. Duchy and her pups (sleeps, sleep) on the back porch.
2. Kermit the Frog or Miss Piggy (is, are) my favorite Muppet.
3. Ted and Victoria (has, have) cameras.
4. Either Mrs. Lunt or her son (walks, walk) the dog every day.

349

5. Neither the girls nor the boys (has, have) the right answer.
6. Everyone and his dog (was, were) there.
7. Seven oranges or one melon (weighs, weigh) three pounds.
8. The swimmers and their coach (practices, practice) every day.
9. Neither the lights nor the phone (works, work).
10. Either Ed or the other boys (is, are) setting up the chairs.

The Words *I* and *You*

Although *I* stands for a single person, the only singular verb forms used with it are *am* and *was*.

I *am* in my room.   I *was* here yesterday.

Otherwise, the verb form is the same as the plural form.

I *do* my work.   I *have* a cold.   I *throw* a good fastball.

The word *you* can stand for one person or for several persons. It may be either singular or plural. Whether it is singular or plural, always use the plural verb form with the pronoun *you*. For example, never say or write *you was*. Always say or write *you were*.

Exercise   Choosing the Right Verb Form

Choose the right form of the verb for each sentence.

1. You (was, were) ready, (wasn't, weren't) you?
2. I (am, is, are) going for a walk.
3. In that closet (is, are) the roller skates.
4. With your new bike, you (rides, ride) faster than before.
5. Among the library aides, I (is, am, are) the youngest.
6. You or anyone else (is, are) welcome at the party.
7. (Has, Have) you brought in the flag?
8. My friend Lucy or I (am, is, are) the best speller in the class.
9. (Was, Were) you afraid?
10. My mother and I (am, is, are) going to the supermarket.

Reinforcement Exercises—Review

Making Subjects and Verbs Agree

A. Using the Right Verb Form

Choose the right form of the verb from the parentheses.

1. (Was, Were) the three of you too hot?
2. Moles by nature (is, are) almost blind.
3. The equipment (has, have) been moved to the attic.
4. The guests (is, are) being shown the doll collection.
5. In the summer all the sheep (huddle, huddles) in the shade.
6. How (do, does) Corinne get to school?
7. All the girls on the team (has, have) been practicing their shots.
8. When (is, are) Uncle Bert arriving?
9. Many trout usually (hide, hides) by this old log.
10. (Isn't, Aren't) there any brownies left?

B. Choosing the Right Verb Form

Choose the right form of the verb for each sentence.

1. Dan and Joanie (take, takes) turns for Saturday chores.
2. Over the door (was, were) carved two huge swords.
3. My pet fish (doesn't, don't) need a lot of attention.
4. Here (is, are) some bigger pieces of pizza.
5. Neither of us boys (has, have) ever shot the rapids.
6. Where (are, is) the cord for this radio?
7. Between the bricks (are, is) a small metal handle.
8. Where (have, has) Maria's hammer and nails been put?
9. Behind the door (was, were) an old umbrella stand and some model planes.
10. Everyone usually (crowd, crowds) into the kitchen.

351

Chapter 23

Using Irregular Verbs

Part 1 Principal Parts of Verbs

Every verb has many different forms. You have seen and used the forms *talked, have talked, had talked, will talk, would have talked,* and others. All of these different forms of a verb are made from just three parts. For this reason, the three parts of any verb are called its **principal parts**.

The principal parts of a verb are the following:

1. **present**
   talk
2. **past**
   talked
3. **past participle**
   talked

353

Here are some examples:

Present	Past	Past Participle
call	called	called
hurry	hurried	hurried
look	looked	looked
paste	pasted	pasted
stop	stopped	stopped
walk	walked	walked

The **present** part of the verb is its present tense. (Add *s* to form the singular.) The present part used with *will* or *shall* forms the future tense.

The **past** part of the verb is its past tense.

The **past participle** is used with helping verbs to make other forms of the verb. Here are some examples of these other forms:

has called	was being called
have called	shall be called
had called	has been called
was called	will have called
were called	should have been called

Regular Verbs

In the list of principal parts given above, the verbs are called **regular verbs**. Every verb that is *regular* forms its past tense by adding *-ed* (*call**ed***) or *-d* (*paste**d***) to the present form. The past participle is the same as the past form and is always used with a helping verb. Most English verbs are regular.

Exercises **Forming Principal Parts**

A. Number your paper from 1 to 10. Write the verb form indicated for each of the following regular verbs. Use one or more helping verbs with each past participle.

1. print (past)
2. decorate (present)
3. paste (past participle)
4. carry (past)
5. use (past participle)

6. help (past participle)
7. confuse (present)
8. list (past)
9. cover (past participle)
10. like (future)

B. Write a sentence for each of the verbs below. Use the verb form indicated.

1. introduce (future)
2. protect (past)
3. wobble (present)
4. add (past participle)
5. trade (past)

6. sound (past participle)
7. develop (past)
8. need (future)
9. improve (past)
10. organize (past participle)

Part 2   Irregular Verbs

Some verbs do not form their second and third parts in a regular way. These five verbs are examples:

Present	Past	Past Participle
feel	felt	felt
go	went	gone
know	knew	known
see	saw	seen
think	thought	thought

These verbs are not regular verbs. They are called **irregular verbs**.

There are about sixty of these irregular verbs in English. The best way to learn about them is to memorize their three principle parts. A list of the most commonly used irregular verbs is given on page 317.

When you are using irregular verbs, you should remember these two rules:

1. The past form is always used by itself, *without* a helping verb.

   We *went* to the library.

2. The past participle is always used *with* a helping verb.

   We *have gone* to the library.

Helping Verbs

The words most often used with the third principal part of all verbs are the forms of *be* and *have*. Here they are, so that you can refer to them when you need to.

Be	**Have**
I am	*I, we, you, they* have
we, you, they — are / were	
he, she, it — is / was	*he, she, it* has
Each of these must be used with one or more additional helping verbs. — be / been / being	(any subject) had

Principal Parts of Common Irregular Verbs

Present	Past	Past Participle
begin	began	begun
break	broke	broken
bring	brought	brought
choose	chose	chosen
come	came	come
do	did	done
drink	drank	drunk
eat	ate	eaten
fall	fell	fallen
fly	flew	flown
freeze	froze	frozen
give	gave	given
go	went	gone
grow	grew	grown
have	had	had
know	knew	known
lay	laid	laid
lie	lay	lain
ride	rode	ridden
ring	rang	rung
rise	rose	risen
run	ran	run
say	said	said
see	saw	seen
sing	sang	sung
sit	sat	sat
speak	spoke	spoken
steal	stole	stolen
swim	swam	swum
take	took	taken
teach	taught	taught
throw	threw	thrown
wear	wore	worn
write	wrote	written

Chapter 24

Improving Your Listening Skills

Listening is part of your everyday life. In school, you listen to reports and assignments. You participate in discussions and conversations. You attend assemblies and movies. Outside of school, you watch TV and listen to radio. You hear commercials along with regular programs. You learn about the world through news shows and specials.

This chapter explores several important listening skills. These skills will help you to be both an accurate listener and a thinking listener.

Part 1 Becoming a Good Listener

Can you tell whether each of these statements is true or false?

1. Good listeners are smarter than poor listeners.
2. Better readers are better listeners.
3. More of your time is spent talking than listening.
4. Most people are good listeners.

All four of these statements are false. Here's why.

Statement 1. Good listeners are not necessarily smarter than poor listeners. However, they do learn more because they take in more information. This might make them seem smarter.

Statement 2. Good listening and good reading require some of the same skills. However, being good at one doesn't make you good at the other. Both must be learned.

Statement 3. Nearly half of all the time you spend communicating is spent listening. Only about a third is spent speaking. The amount of information you take in depends to a great degree on how well you listen.

Statement 4. Most people are *not* good listeners. They spend little time developing the art of good listening.

Listening is an important way to increase your knowledge of the exciting world in which you live. Being a good listener requires effort. It requires energy directed toward polishing your listening skills.

Overcoming Communication Barriers

A **communication barrier** is something that interferes with the messages traveling from speaker to listener. Some barriers are created by listeners. For example, a listener might daydream or might reject all new ideas. Other barriers are created by speakers. For example, a speaker might present a confusing jumble of ideas or might make distracting gestures.

This chart lists some communication barriers. It also tells how good listeners deal with these barriers.

Barrier	Overcoming the Barrier
Wandering thoughts	Good listeners pay attention. They save daydreaming for quiet moments alone.
Distracting noises	Good listeners concentrate on the speaker. They tune out distractions.
Confusing nonverbal signals	Good listeners ignore most nonverbal signals. They listen instead to the main message.
Information overload	Good listeners sort information. They recognize and remember main ideas. They devote less effort to remembering details.
Lazy listening	Good listeners work hard to get the most out of what they hear. They pay attention even when what they hear doesn't seem especially important.
Hasty conclusions	Good listeners are careful not to jump to conclusions or to get carried away with words or ideas. They make thoughtful judgments at the end of a presentation.
Narrow thinking	Good listeners are open to new ideas.

Exercises **Practicing Listening Skills**

A. Close your eyes and spend the next few minutes listening only to certain sounds. As your teacher directs, listen to each of these:

Sounds outside the building
Sounds in the hallway
Sounds in the classroom
Your own sounds (heartbeat, breathing)

B. In pairs, act out the following situations. After a few moments, discuss the communication barriers that you notice in each situation.

1. A student comes home from school two hours late and meets a parent at the door.
2. Brother and sister both believe it is the other's turn to do the dishes.
3. One student has lost another student's book. The second student did not even know the first had borrowed the book.

Part 2 Listening to a Speaker

Sometimes you listen to a speaker taking his or her turn in a discussion or conversation. Other times you listen to a speaker making an individual presentation. In both cases, you exercise the same basic listening skills. You concentrate on the speaker. You work to overcome communication barriers. In addition, when one person speaks at length, you should exercise certain other listening skills. These will enable you to hear ideas exactly and to make intelligent judgments.

Following a Presentation

Some speakers present information organized according to a definite outline. Therefore, to get the most out of what you hear, you must be able to follow an orderly flow of ideas. These six suggestions will help you.

1. **Listen closely to the speaker's opening remarks.** They will give you an idea of the speaker's approach.
2. **Listen for the introduction of each new idea.** Pay attention to pauses. They might mark the end of one idea and the beginning of the next.
3. **Listen for the main ideas.** Ask yourself: Which ideas are repeated? Which are explained? Does the speaker's voice become louder when stating certain ideas?

4. **Listen for connecting words.** Here are some examples: *first, next, then, finally, therefore, and so,* and *however.*
5. **Always keep the speaker's subject in mind.** That way, you will not get lost in a tangle of details.
6. **Listen to the speaker's final remarks.** They might highlight or summarize main points.

Exercise   Listening to a Speaker's Ideas

Choose a short article from a newspaper or magazine. Read the article aloud to a partner. Then have your partner answer this question: What are the main ideas in the article? Repeat the activity with a second article, this time with your partner as the reader and you as the listener.

Looking Beyond the Message

Good listeners focus on the message. They also focus on the person presenting the message. They know that the feelings and aims of a speaker affect what that person says.

Here are three questions that a good listener might ask.

Question 1: What is the speaker's motive?

Motive refers to a person's reason for doing or saying something. A speaker's motive influences his or her choice of details. For example, a speaker who wants to *inform* listeners about caring for a pet parakeet will present many facts. A speaker who wants to *entertain* an audience might tell humorous stories about a pet parakeet. A speaker who want to *persuade* a listener to buy a parakeet will talk about the joys but not the problems of owning this pet.

Question 2: What is the speaker's point of view?

Point of view describes a person's own special way of looking at the world. Likes and dislikes, feelings and experiences all influence point of view. Point of view, in turn, influences how a speaker treats a subject.

For example, two students might review the same science fiction film. One of the students likes technically accurate science fiction. The other doesn't mind if the film wanders from reality. Each reviewer's point of view will affect whether he or she reviews the film with approval or disapproval.

Question 3: Does the speaker show bias?

Bias is a strong opinion based on a personal like or dislike. Bias can cause a speaker to explain only one side of a many-sided subject or to ignore key facts. A student whose father works for a certain computer company, for example, might believe that only her father's make of computers is worth buying. If she gave a speech on computers, her bias would show in her statements.

Bias on the part of a listener, too, is a communication barrier. The student biased in favor of one computer might find it hard to listen to someone else discussing the good points of other computers. To overcome the barrier, a listener must attempt to be open to new ideas.

Exercise **Thinking About Motive, Point of View, and Bias**

Describe how you think and feel about each subject listed below. Decide whether you have a bias for or against the subject. Then choose one subject. Explain briefly what you might say about the subject if your purpose were to inform your listeners. Do the same for these two motives: to entertain and to convince.

1. monster movies
2. spaghetti
3. gym class
4. stamp collecting

Part 3 Listening for Fact and Opinion

A **fact** is a statement about something that has really happened or is true. It can be proved. An **opinion** is one person's idea about something or someone. An opinion cannot be proved.

Every speaker uses a mixture of facts and opinions. A good listener must be alert to separate them. This may be difficult because some speakers use opinions in a way that makes them look like facts. Watch out particularly for **over-generalizations** and **propaganda**.

Understanding Generalization

A **generalization** is a statement of fact based on details. For example, Janet asks one class of sixth graders, "What is your favorite carnival ride?" Nineteen students answer, "Tilt-a-Whirl." Five answer, "Octopus." Four answer, "Bumper Cars." Two say, "Ferris Wheel." These answers are details. From them, Janet might generalize: Most sixth graders like the Tilt-a-Whirl better than other rides.

Generalizing is a useful way of pulling together facts. Over-generalizing, however, is an error. For example, Janet might have said, "Everyone's favorite ride is the Tilt-a-Whirl." A careful listener would question this statement. Did Janet talk to any young children? any teenagers? any adults? The listener would conclude that the statement is too broad. The details did not support the conclusion.

Spotting Over-Generalizations: Words To Listen For			
everyone	never	nobody	all the time
always	every	everybody	no one

Recognizing Propaganda

Propaganda is an effort to spread an opinion or belief. The motive behind propaganda is to convince listeners to think or act in a certain way. The speaker wants the listeners to end up agreeing with his or her bias.

How do you know when you are hearing propaganda?

First, think about what the speaker is saying.

Does the speaker present opinion as facts?
Does the speaker over-generalize?
Does the speaker make vague statements that say little?

Next, think about how the speaker is saying it.

Does the speaker use many strong adjectives, such as *worthwhile, grim, sleek?*
Does the speaker present only one point of view?
Does the speaker use catchy slogans?

Then, think about the speaker's motive.

What is the speaker trying to do?

Finally, think about the way you feel.

Do you find yourself being carried away by the presentation?

Exercise **Practicing Listening Skills**

Together with a partner, make up a commercial to sell a product. Model your commercial after one that you hear on radio or TV. Present your commercial for the class.

The class should do the following for each commercial.

1. Describe the speakers' motive, point of view, and bias.
2. Identify any over-generalizations.
3. Pick out signs of propaganda.

Part 4   Following Directions

As you get older, your world becomes more complicated. It is important for you to listen carefully while something is being explained. Your school assignments are becoming longer, with more complex directions. You may want to learn a new game or take a message. You may wish to try a new recipe or find a new park. Like other types of listening, following directions takes concentration.

Practice in Following Directions

One good way to practice following directions is to use a map. Take a moment to examine the imaginary neighborhood map on the next page. Notice the names of the streets, the locations of landmarks, and the compass direction marker. Ask someone to read aloud the sets of directions below while you try to follow them. Compare results with others.

1. You are at the corner of Adams and Scott. You travel north two blocks and make a left turn. You continue two blocks and then turn north again. After walking one half block more, where will you be?

2. You leave Ivy Elementary School to go home, but must do a few errands on the way. You walk east three blocks and stop to mail a letter. You then turn around and go back one block. You go south on Lincoln for two blocks. After buying a loaf of bread, you walk west on Matthew one block and then turn left. When you reach the northwest corner of Scott and Jefferson you are home. What landmark is across the street from where you live?

3. You and your friends meet in front of the Park District Office on Scott. You walk to the corner of Scott and Madison and go north until you get to the Owens Parkway. You turn right and continue one block. You turn left on Jefferson Street. After walking about one half block north, where will you be?

367

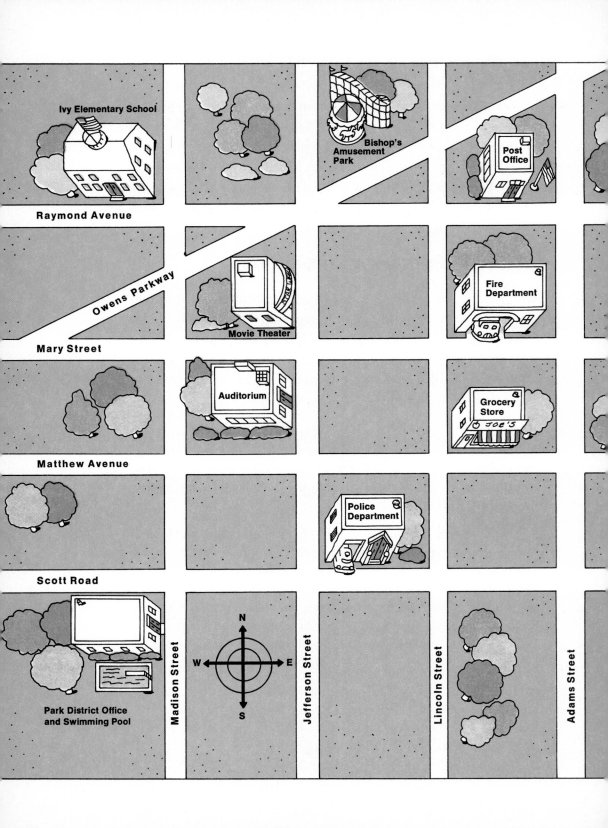

Ivy Elementary School

Bishop's Amusement Park

Post Office

Raymond Avenue

Owens Parkway

Movie Theater

Fire Department

Mary Street

Auditorium

Grocery Store

JOE'S

Matthew Avenue

Police Department

Scott Road

Park District Office and Swimming Pool

Madison Street

Jefferson Street

Lincoln Street

Adams Street

N
W E
S

How well were you able to follow directions? Were there any barriers to your listening? What did you do about them? Was it necessary for the direction-giver to repeat any part of the directions?

Sometimes the listener can help the speaker or direction-giver to do a better job. If the speaker's volume is too low, the listener should politely ask the speaker to talk more loudly. If some part of the speaker's message is unclear, the listener should ask questions.

Following directions is an active process. Try to follow the good listening habits suggested earlier in this chapter.

Exercises   Following Directions

A. Make a set of directions, using the map on page 368. Have classmates practice their listening skills while you read the directions aloud. As a direction-giver, be sure you are polite and clear, and your directions are complete.

B. Place two chairs back to back. In one chair the speaker gives directions for drawing one of the suggested figures. In the second chair, the listener tries to draw the figure. The listener may not ask the speaker to repeat any directions. When the drawing is finished, compare it with the original. Is the drawing accurate? If not, what might have been the problem? If it is accurate, what helped it to be that way?

Suggested figures:

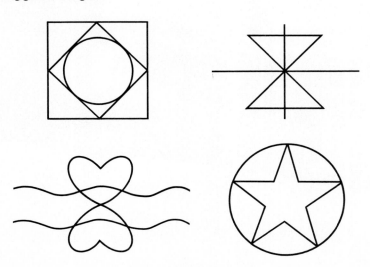

Chapter 25

Improving Your Speaking Skills

Everywhere you go you hear people talking. They may be talking about their hobbies or planning a trip. They may be asking about an assignment or just talking with a friend. There are many reasons for talking. Here are some of them:

To fill a need to share our feelings

To communicate our ideas

To control the things around us

To get a response from others

To gain understanding

To satisfy our physical needs

However, most people talk just because they like to talk. They seldom stop to think about all the things that make human speech more than just a mixture of sounds. This chapter will discuss some of the basics of spoken language. It will give you a chance to improve your speaking skills.

Part 1 Verbal and Nonverbal Communication

Much of what we say to each other comes out in words or sounds called **verbal** messages. Sometimes, however, all or part of our message is sent through silent but visible signals. These signals are called **nonverbal** communication. Look carefully at these pictures:

What messages do you receive from each picture? What gives you the message?

You can also say things with body movements. While riding your bike down the street, you might say hello to a friend with the wave of a hand. While listening to someone tell a story, you might show you understand by nodding your head. Expressions on your face give messages, too. A smile tells your aunt you're glad to see her. A frown tells your mom that salmon is not your favorite meal.

As you can see, an important part of your daily communication is completely silent. Can you think of other examples of nonverbal messages you use or see every day?

Exercises Sending Nonverbal Messages

A. Show these sounds but don't make them.

shout	growl	laugh	whisper
sneeze	cheer	scream	cry

B. Show these emotions on your face.

fear	anger	happiness
sorrow	confusion	excitement

C. Act out these short nonverbal messages.

Wait for me!	Where are you?
Come on.	I don't understand.
Get out!	Forget it!
Who cares?	Stop.
Isn't it hot?	What do you want?

D. Walk into a room and sit down in a chair as each of these characters might.

a fashion model	a heavyweight wrestler
a four-year-old	an old person with a cane

The Whole Message

Most communication is a mixture of verbal and nonverbal signals.

A good speaker tries to be sure that the message sent verbally is the same as the message sent nonverbally. If you pat your teammate on the back as you say "Good play," your message is clear. Try not to confuse your listener by saying one thing verbally and something else nonverbally. For example, saying "This is a really interesting movie" and yawning at the same time send opposite messages.

Exercises **Sending the Whole Message**

A. Count to ten these ways:

Measuring teaspoons of sugar and adding them to a cake mix
Counting pennies on a table
Doing a physical exercise
Counting out a fighter like a referee
Counting people in a room

B. Give these messages, using verbal and nonverbal signals together:

Hurrah!   No.   Not me!
Ouch.   Who cares?   This doesn't make sense.

C. Say each of the following messages verbally but give the *opposite* message nonverbally:

This is delicious.   Oh, that's terrible.
Just what I wanted!   This movie isn't scary at all.
Sure, you can come with me.

D. Choose a partner and act out the following situations. Be sure to communicate both verbally and nonverbally.

You are in a movie theater saving a seat for a friend who went to buy popcorn. Someone comes, pays no attention to you, and tries to take the seat.

You are in the dentist's waiting room with a toothache. You don't feel like talking to anyone. A very chatty person sits down next to you and starts to drive you crazy.

You answer the door to a pushy salesperson who won't take your polite "No, thank you" and go away.

374

E. Give examples of times when you have said one thing in words and meant just the opposite.

Part 2 Using Your Voice Effectively

Volume

While you are watching your favorite TV show, your brother turns on the vacuum cleaner. Your dog begins to bark. You can no longer hear the program. What can you do? You probably go to the set and turn the knob labeled "Volume." Ah! That's better. Now you can enjoy the show.

Volume is the strength or power of a sound. When you are speaking, you must be sure that your volume is at the right level for others to understand you. It must not be too high or too low. Practice speaking with reasonable volume.

Exercises Controlling Your Volume

A. Make a list of things that have a volume control. When are you likely to adjust them to a low or soft level? When might you have them at a higher or louder level?

B. Practice volume control with a partner. One person repeats the sentence, "I am learning to control my volume." The other person controls the speaker's volume by raising (louder) or lowering (softer) a hand. Take turns being a speaker and volume controller.

C. Whisper this sentence: "Can you hear me?" Can you make the whisper louder but still keep it a whisper? What happens when you reach the highest volume of a whisper? What is the next higher level? How is it different from a whisper?

375

D. Say, "Go all the way down," to someone next to you. Ten feet away. Fifty feet away. One hundred feet away.

Rate and Articulation

Have you ever put a record on a record player and when it started to play, discovered it was at the wrong speed? The result is a strange listening experience. To enjoy the record, you must play it at the correct rate of speed.

To communicate in the best way you can, you must pay attention to your **rate** of speaking. How quickly or slowly you speak can affect your meaning. If you speak too slowly, your listener may become bored. If you speak too quickly, your listener may have trouble understanding you.

Articulation is the forming of sounds into separate words. To be able to articulate clearly, you must first know how to pronounce the words you use. A good dictionary will provide the standard American pronunciation of a word. However, people in different parts of the country or of different backgrounds may pronounce words in other ways.

These variations are called **dialects.** As a speaker, use the speech that you are most comfortable with and that your audience will best be able to understand. At all times, speak clearly and distinctly.

Exercises Rate and Articulation

A. Read the following tongue twisters slowly. Then increase your rate. What begins to happen as the rate gets faster?

Please paint the post purple, Polly.
Much whirling water makes the water wheel work.
She makes a proper cup of coffee in a copper coffee pot.
Six thick thistles stick through the fence.

B. Say the following word pairs several times, starting at a slow rate and gradually increasing your speed. What happens if each word is not carefully articulated?

my trip   my twin   my crushes   I scream   great rain

C. Choose a partner. Ask your partner to listen to you talk for a minute. Any subject will do. As you talk, experiment with different rates of speaking. Ask your partner to tell you what the best rate seems to be for you. Continue talking for another minute, trying to maintain your best rate.

D. Practice careful articulation with these word pairs:

can't you   let me   don't you   give me   want to

E. Say these tricky tongue twisters slowly and distinctly:

Penny picked the peppers perfectly.
Pearl joined the boys and girls.
Brown bears wandered around the park grounds.
Tent tops and ten tops are tip top.

Stress and Phrasing

As you have learned, it is important to say individual words distinctly. To get your meaning across to your listener, you must also emphasize words of importance. **Stress** is emphasis. Read the following sentences aloud. Emphasize each underlined word.

<u>I</u> want some ice cream.   I want <u>some</u> ice cream.
I <u>want</u> some ice cream.   I want some <u>ice cream</u>.

Did you notice that the meaning of each sentence is slightly different? What situation might suggest each of the above responses?

Phrasing is putting words together into meaningful groups. Read the following two sentences aloud. Group the words as the punctuation suggests.

The boy says his sister is a fool.
"The boy," says his sister, "is a fool."

377

If you read each sentence correctly, you should have discovered that the meaning of the second is the opposite of the first. Who is the fool, according to each sentence?

Exercises Stress and Phrasing

A. Show the difference in meaning as you say these pairs of sentences.

"You hope," she said, "too much."
You hope she said too much.

What do you think? I will invite you to my party.
What? Do you think I will invite you to my party?

Ms. Sanders, our teacher, was late.
Ms. Sanders, our teacher was late.

B. Use the statement, "You're my friend." Say it three times, each time placing the stress to give the following different meanings:

But she's not.
You're not his friend.
You're not my enemy.

Do the same with each of the following statements.

"José walked to school."

Not Alice.
He didn't run.
Not to the park.

"She found the money."

Not he.
She didn't earn it.
She didn't find the wallet.

C. Stress the underlined words and explain why the phrases have different meanings.

green <u>house</u>—<u>green</u>house
<u>sing</u>ing teacher—singing <u>teacher</u>
<u>play</u>ing cards—playing <u>cards</u>
<u>sail</u>boats—sail <u>boats</u>
<u>White</u> House—white <u>house</u>

Part 3 Reading Poems and Stories Aloud

An excellent way to practice the effective use of your voice is reading aloud. Everyone enjoys hearing an interesting story or a good poem. With some planning you can share some of your favorites with your friends.

Preparing To Read Aloud

> I took a deep breath and ran right up to the diving board and jumped into the swimming hole. This time I held my breath and kept my mouth shut as I paddled and kicked my way to the surface. Then I began paddling furiously with my arms and kicking my legs. The next thing I knew I had reached the river bank. All the kids ran up to congratulate me. It was the proudest moment of my life. I wasn't afraid of the water anymore. As soon as I got my wind I ran and jumped off the diving board again.
>
> —JOHN D. FITZGERALD

This paragraph is a good selection for sharing. Prepare it for reading aloud by following a few simple steps:

1. Silently read the selection *twice*.
2. Copy the selection on paper, leaving space between the lines.
3. Look up the meaning and pronunciation of any unfamiliar words.
4. Decide on the meaning of each phrase, sentence, paragraph, or stanza.
5. On your own copy, make any marks that will help you to remember particular pronunciations, stresses, or pauses needed to get the meaning across to the listener.
6. Practice reading the selection aloud many times. Think about the nonverbal signals you convey. Be sure they add to the reading.

When several members of the class are ready, take turns reading the selection aloud. How well has each reader followed the steps?

Choosing a Selection

When you choose material to read aloud, choose a selection you enjoy. Also consider who will be listening to you. If your audience is going to be young children, you may want to select something different from what you would read to your classmates.

Select one of the following story excerpts or poems. Prepare it for presentation to the class.

There was no trace of the fog now. The sky became bluer and bluer and now there were white clouds hurrying across it from time to time. In the wide glades there were primroses. A light breeze sprang up, which scattered drops of moisture from the swaying branches and carried cool, delicious scents against the faces of the travelers. The trees began to come fully alive. The larches and birches were covered with green, the laburnums with gold. Soon the beech trees had put forth their delicate, transparent leaves. As the travelers walked under them, the light also became green. A bee buzzed across their path.—C. S. LEWIS

DREAMS

Hold fast to dreams
For if dreams die
Life is a broken-winged bird
That cannot fly.

Hold fast to dreams
For when dreams go
Life is a barren field
Frozen with snow.

—LANGSTON HUGHES

380

SPAGHETTI

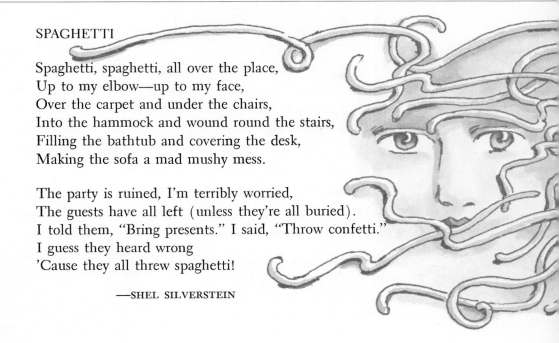

Spaghetti, spaghetti, all over the place,
Up to my elbow—up to my face,
Over the carpet and under the chairs,
Into the hammock and wound round the stairs,
Filling the bathtub and covering the desk,
Making the sofa a mad mushy mess.

The party is ruined, I'm terribly worried,
The guests have all left (unless they're all buried).
I told them, "Bring presents." I said, "Throw confetti."
I guess they heard wrong
'Cause they all threw spaghetti!

—SHEL SILVERSTEIN

Exercises   **Reading Poems and Stories Aloud**

A. A person who is reading aloud should help the listeners understand and enjoy the selection. List some of the ways a reader can do this. Compare your list with those of others in your class.

B. Most newscasters read the news on their programs. Listen to several different newscasters. Compare the way they read aloud. Do some sound better to you than others? Does there seem to be any difference between the way local and national newscasters read aloud? Discuss your observations with the class.

C. Find a poem or story that you think a young child might enjoy. Prepare it for reading aloud. If you can, actually read it to a child.

D. Collect a notebook of selections you think you would enjoy sharing aloud with others. Include both poetry and story material. Plan a reading-aloud day in class.

381

Part 4 Giving a Report

When you give a report, you present organized information to a group of listeners. One key to a successsful report is careful preparation. To get ready for a report, research your subject carefully. Think through your ideas and note the points you want to stress. Gather materials such as pictures, maps, and models. Then practice your report until you feel confident and relaxed.

Your report may be interesting and well prepared. However, unless you present it in an appealing way, you will not reach your listeners. Following are some suggestions to help you put your ideas across.

1. **Be aware of nonverbal communication.** Stand still. Gesture with a purpose. Look directly at your listeners.
2. **Use your voice effectively.** Speak clearly and at a comfortable rate for you and your listeners. Stress important points.
3. **Speak in simple, correct English.**
4. **Be sensitive to your listeners.** Stop to explain anything that seems to confuse them.

Exercise Giving Reports

For the report and discussion parts of these activities, work in groups of four or five. Each student should do the following.

A. Choose an activity to observe, for example, a squirrel storing nuts, a group of children playing a game, or shoppers waiting in a checkout line. Prepare a brief report on what you see. Then present the report to your group.

B. Comment on each report given in your group. Note the speaking skills that each speaker has mastered. Note those that need improvement.

382

Part 5 Taking Part in Conversation and Discussion

How often do you talk on the phone? answer questions? share experiences with friends? make plans with your parents? You probably talk with other people dozens of times each day. These conversations just happen. They are unplanned and unstructured, moving naturally from one idea to the next.

Not all speech, however, is quite so free in its form. For example, planning sessions, panel discussions, and club meetings all demand more preparation and more thoughtful expression of ideas.

In this Part, you will learn some guidelines for participating effectively in both informal conversations and more structured discussions.

Taking Part in a Conversation

Conversation is a sharing of ideas. It is a way of getting to know people better and of learning new things. Good conversation is lively. The participants pay attention to each other and are considerate. When speaking, they use their voices effectively. They send clear nonverbal signals. When listening, they think about what the speaker is saying. Participants do not allow one person to do all the talking or to interrupt other speakers.

Interesting conversation flows from one idea to the next. Notice the way that each person in the following conversation keeps things going.

JOHN: I wish you could have seen my crazy dog Bif last night.

BETH: Why, what did he do?

JOHN: Well, he was sound asleep on the floor in his usual position — on his back with all four paws in the air. I turned on the TV and the sound was really loud. Old Bif jumped up, gave me a dirty look, and pushed the "Off" button with his nose!

KARL: Did you teach him to do that?

JOHN: Nope. It was a complete surprise.

BETH: Karl, doesn't your cat do some funny things, too?

To be good at carrying on a conversation, you must listen and think as well as speak. The following guidelines will help you in future conversations.

Guides for Taking Part in a Conversation

1. Listen carefully to what others are saying.

2. Respect and accept ideas that differ from your own.

3. When you don't agree with another's point of view, don't interrupt. Wait your turn and then tell your reasons for disagreeing and your point of view.

4. Pay attention to the reactions of your listeners.

5. Avoid remarks that will hurt a listener's feelings.

6. Respond to your listeners' questions by repeating, explaining, or adding new ideas.

7. Ask questions for the sake of understanding.

8. Encourage others to speak by asking questions.

9. When one topic is growing stale, think of new topics to interest others.

10. Give everyone a chance to speak.

Exercises   Practicing Conversation

A. Choose one of the following situations. With two partners, act out a two-minute conversation. Practice good conversation techniques.

1. Three close friends talk about their favorite TV shows.
2. A parent and child welcome a new neighbor.
3. Two children describe a sport or video game for a grandparent.

B. Make a list of several topics that might be appropriate for conversation with each of the following groups:

A few close friends   The parents of a friend
Several elderly relatives   A stranger on a bus
A new neighbor   Your teacher

C. Choose a partner. Act out a solution for each of the following conversation problems.

1. One person has been talking for several minutes.
2. One person has listened carefully but has not talked.
3. You and another person begin to speak at the same time.
4. Someone makes a statement you know to be incorrect.
5. Someone begins to change the topic before the original topic has been completed.

Taking Part in a Discussion

Like conversation, discussion is an exchange of ideas. A discussion, however, has a definite purpose. For example, a group of students might get together to plan a mural, to decide the rules of a contest, or to talk about a book.

The basic rules of conversation apply to discussion. Participants must be polite and respectful. They must speak and listen, must ask and answer questions. In addition, the participants must be ready to suggest ideas and solutions if at all possible.

385

Every participant in a discussion has the following responsibilities:

Guides for Participating in a Discussion

1. Prepare for the discussion, if possible.

2. Listen and respond to other participants.

3. Add ideas and make suggestions.

4. Ask questions for specific reasons:
   a. to clarify points
   b. to get information
   c. to move the discussion forward

5. Be polite.

One participant in a discussion group acts as the leader, or chairperson. The leader guides the discussion. He or she makes sure that what is said is orderly and purposeful. The leader keeps the participants on the subject and sees that everyone contributes ideas.

Responsibilities of a Discussion Leader

1. State the problem or ask another participant to do so.

2. Restate the problem if the talk strays from the subject.

3. Draw participants into the discussion through questions.

4. Remind the participants of the rules of conversation, if necessary.

Exercises Conducting Discussions

A. Read this discussion. Then answer the questions that follow.

Jackson School has a problem. Students are not using the school's library often enough. Mr. Carroll's homeroom discusses the problem.

MR. CARROLL: Mrs. Campbell, the new librarian, would like your ideas about ways she can encourage library use. Any suggestions?

SALINA: I think that the library should be open later. Now, most students go to the library where they can stay...

MATT: Ha! Who wants to hang around after school?

SALINA: Not you, that's for sure!

MR. CARROLL: Matt, Salina, students *do* have different ideas about ways to spend after-school time. Let's get back on the track. Salina has a good idea — lengthening library hours. Paul, have you come up with any ideas since we talked yesterday?

PAUL: Many students don't know their way around the school library. Could Mrs. Campbell arrange for small groups to visit the library?

LISA: Mrs. Campbell might be willing, but what about the teachers? Would they let groups of students leave their classes?

MR. CARROLL: Good question, Lisa. I'll try to find out. Now, let's talk a little about the kinds of books you think should be added to the library's collection.

1. Which of the participants carry out their responsibilities? Explain.

2. Which of the participants do not follow the rules of good discussion? Explain how they failed.

3. Who is the discussion leader? Explain how this leader guides the discussion.

B. Have a class discussion about a problem involving your own school library. Choose a leader. Set a time limit. After the discussion, write a report explaining what was done well in the conversation and what could have been done better.

387

Chapter 26

Understanding Literature

The word *literature* has many meanings. In one sense, it means everything that is written. However, when we talk about reading or studying literature, we mean something different. Then *literature* means writing that makes us think and feel. Literature gives us new ideas or makes us see things in a new way. It helps us to understand others and ourselves.

Literature that is written in sentences and paragraphs is called *prose*. Another type of literature is called *poetry*.

The two main categories of prose writing are **fiction** and **nonfiction**. Fiction is writing that comes from the imagination. Nonfiction is writing that tells of facts. The writer of fiction invents stories, while the writer of nonfiction records the happenings of the real world.

In this chapter, you will study examples of fiction, nonfiction, and poetry. You will examine the ways that writers shape language to express their ideas. Then, in your reading, you can recognize these techniques. In your writing, you can put their techniques into practice.

Part 1   Fiction

Fiction originates in the imaginations of writers. A work of fiction is called a **story**. Some stories, such as **folktales** and **tall tales**, were created by groups. Most stories, however, can be traced back to individual authors.

Some writers of fiction write about people who never lived but *could* live, and about events that have not happened but *could* happen. This is called **realistic fiction**, for it is rooted in the real world. Other writers create new worlds different from the real world. This kind of fiction is called **fantasy**.

All works of fiction have three basic elements:

> **Characters** are the people or animals in a story.
> **Setting** is where and when a story takes place.
> **Plot** is what happens in a story.

The action of most stories begins with a short introduction that presents the characters, the setting, and the **conflict**, or problem faced by the characters. The events of the story follow, building to a **climax**, or turning point. The climax is the most surprising or exciting moment in a story. The story ends soon after the climax.

The Folktale

Folktales are stories made up by groups of people. Many are thousands of years old. These simple tales provide information and entertainment. In addition, they teach the listener or reader about the behavior that the group admires and values and about the behavior that it dislikes and discourages.

In the past, before printing became easy and inexpensive, folktales were told and retold by skilled storytellers. Each storyteller had the freedom to change the tale a little, according to the audience's beliefs and customs. In this way, many versions of the same story were created.

Following is an example of a folktale. Notice that the author is a group, not an individual. As you read, think about the behavior that this group might admire.

THE STORYTELLER

Once there was a king in the land of Shoa who loved nothing so much as listening to stories. Every moment of his spare time was spent in listening to the tales told by the storytellers of the country but a time came when there were no stories left that he hadn't heard. His hunger for stories came to be known in the neighboring kingdoms, and wandering singers and storytellers came to Shoa to be rewarded for whatever new tales they could bring. But the more tales the king heard the fewer were left that he had not heard. And so, finally, in desperation he let it be known throughout the land that whatever storyteller could make

391

him cry, "Enough! No more!" would receive a great piece of land and the title of Ras, or prince.

Many men, inspired by the thought of such wealth and honors, came to tell him stories, but always he sat and listened eagerly without ever protesting that he had had too much.

But one day a farmer came and offered to tell stories until the king was so full of them that he would cry out in protest. The king smiled.

"The best storytellers in Ethiopia have come and gone without telling me enough," he said. "And now you come in your simple innocence to win the land and the title of Ras. Well, begin, you may try."

And so the farmer settled himself comfortably on a rug and began:

"Once there was a peasant who sowed wheat," he said. "He mowed it when it was grown, threshed it, and put all the precious grain in his granary. It was a rich harvest, one of the best he had ever had.

"But, and this is the irony of the tale, in his granary there was a tiny flaw, a hole big enough to pass a straw through. And when the grain was all stored an ant came and went through the hole and found the wheat. He carried away a single grain of it to his anthill to eat."

"Ah-ha!" the king said, showing interest. For this story was one that he hadn't heard.

"The next day," the farmer continued, "another ant came through the hole and found the wheat, and he, too, carried away a grain of it."

"Ah-ha!" the king said.

"The next day another ant came and carried away a grain," the farmer said.

"Ah-ha!"

"The next day still another ant came and carried away a grain."

"Yes, yes, I understand, let us get on with the story," the king said.

392

"The next day another ant came, and carried away another grain. And the next day another ant came and carried away another grain."

"Let us not dally with the details," the king said. "The story is the thing."

"The next day another ant came," the farmer continued.

"Please," the king said, "please!"

"But there are so many ants in the story," the farmer said. "And the next day another ant came for a grain of wheat, and . . ."

"No, no, it must not be!" the king said.

"Ah, but it is the crux of the story," the farmer replied. "And the next day another ant came and took away a grain . . ."

"But I understand all this," the king protested. "Let us pass over it and get on with the plot."

"And the next day another ant came and took his grain. And the next day . . ."

"Stop, I want no more of it!" the king shouted.

"The story must be told in the proper way," the farmer said. "Besides, the granary is still nearly full of wheat, and it must be emptied. That is in the story. And the next day . . ."

"No, no, enough, enough!" the king shouted.

"And the next day another ant . . ."

"Enough, enough, you may have the land and the title of Ras!" the king shouted, jumping up and fleeing from the room.

So the farmer became a prince and owned a great parcel of land.

This is what people mean when they say: "One grain at a time brings good fortune."
—HAROLD COURLANDER

393

The characteristics, or qualities, of a folktale are these:

1. The characters are not described in detail.
2. Few details about the setting are given.
3. The plot is the most important element.
4. The ending is satisfying. Goodness is rewarded. Evil is punished. Wisdom wins over foolishness.
5. A moral, or truth, often appears at the end.

Think about how these characteristics are shown in "The Storyteller."

Exercises **Understanding the Folktale**

A. Answer these questions about "The Storyteller."

1. Who are the two most important characters?
2. What details about setting are given?
3. What conflict, or problem, is faced by the king?
4. List the events that take place. Which event is the climax, or turning point?
5. How is the farmer rewarded? Does he deserve the reward? Why or why not?
6. What moral appears at the end of the folktale? Explain the moral in your own words.
7. What qualities does this group of Africans seem to admire? What qualities does the group seem to dislike?

B. Write a new folktale using "The Storyteller" as a model. Invent new characters (human or animal), and change the setting. You might want to use a modern setting with modern characters. Leave the plot the same. Decide on a logical reward or punishment for one of your characters.

The Tall Tale

A tall tale is a humorous exaggeration of facts. It is told with absolute seriousness, as if it were the truth. A tall tale is similar to a folktale in that it is created by a group of people. A major difference is that a tall tale is pure entertainment.

A tall tale can be long and complicated or short and simple. It may present one incredible event or a series of events, as in the following tall tale.

THE COLD

It got so cold that winter, a boy's shadow froze right to the side of his house and he had to leave it behind.

The air also froze. And when people spoke, their words froze. One man was strong enough to break the air with his fists, which enabled him to speak. But most people were not that strong.

When one woman tried to call her son, her words froze before they reached him. As a result, he did not come home for two months—not until they finally thawed, and at last he heard her calling.

When two girls tried to quarrel, they couldn't. Instead of insults, ice cubes tumbled from their mouths, one for each word. But they were so angry, they collected the ice cubes in sacks and took them home. Then they melted them and listened to their words and enjoyed a good fight. —ALVIN SCHWARTZ

In a tall tale, what happens is the most important element. The plot is often quite simple, consisting merely of a collection of incidents. In some tall tales, such as "The Cold," neither the characters nor the settings are well developed because they are not important to the plot. In others, such as the stories of Paul Bunyan and Pecos Bill, the character and setting are better developed because they are more important to the plot.

395

Exercises Understanding the Tall Tale

A. Review the characteristics of a tall tale explained in this section. Then tell how "The Cold" fits these characteristics.

B. The weather is a good subject for tall tales. Heat, cold, fog, wind, snow—all of these can be exaggerated enough to be funny. Write two short tall tales about the weather. You can use this beginning sentence or one like it: One day the wind was so strong that. . . .

C. Tall tales can be written about people or animals with unusual qualities, such as great size, tremendous speed, and superhuman strength. Write a tall tale about a character with one of these qualities. Remember that your story need not make sense. It can be just plain silly.

Realistic Fiction

Realistic fiction tells a story that could possibly happen. Its characters are believable. They may remind you of your family or friends. The setting is realistic. It may be a familiar neighborhood or an unfamiliar but believable setting, such as an island or an Arctic wilderness.

The plot usually centers on problems that many people experience. By seeing how the characters face their problems, readers gain an understanding of other people. They also may discover possible ways of solving their own problems.

Following is an example of realistic fiction. As you read, notice how the writer places the story firmly in the real world.

396

HARRY THE HEAVYWEIGHT

This kid Bruno Heckenberg always seemed to be a million steps ahead of everyone else—including me. He was bigger, tougher, and louder than any of us other kids. He was always ready to lean on one of us. He was like a tornado running a relay race. He'd give you a quick little shove from behind, scatter your books, or grab your hat right off your head. Then he'd dare you to start something.

I was thinking about this very thing while I was delivering papers on the last day of school in June. My last house was the Biddle place. I tossed the paper on the porch lightly, keeping an eye out for their dog. Just as I was turning away, the front door crashed open, and out came a burst of angry shouts along with a large cat. I don't know whether he was thrown out or what, but by the time he hit the steps he was streaking, tail up and ears back.

The cat shot by me, a rippling, grayish blur. The door slammed shut. I backed away, looking for that high-speed cat. He was waiting for me at the corner, sitting on a low stone wall, washing himself as if nothing had happened. Was he a rough-looking brute! Both ears above his wide, flat face were chewed up and cauliflowered. He had a healed-up cut over his right eye. The scar pushed his eyebrow down until it almost covered his eye. This gave him a cockeyed squint and made him look a cross between a sleepy owl and a wide-awake hawk. His coat was either dirty gray with white spots, or dirty white with gray spots. I couldn't decide which. Either way, he looked like he'd just crawled up out of the smokestack of a steam engine.

397

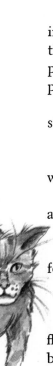

From my pocket I dug out a piece of soft candy still wrapped in paper. I pushed it toward him. He sniffed it and ate the whole thing, paper and all. "Let's go, Harry," I said. The name just popped up. I suppose it was because of my Uncle Harry who plays professional hockey.

I hung my paper sack in the garage, waiting for Harry. He strolled in and gave my legs a rub-around. I went inside.

"Mom," I said, "a big cat followed me home."

"Never mind about the size," she said. "I hate cats. And we're not interested in such an animal, Bryan."

"But he's hungry, Mom! Harry ate a piece of candy, paper and all."

"What about Harry?" asked Pop, coming in just then.

"He's sitting on the hood of our car right now, washing his feet," I said.

"My brother Harry?"

"No—Harry the cat. Take a look, Pop."

In the garage Harry eyed Pop like a seasick pirate. Then he flicked his tail and gave Pop's legs a rubbing. "He's as ugly as a beat-up lid of a garbage can," said Pop, "but friendly. Where'd you get him?"

I told Pop. He rubbed Harry under the chin, and the cat hissed. "Hey," said Pop. "He can't meow. You've got a speechless beast here, Bryan."

"I know," I said, as Harry curled up his front paws into furry fists and jabbed at Pop with his left. "Something else is weird too. He belches a lot. I never heard a cat belch—never. Do you think there's something wrong with him?"

Pop grinned and said, "No, but of his nine lives, I'd say it's six down and three to go."

"He needs someone to look after him," I suggested. "Do you suppose I can keep him, Pop?"

"Well, if you can't find his owner—and if he'll stay—but he belongs in the garage. Your mother has her opinion of cats, so don't expect any improvement when she sees this one. Feed him, Bryan."

I put a lost-and-found ad in the paper, but no one called or came to claim Harry. So he stayed. By August, after eating regu-

398

larly, he weighed almost seventeen pounds. We got used to his hissing, which he couldn't help, and his belching, which he seemed to enjoy.

I was the only kid in town with a pet like Harry. I tied a piece of old throw rug over the rear carrier on my bike. Harry would ride along, hanging on with his claws dug into the rug like a bundle of fishhooks. He'd turn his head and hiss at passing cars. Other times we guys would form a circle and hiss at him. Harry would stand up on his hind legs, double up his front paws, and jab away like a heavyweight. I've had three dogs, and I was crazy about each one. But, believe me, I loved that Harry better.

Then along came Labor Day. I'd be starting sixth grade and going to the new school that had been built. Opening day was supposed to be something special. Pop made me dress up a little more, which I hated. The mayor herself and a lot of other bigwigs were all over the place. In the afternoon there was a special assembly. Afterwards, at about two-thirty, everyone headed home.

I was jogging along, anxious to get out of my school clothes. Suddenly I heard this "Clomp! Clomp!" behind me. It sounded like some giant creature from a monster movie. I didn't have to look. I knew who it was—Bruno Heckenberg, looking bigger and meaner than last June.

"Hey, pretty-boy Bryan," he hooted, coming up beside me. "Your shoes are on backwards. You're going to trip and hurt yourself, dummy." He moved closer to me. Then slick as a whistle he put one foot down right in my path. I tripped on it, falling flat in the dirt, losing my glasses. Angry and scared, I looked up at Bruno. "Told you," he said, grinning. "Warned you, but—"

I never saw Harry, but I heard his hiss. Next thing I knew, he was up on Bruno's back and shoulders, clawing away at his

399

head ratatat-tat, triple time. When Bruno turned his head to see what was after him, Harry leaned over and let go a combination belch, hiss, and scream right in Bruno Heckenberg's ear. I could see the blood drain from Bruno's face, turning it as pale as a bleached sheet. Bruno ran, old Harry hanging on, still using his head for a bongo drum.

"Harry!" I called. Harry let go of Bruno's shoulder and jumped to the ground. He came loping back to me, still hissing softly.

I told Mom and Pop about what had happened. Pop said, "I hope Harry didn't hurt Bruno."

"No," I said, "But he sure scared him."

Then Mom said something that made me think she wasn't the cat-hater she pretended to be. "Bryan, let's ask the vet why Harry can't meow," she suggested. "It's the least we can do for him."

At the vet's I put Harry on the examining table and held him down. Just then the vet walked in. She took one look at the cat and yelled, "Hey, where'd you find him, Bryan?"

"Find who?" My heart sank.

"Rocky, my crazy cat! He hung around here for a couple of years. I tried to find a home for him; but, of course, no one wanted him. Finally he got so frightful I had to put him in a cage. He wasn't cockeyed then, but one way I'd always recognize him. He couldn't meow, so he hissed. Say there, old Rocky! Want to hiss for me?"

Old Harry sat crouched on the table. His ears were twitching, and his eyes were flashing. No doubt he was thinking about his time in the cage out back. Then he straightened up, flicked his crooked tail, opened his mouth, and meowed. Just once, no more.

The vet scratched her head in amazement. "Well, I never! Boy, he sure looks like Rocky. Why did you bring him in to see me?"

"Never mind," I said, picking Harry up carefully. "Let's go, Mom."

400

Harry never meowed again, but that once was enough. You'll never find a cat smarter than old Harry. In my book, he was a heavyweight in more ways than one.   —A. R. SWINNERTON

The writer of this story creates true-to-life characters who exchange realistic **dialog**, or conversation. Bryan, the main character, tells the story. The story is told from his **point of view**. The reader learns about Bryan through his words and actions, through his thoughts, and through the comments of other characters about him.

Exercises **Understanding Realistic Fiction**

A. Answer the following questions about "Harry the Heavyweight."

1. Describe Bryan. Then describe Harry. Find parts of the story that gave you the information you needed for your descriptions.
2. What is the setting? Find details in the story that describe or suggest the setting.
3. Find one example of realistic dialog in the story.
4. What is the climax, or turning point, in the story?

B. Write a short realistic story. Describe your characters and setting using realistic details. Include at least one conversation. Keep in mind that it is often easiest to write about people and places similar to ones you know.

Fantasy

Writers of fantasy create worlds in which the impossible happens. In strange new places, animals speak, people move back or ahead in time, children find magic objects.

The characters in a fantasy accept the unusual as normal or at least possible. Readers, too, must forget the rules of life in the real world. They must accept new sets of rules.

Fantasies often include realistic details which describe the characters and the setting. The fantastic events then seem more believable, as they happen to normal people in everyday surroundings.

401

As you read the following story, notice the mingling of realistic and fanciful details.

ZOO

The children were always good during the month of August, especially when it began to get near the twenty-third. It was on this day that the great silver spaceship carrying Professor Hugo's Interplanetary Zoo settled down for its annual six-hour visit to the Chicago area.

Before daybreak the crowds would form, long lines of children and adults both, each one clutching his or her dollar and waiting with wonderment to see what race of strange creatures the Professor had brought this year.

In the past they had sometimes been treated to three-legged creatures from Venus, or tall, thin men from Mars, or even snake-like horrors from somewhere more distant. This year, as the great round ship settled slowly to earth in the huge tri-city parking area just outside of Chicago, they watched with awe as the sides slowly slid up to reveal the familiar barred cages. In them were some wild breed of nightmare—small, horse-like animals that moved with quick, jerking motions and constantly chattered in a high-pitched tongue. The citizens of Earth clustered around as Professor Hugo's crew quickly collected the waiting dollars, and soon the good Professor himself made an appearance, wearing his many-colored rainbow cape and top hat. "Peoples of Earth," he called into his microphone.

The crowd's noise died down and he continued. "Peoples of Earth, this year you see a real treat for your single dollar—the little-known horse-spider people of Kaan—brought to you across a million miles of space at great expense. Gather around, see them, study them, listen to them, tell your friends about them."

The crowds slowly filed by, at once horrified and fascinated by these strange creatures that looked like horses but ran up the walls of their cages like spiders. "This is certainly worth a dollar," one man remarked.

All day long it went like that, until ten thousand people had filed by the barred cages. Then, as the six-hour limit ran out, Professor Hugo once more took microphone in hand. "We must go now. Tomorrow we will land in New York and next week on to London, Paris, Rome, Hong Kong, and Tokyo. Then on to other worlds!"

As the ship rose from the ground the Earth peoples agreed that this had been the very best Zoo yet. . . .

Some two months and three planets later, the silver ship of Professor Hugo settled at last onto the familiar jagged rocks of Kaan, and the horse-spider creatures filed quickly out of their cages. Professor Hugo said a few parting words, and then they scurried away in a hundred different directions, seeking their homes among the rocks.

In one, the she-creature was happy to see the return of her mate and offspring. She babbled a greeting in the strange tongue and hurried to embrace them. "It was a long time you were gone. Was it good?"

The he-creature nodded. "The little one enjoyed it especially. We visited eight worlds and saw many things."

The little one ran up the wall of the cave. "On the place called Earth it was the best. The creatures there wear garments over their skins, and they walk on two legs."

"But isn't it dangerous?" asked the she-creature.

"No," her mate answered. "There are bars to protect us from them. We remain right in the ship. Next time you must come with us. It is well worth the nineteen commocs it costs."

And the little one nodded. "It was the very best Zoo ever. . . ."

—EDWARD D. HOCH

403

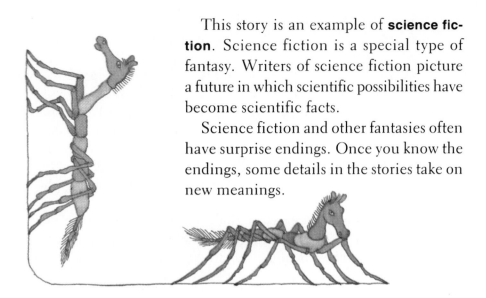

This story is an example of **science fiction**. Science fiction is a special type of fantasy. Writers of science fiction picture a future in which scientific possibilities have become scientific facts.

Science fiction and other fantasies often have surprise endings. Once you know the endings, some details in the stories take on new meanings.

Exercises **Understanding Fantasy**

A. Answer these questions about "Zoo."

1. Who are the characters in this story? Where is the setting at the beginning of the story? At the end? When does the story take place?

2. What impossible things happen in this story?

3. Find two realistic details in the story.

4. Do the characters accept the possibility of travel between planets? Give proof for your answer from the story.

5. What makes this story science fiction?

6. After you have read the ending, what details take on new meaning?

404 B. Write a short fantasy. Include both realistic and fanciful details. If you wish, you may write about one of the following: a time machine, a magic formula, the exploration of a newly discovered planet, a human-like animal.

Part 2 Nonfiction

Nonfiction is prose writing that deals with reality. Like fiction, most works of nonfiction have characters and settings. Many relate events, although these events may not be shaped into a plot.

Writers of fiction are free to invent characters, settings, and plots. In contrast, writers of nonfiction must stick to the truth. Each element in a work of nonfiction must be factually accurate.

On the following pages, you will study three kinds of nonfiction: the **biography**, the **autobiography**, and the **journal**. In a biography, an author writes about the life of a real person. In an autobiography, a writer tells his or her own life story. In a journal, a writer records daily happenings, often for a limited period of time only.

Biography

A biography is the true story of someone's life. Most full-length biographies discuss the subject's early life as well as important events in later years.

Writers of biography research their subjects thoroughly. They study letters and other writings by the subject. They read the writings of others about the subject. Sometimes they even visit the areas where their subjects once lived.

Following is a selection from a biography of Benjamin Franklin. As you read, notice the details that the writer gives about Franklin and his experiment.

BENJAMIN FRANKLIN

Since little was known about electricity, Franklin, without knowing it, performed many dangerous experiments. In one experiment, he almost electrocuted himself. He thought, wrongly, that the meat of an animal would be more tender if the animal were killed by an electric shock rather than by conventional means. With this theory in mind, he tried to kill a turkey by

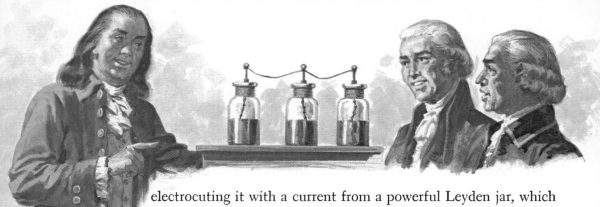

electrocuting it with a current from a powerful Leyden jar, which was used to store electricity. Franklin tried to hold the bird between his feet and apply the electrodes to its wings. The turkey, of course, had other ideas. The turkey squirmed from Ben's grasp, and the electrodes slipped into his hands. He wrote what happened next: "I then felt what I know not well how to describe: a universal blow throughout my whole body from head to foot."

Franklin was shaken up by the experience, but he survived. Later, he said about his attempt to kill the turkey by electricity: "I meant to kill a turkey, and instead, almost killed a goose."

—CONRAD STEIN

A well written biography makes you feel as if you know the subject. As you read, you begin to see the subject as a real, living person. Believable dialogue is one way that a biographer brings characters to life. Through careful research, the biographer gains a good idea of what the subject and other characters might say. He or she then uses this knowledge as the basis for creating realistic conversations.

The writer of Franklin's biography uses a different technique. He includes Franklin's own words, selected from the famous man's own writings. Franklin's statements are enclosed in quotation marks.

Exercises Understanding Biography

A. Answer these questions about the sample biography.

406

1. How would you describe Franklin after reading this selection? Find reasons for your answer in the selection.

2. Find the two quotations in this selection. What does each suggest about Franklin?

B. Choose a famous person as a subject, and find a full-length biography about that person. Choose one incident in the person's life and read about it. Then read an encyclopedia article about the person. Write an addition to the article, telling about the incident. Use the biography of Franklin as a model. If the original article mentions the incident, add details. Include a quotation, if possible.

Autobiography

An autobiography is the true story of a person's life, written by that person. In a full-length autobiography, the writer tells, in order usually, the important or memorable happenings in his or her life.

An autobiography is similar to a biography in several ways. However, while the writer of a biography often must guess at the exact thoughts and feelings of the subject, the writer of an autobiography knows them for certain.

Following is a selection from the autobiography of Helen Keller, a woman left deaf and blind by a childhood illness. The selection features two characters, the writer as a six-year-old child and Anne Mansfield Sullivan, her teacher. As you read, be aware of the writer's thoughts and feelings.

THE STORY OF MY LIFE

The morning after Miss Sullivan came, she led me into her room and gave me a doll. When I had played with it a little while, she slowly spelled into my hand the word "d-o-l-l." I was at once interested in this finger play and tried to imitate it. When I finally succeeded in making the letters correctly, I was flushed with childish pleasure and pride. Running downstairs to my mother, I held up my hand and made the letters for doll. I did not know that I was spelling a word or even that words existed; I was simply making my fingers go in monkey-like imitation. In the days that followed I learned to spell in this way a great many words, among them *pin, hat, cup* and a few verbs like *sit, stand*

407

and *walk*. My teacher had been with me several weeks, however, before I understood that everything has a name.

One day, while I was playing with my new doll, Miss Sullivan put my big rag doll into my lap also, spelled "d-o-l-l" and tried to make me understand that "d-o-l-l" applied to both. Earlier in the day we had had a struggle over the words "m-u-g" and "w-a-t-e-r." Miss Sullivan had tried to impress it upon me that "m-u-g" is *mug* and that "w-a-t-e-r" is *water*, but I persisted in confusing the two. In despair she had dropped the subject for the time, only to renew it at the first opportunity. I became impatient at her repeated attempts and, seizing the new doll, I dashed it upon the floor. I was keenly delighted when I felt the fragments of the broken doll at my feet. Neither sorrow nor regret followed my outburst. I had not loved the doll. In the still, dark world in which I lived there was no strong sentiment or tenderness. I felt my teacher sweep the fragments to one side of the hearth, and I had a sense of satisfaction that the cause of my discomfort was removed. She brought me my hat, and I knew I was going out into the warm sunshine. This thought, if a wordless sensation may be called a thought, made me hop and skip with pleasure.

We walked down the path to the well-house, attracted by the fragrance of the honeysuckle with which it was covered. Someone was drawing water and my teacher placed my hand under the spout. As the cool stream gushed over one hand she spelled into the other the word *water*, first slowly, then rapidly. I stood still, my whole attention fixed upon the motions of her fingers. Suddenly I felt a misty consciousness as of something forgotten—a thrill of returning thought; and somehow the mystery of language was revealed to me. I knew then that "w-a-t-e-r" meant the wonderful cool something that was flowing over my hand. That living

408

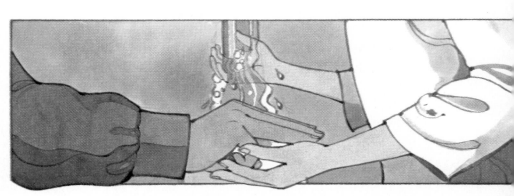

word awakened my soul, gave it light, hope, joy, set it free! There were barriers still, it is true, but barriers that could in time be swept away.

I left the well-house eager to learn. Everything had a name, and each name gave birth to a new thought. As we returned to the house, every object that I touched seemed to quiver with life. That was because I saw everything with the strange, new sight that had come to me. On entering the door, I remembered the doll I had broken. I felt my way to the hearth and picked up the pieces. I tried vainly to put them together. Then my eyes filled with tears; for I realized what I had done, and for the first time I felt regret and sorrow.

—HELEN KELLER

In this autobiography, the writer describes events and the thoughts and feelings that went along with the events. The writer also provides reasons for her actions. Although the autobiography was written many years after the events occurred, the writer recalls her experiences vividly. She brings her memories to life through carefully chosen words and precise details.

Exercises   Understanding Autobiography

A. Answer these questions about the sample autobiography.

1. Name two ways in which an autobiography is similar to a biography. Name two ways in which an autobiography differs from a biography.

2. What is the setting of this selection? Write the events in the plot in order.

3. Find three sentences in which Helen Keller expresses her private thoughts and feelings.

4. Why do you think Helen Keller included this incident in her autobiography?

409

B. Write about one experience in your life. Choose an incident you remember well. Tell what happened and your feelings about it.

The Journal

A journal is a record of daily happenings, much like a diary. A journal often is written on a long trip so that, at the end of the trip, the traveler can remember what happened each day.

Like an autobiography, a journal is a personal account. The writer describes the experiences that he or she feels should not be forgotten. Unlike a full-length autobiography, a journal does not concentrate on only a few important events. The writer makes entries soon after events occur, before he or she has had time to think about their importance.

In 1804, Meriwether Lewis and William Clark set off on a journey west, across the unexplored American continent. They recorded their experiences in journals. Following is an entry from Lewis's journal. Lewis gives the reader a factual reporting of events. He also reveals his thoughts and feelings.

> May 29
>
> Last night we were all alarmed by a large buffalo bull, which swam over from the opposite shore and coming alongside of the white pirogue (canoe) climbed over it to land. He, then alarmed, ran up the bank in full speed directly towards the fires and was within eighteen inches of the heads of some of the men who lay sleeping before the sentinel could alarm him or make him change his course. Still more alarmed, he now took his direction immediately towards our lodge, passing between four fires and within a few inches of the heads of the men as they yet lay sleeping. When he came near the tent, my dog saved us by causing him to change his course a second time, which he did by turning a little to the right, and was quickly out of sight, leaving us by this time all in an uproar with our guns in our hands, inquiring of each other the cause of the alarm, which after a few moments was explained by the sentinel. We were happy to find no one hurt. The next morning we found that the buffalo in passing the pirogue had trodden on a rifle. The rifle was much bent. With this damage I felt well content, happy indeed that we had sustained no further injury.　　—MERIWETHER LEWIS

Journals are sometimes difficult to read. They often include details that are not interesting to every reader. Often, therefore, other writers retell the events in journals in a more storylike form. Here is a retelling of the entry from Lewis's journal. As you read, notice the difference between this selection and the original journal.

Suddenly, one night, the camp was roused by Scannon's (Lewis's dog) barking and a terrific rushing about in the darkness. A buffalo bull had swum the river and blundered into one of the canoes. Mad with fright, he was charging about the camp among the sleeping men, barely missing trampling on their heads. Finally the bull rushed off into the darkness with Scannon snapping at his heels. —DAVID FREEMAN HAWKE

The retelling is shorter and easier to read than the journal. However, it does not give the reader the same feeling of being an eyewitness to the past.

Exercises   Understanding the Journal

A. Answer these questions about the two selections in this lesson.

1. Compare the vocabulary in Lewis's journal with the vocabulary in the retold version. Which difficult words from the journal are left out or changed in the retelling?

2. Find sentences in Lewis's journal that express his thoughts and feelings. Does the writer of the retold version include thoughts and feelings?

B. Reread the selection about Benjamin Franklin in the lesson on biography. Write an entry to a journal for that day, as if it were written by Franklin himself. Remember to include Franklin's thoughts and feelings.

Part 3 Poetry

When you read a poem, the words take you into another person's mind. You may share that person's memories. You may see a familiar sight in a new way.

Poetry looks different from prose writing. Writers of fiction and nonfiction write sentences. They arrange the sentences into paragraphs. Poets write in **lines**. They group the lines into **stanzas**.

Poets choose their words carefully. They choose words for their sounds and for the special feelings the words create. They pack as much meaning as possible into their lines and stanzas.

Sound in a Poem

Words that **rhyme** end with the same sound. *Kite* and *right* are examples. Rhyming words often are used in a pattern. See if you can find the pattern of rhyme in the following poem.

A TREE HOUSE

A tree house, a free house,
A secret you and me house,
A high up in the leafy branches
Cozy as can be house.

A street house, a neat house,
Be sure and wipe your feet house
Is not my kind of house at all.
Let's go live in a tree house.

—SHEL SILVERSTEIN

In the first stanza, the rhyming words are *tree*, *free*, *me*, and *be*. In the second stanza, the words *street*, *neat*, and *feet* rhyme. One word in the last line of the second stanza picks up the rhyme of the first stanza. Can you find that word?

Poems usually have a **rhythm**, or pattern of strong beats. The reader can feel the strong beats in each line.

The strong beats in the first two lines of "A Tree House" are marked here. Read the lines aloud, stressing the marked words.

A tree house, a free house,

A secret you and me house,

Reread the second stanza of "A Tree House." Feel the strong beats in these lines.

However, rhythm is not only the strong beats. The pattern of strong and weak beats is what is important. In "A Tree House," for example, the first six lines end in weak beats. Then the seventh line leaves off that final weak beat and ends with a strong beat. Notice what that does to the sound of the eighth line.

The rhythm of the following poem is different from the steady beat in "A Tree House." The smooth, free-flowing rhythm makes you think of the graceful movements of a cat and the quiet beauty of moonlight. Notice, too, that there is no pattern of rhyme to limit that feeling.

MOONLIGHT

Like a white cat
Moonlight peers through windows,
Listening, watching.
Like a white cat it moves
Across the threshold
And stretches itself on the floor;
It sits on a chair
And puts white paws on the table.
Moonlight crouches among shadows,
Watching, waiting
The slow passing of night.
—MAUD E. USCHOLD

The rhythm of the next poem is the natural rhythm of a person talking.

MOOCHIE

Moochie likes to keep on playing
That same old silly game
Peeka   Boo!
Peeka   Boo!

I get tired of it
But it makes her laugh
And every time she laughs
She gets the hiccups
And every time she gets the hiccups
I laugh

—ELOISE GREENFIELD

What is this poem about? How does the rhythm match this subject?

Rhyme is one way that poets repeat sounds. Another way is called **alliteration**. Alliteration is the repetition of a consonant sound. Here is an example of alliteration.

Windshield *w*ipers *w*ipe the *w*indshield

The repetition of sounds, words, and phrases can emphasize the meaning of a poem. Notice in this poem how repetition, especially of the *s* and *w* sounds, creates the sound of a windshield wiper at work.

Windshield wipers wipe the windshield
   Wipe the water off the pane
This way   That way
This way   That way
This way   That way
   In the rain

—MARY ANN HOBERMAN

The rhythm of this poem sounds like the rhythm of windshield wipers. Alliteration and the repetition of *windshield, this way*, and *that way* help to create this rhythm.

Pictures in a Poem

Poets create pictures with words. One way to do this is by comparing one thing with another. The comparison helps readers see how things are similar in a new or different way. If a poet uses *like* or *as* in a comparison, he or she is writing a **simile**. Following is a simile from the poem "Moonlight" on page 413.

> *Like* a white cat
> Moonlight peers through windows.

This simile compares moonlight to a white cat peering through a window. Find another simile in this poem.

A **metaphor** also compares one thing with another. However, a metaphor does not use *like* or *as*. A metaphor says that one thing *is* another.

Read the following poem. Can you find the metaphor?

> The dark gray clouds,
> the great gray clouds,
> the black rolling clouds are elephants
> going down to the sea for water.
> They draw up the water in their trunks.
> They march back again across the sky.
> They spray the earth again with the water,
> and men say it is raining.
> —NATALIA M. BELTING

The specific metaphor is stated in the third line. The entire poem, however, compares the actions of clouds to the actions of elephants.

415

Mood and Meaning in a Poem

The sounds and word pictures in a poem join to create a **mood**. Mood is the feeling experienced by the reader. "A Tree House" has a cheerful mood, which reflects the happiness of children in a tree house. In "Moonlight" the mood is quiet and mysterious, as are the cat and moonlight. In the poem comparing clouds to elephants, the mood is awed and respectful. The mood of each poem fits the subject of the poem.

The subject of "Moochie" is a game played with a baby. The attitude of the speaker is reflected in the mood, which is free and playful. The mood of the poem about windshield wipers also is lighthearted. Notice that, in all five poems, sounds and word pictures together bring out meaning.

Exercises **Understanding Poetry**

A. Read this poem. Then answer the questions.

JANUARY

The days are short,
    The sun a spark
Hung thin between
    The dark and dark.

Fat snowy footsteps
    Track the floor.
Milk bottles burst
    Outside the door.

416

The river is
　A frozen place
Held still beneath
　The trees of lace.

The sky is low.
　The wind is gray.
The radiator
　Purrs all day.
　　　　—JOHN UPDIKE

1. Find the words that rhyme in this poem. Is there a pattern to the rhymes?

2. Choose any stanza. Find the strong beats. Count the strong beats in each line. Can you see a pattern to them?

3. To what does the poet compare the radiator? Is this comparison a simile or a metaphor?

4. Find one example of alliteration.

5. How would you describe the mood of this poem?

B. Write a poem on any subject. The poem may rhyme but it does not need to rhyme. The rhythm can be steady and strong, free-flowing, or conversational. Use alliteration and, if you like, repeat a word or phrase at least once. Include a simile or a metaphor.

Chapter 27

Capitalization

The use of capital letters is called **capitalization**. When you use a capital letter at the beginning of a word, you **capitalize** the word.

Capital letter are used to make reading easier. They call attention to the beginnings of sentences and to certain special words.

Part 1 Proper Nouns and Adjectives

> Capitalize **proper nouns** and **proper adjectives**.

A **common noun** is the name of a whole group of persons, places, or things.

man   country   book

A **proper noun** is the name of a particular person, place, or thing.

Queen Victoria   Sweden   Bible

419

A **proper adjective** is an adjective formed from a proper noun.

Victorian   Swedish   Biblical

There are many different kinds of proper nouns. The following rules will help you recognize many proper nouns which need to be capitalized.

Capitalize the names of people and pets.

Begin every word in a person's name with a capital letter. An initial stands for a name. Write initials as capital letters. Put a period after every initial.

Susan B. Anthony   A. J. Foyt

Often, a word for a family relation is used as the name of a particular person or as part of the name. *Mom* and *Grandfather Lewis* are two examples. Capitalize a word used in this way.

Capitalize a title used with a person's name.

In assembly today, Dr. Martin and Coach Brown talked about food, rest, and exercise.

Have you seen Ms. Gray or Mr. Townsend?

Capitalize words referring to God and to religious scriptures.

the Deity   the Bible   the Gospel
Allah   the Talmud   the Book of Genesis
the Lord   the Koran   the New Testament

420

Capitalize the word *I*.

Mary and I planted sunflower seeds.

Exercises   Using Capital Letters Correctly

A. Number your paper from 1 to 10. Copy the following sentences. Change small letters to capital letters wherever necessary.

1. A television series was based on books by laura ingalls wilder.

2. The names linda ann rigby and spencer a. marks were engraved on the plaque.

3. Some people think that thomas edison was a genius.

4. The name nadine means "hope."

5. This famous scientist, dr. george washington carver, was born a slave.

6. In church last week, i heard a reading from the book of genesis.

7. Stacy and i played tennis against kenny and maria.

8. We live next door to mr. and mrs. torres.

9. The best teacher i ever had was professor eileen black.

10. Aunt annette made an appointment with our family dentist, dr. means.

B. Follow the directions for Exercise A.

1. The Indian chiefs william brant and red jacket signed a treaty with moses cleaveland.

2. Tomorrow, grandpa and i will cut miss quinlan's lawn.

3. Years later, president lincoln met harriet beecher stowe.

4. The twins, sandy and dennis, went to the store with their father, mr. cage.

5. The leader of althea's Bluebird group is mrs. hartley.

6. After adopting the Muslim religion, the boxer cassius clay changed his name to muhammed ali.

7. For years, researcher jane goodall lived with a band of apes.

8. One of the speakers was the artist, andrew wyeth.

9. Either lottie or i can take you to ms. franklin's office.

10. When did marian anderson begin her career?

Capitalize the names of months, days, and holidays.

Do not capitalize names of seasons (spring, summer).

Examples:

On Friday, December 16, our Christmas vacation begins.
My favorite season is winter.

Capitalize the names of particular places and things.

a. Cities, states, and countries.

Examples:

Which is larger, Portland, Oregon, or Detroit, Michigan?
Brazil is the largest country in South America, and Canada is the largest country in North America.

b. Streets, bridges, and buildings.

Examples:

The Chambers Building is at the corner of Greenlawn Avenue and High Street.

c. Geographical names. Capitalize all geographical names. Also capitalize the words *north, south, east,* and *west* when they refer to a section of a country. Do not capitalize them when they refer to a direction.

Examples:

Most of the area between the Rocky Mountains in the West and the Appalachian Mountains in the East is drained by three rivers, the Mississippi, the Ohio, and the Missouri.

The boat sailed west, toward the island.

Exercises **Using Capital Letters Correctly**

A. Number your paper from 1 to 10. Copy the following sentences. Change small letters to capital letters wherever necessary.

1. If you can't come at easter, come next summer.
2. We could see long island and new jersey from the top of the empire state building.
3. Is the amazon river in brazil or in argentina?
4. Dean's dairy bar isn't open on holidays.
5. Doreen was in the west, visiting relatives in arizona.
6. We rode north from the lazy l ranch just before sunset.
7. The first king of hawaii was king kamehameha.
8. Interstate highway 80 carries heavy traffic.
9. The famous irwin hospital is in the east.
10. Five states border the gulf of mexico.

B. Number from 1 to 10. Copy each of the following groups of words. Wherever necessary, change small letters to capitals.

1. in the twentieth congressional district
2. the most powerful tribes in the west
3. ten miles east of pike's peak
4. in houston on tuesday
5. the altitude of denver, colorado
6. the golden gate bridge in san francisco
7. the spring holidays in florida
8. special thanksgiving celebrations at plimoth plantation
9. on cathedral square in the kremlin in moscow
10. in puerto rico on thursday, july 12

Capitalize the names of races, religions, nationalities, and languages.

Modern American Indian artists often use traditional designs in their work.

Judaism, Christianity, and the Muslim religion share a belief in one God.

The Russians and the Chinese have frequent arguments about their border.

Does this junior high school offer French?

Capitalize the names of clubs, organizations, and business firms.

My aunt belongs to the Centerville Garden Club.

Where is the headquarters of the Boy Scouts of America?

Don's father works for General Motors.

Exercises Using Capital Letters Correctly

A. Number from 1 to 10. Copy each of the following groups of words. Wherever necessary, change small letters to capitals.

1. a dutch windmill
2. african art
3. a jewish temple
4. the cub scouts
5. polish sausage
6. an anglican minister
7. filipino traditions
8. the campfire girls
9. bell telephone company
10. the arab oil fields

B. Number from 1 to 10. Copy each of the following sentences. Wherever necessary, change small letters to capitals.

1. Some of the Romance languages are french, italian, and spanish.

2. The olmecs were an ancient indian tribe in mexico.

3. Gabriel joined the united states marine corps.

4. Were those tourists speaking japanese?

5. Many people of india practice hinduism.

6. Dolores's mother tests computers for the digital equipment company.

7. The elmwood photography club meets every monday in the carnegie library.

8. Roberto became an officer of a junior achievement business.

9. The museum exhibits include an egyptian mummy and several roman statues.

10. The irish writer jonathan swift wrote a great english novel about a man named gulliver.

Part 2 First Words

Sentences

Capitalize the first word of every sentence.

Workers digging the foundation found a mastodon bone.

When will the eclipse begin?

Look out!

Poetry

Capitalize the first word in most lines of poetry.

I'll tell you how the sun rose
A ribbon at a time,
The steeple swam in amethyst,
The news like squirrels ran.

EMILY DICKINSON, "I'll Tell You How the Sun Rose"

425

Sometimes, especially in modern poetry, the lines of a poem do not always begin with a capital letter.

so much depends
upon

a red wheel
barrow

glazed with rain
water

beside the white
chickens.

WILLIAM CARLOS WILLIAMS, "The Red Wheelbarrow"

Exercises Using Capital Letters Correctly

A. Number your paper from 1 to 10. Find the words in the following sentences that should be capitalized. Write the words after the proper number, using the necessary capital letters.

1. the third sunday in june is father's day.
2. is cotton still an important crop in the south?
3. a bird came down the walk:
   he did not know i saw;
   he bit an angleworm in halves
   and ate the fellow, raw.

   EMILY DICKINSON, "A Bird Came Down the Walk"

4. last year we had a dry summer and a rainy fall.
5. do you like italian food? we can get pizza at tina's restaurant.
6. there is a program on television tonight about japan.
7. dr. frances gilbert teaches english literature at carroll university.
8. this month has five saturdays.
9. have you seen any movies by d. w. griffith?

426

10. whose woods these are i think i know.
   his house is in the village though;
   he will not see me stopping here
   to watch his woods fill up with snow.
   ROBERT FROST, "Stopping by Woods on a Snowy Evening"

B. Follow the directions for Exercise A.

1. the school orchestra will play two works by wolfgang amadeus mozart.

2. whenever richard cory went down town,
   we people on the pavement looked at him:
   he was a gentleman from sole to crown,
   clean favored, and imperially slim.
   EDWIN ARLINGTON ROBINSON, "Richard Cory"

3. on wednesday i'll be late for dinner. the girl scouts are having a meeting at four o'clock.

4. what is the spanish word for *table?*

5. brown and furry
   caterpillar in a hurry;
   take your walk
   to the shady leaf or stalk.
   CHRISTINA GEORGINA ROSSETTI, "The Caterpillar"

6. we celebrate flag day on june 14.

7. are you visiting montreal, in quebec? there, canadians speak french.

8. the Rhino is a homely beast,
   for human eyes he's not a feast,
   but you and i will never know
   why Nature chose to make him so.
   farewell, farewell, you old rhinoceros,
   i'll stare at something less prepoceros.
   OGDEN NASH, "The Rhinoceros"

427

Outlines

Capitalize the first word of each line of an outline.

Capitalization and Punctuation

I. Use of capital letters

   A. Proper nouns and adjectives

   B. First words

     1. Sentences
     2. Poetry
     3. Outlines
     4. Titles

II. Use of periods

Titles

Capitalize the first word, last word, and any other important words in a title.

Do not capitalize a little word such as *the, in, for, from, a,* or *an,* unless it comes first or last.

Steven Spielberg, *Close Encounters of the Third Kind* (book)

Anne Morrow Lindbergh, *Gift from the Sea* (book)

Lewis Carroll, "The Walrus and the Carpenter" (poem)

Underline the title of a book, magazine, or motion picture.

Mary Poppins   (book title in handwriting)

When these titles are printed, they are in *italics.*

428

Mary Poppins, by P. L. Travers (book title in print)
Ebony Junior (magazine)
Star Wars (motion picture)

Underline the title of a painting or the name of a ship.

Washington Crossing the Delaware (painting)
Queen Elizabeth II (ship)

Put quotation marks around the titles of stories, television programs, poems, reports, articles, and chapters of a book.

"The Little Match Girl" (story)
"The Complete Hen" (poem)
"How Plastic Is Made" (student's report)
"Cubs Take Double-Header" (newspaper article)

Exercise   Using Capital Letters Correctly

Copy the following titles and outline. Capitalize them correctly.

1. "highwire trapeze artist breaks record" (newspaper article)
2. *the peaceable kingdom* (painting)
3. "the brain is wider than the sky" (poem)
4. "how the mob is grabbing the mines" (magazine article)
5. *pets of the world* (magazine)
6. *the return of the king* (book)
7. "what makes the aurora" (student's report)
8. "the world's deepest caves" (article)
9. "the kiteflying tournament" (pupil's report)
10. (outline) indians of the northeast

    I. groups
      A. lake indians
      B. woodland indians
    II. important foods
      A. lake indians
        1. wild rice
        2. fish
      B. woodland indians
        1. corn
        2. deer and other game

429

Reinforcement Exercises—Review

Capitalization

A. Capitalizing Proper Nouns and Adjectives Correctly

Number your paper from 1 to 10. Copy the following sentences. Change small letters to capital letters wherever necessary.

1. At the bus stop pam met josé and ursula.
2. The hostess, ms. barrett, introduced me to dr. and mrs. taylor.
3. Tomorrow i will go shopping.
4. Will october 31 fall on a friday this year?
5. The school year usually ends around memorial day.
6. The grand canyon is in the state of arizona.
7. The sears tower is the tallest building in chicago, illinois.
8. This restaurant serves delicious hungarian goulash.
9. The slavic languages use an alphabet different from ours.
10. Gladys's uncle is a member of the chamber of commerce.

B. Using Capital Letters Correctly

Number your paper from 1 to 10. In each of the following sentences, poems, and outline, find the words that should be capitalized. Write the words after the proper number, using the necessary capital letters.

1. *optricks, a book of optical illusions* is a book by wentzell and holland.
2. this newspaper has an article called "runaway horse stops traffic."

3. I based my report on the article "deserts" in the *world book encyclopedia*.

4. rosalie subscribes to the magazine *skateboard world*.

5. the movie *the wizard of oz* is shown on television almost every year.

6. today monica presented a report entitled "visiting a live television show."

7. have you ever read the story "the little mermaid"?

8. when i was in kindergarten, i watched "sesame street" every day.

9. cats sleep fat and walk thin.
    cats, when they sleep, slump;
    when they wake, pull in —
    and where the plump's been
    there's skin.
    cats walk thin.

ROSALIE MOORE, "Catalog"

10. (outline) some famous paintings

    I. american

        a. early

            1. *death of wolfe*

            2. west's portrait of george washington

        b. modern

            1. *american gothic*

            2. *christina's world*

    II. european

Chapter 28

Punctuation

When you talk with someone, you put words together in a certain way to express your thoughts. Sometimes you drop your voice. That tells your listener you have finished a thought. Sometimes you raise your voice. That tells your listener you are asking him or her a question. If you are excited, perhaps you shout. Sometimes you pause.

What happens when you write? There is no change in voice to guide the reader. Instead, there are capital letters and punctuation marks to guide him or her. They help in the same way that pauses and changes in voice help your listener.

Part 1   End Marks

The signal that shows where a sentence begins is a capital letter. The punctuation marks that show where a sentence ends are called **end marks**.

There are three important end marks: (1) the **period;** (2) the **question mark;** (3) the **exclamation point** (or **exclamation mark**).

433

The Period

Use a period at the end of a declarative sentence.

A **declarative sentence** tells something.

This is my poster for the exhibit.

Use a period at the end of most imperative sentences.

An **imperative sentence** requests, instructs, or orders.

Put your poster on the bulletin board.

Use a period after an abbreviation or after an initial.

We often write words in a shortened form to save time and space. These shortened forms of words are called **abbreviations**. On calendars the names of the days are often abbreviated. For example, *Mon.* stands for *Monday.* Except for such abbreviations as *Mr.*, *Mrs.*, *Ms.*, *A.M.*, and *P.M.*, avoid using abbreviations when you write sentences.

We use the abbreviation A.M. to stand for the two Latin words, *ante meridiem,* which mean "before noon." The abbreviation P.M. stands for *post meridiem,* "after noon."

Here are examples of other common abbreviations. Notice how some abbreviations have two or three parts, with each part standing for one or more words. A period is then used after each part of the abbreviation.

St.	Street or Saint	in.	inch
Mt.	Mount or Mountain	doz.	dozen
R.R.	Railroad	Dr.	Doctor
P.O.	Post Office	Mr.	Mister
U.S.A.	United States of America	Mrs.	Mistress
D.C.	District of Columbia	Ms.	(no longer form)

434

Periods are not used after some abbreviations:

CB   citizens' band   PBS   Public Broadcasting System
FM   frequency modulation   USAF   United States Air Force
M   meter   ml   milliliter

The two-letter state abbreviations, such as IL, OH, and CA, are written with capitals and no periods.

If you are not sure whether an abbreviation should be written with or without periods, look up the abbreviation in a dictionary.

We often shorten a name to its first letter, which is called an **initial.** Always use a period after an initial.

P. L. Travers (Pamela Lyndon Travers)

J. C. Penney (James Cash Penney)

Use a period after each number or letter that shows a division of an outline or that precedes an item in a list.

Punctuation (an outline)   Talent Show Acts (a list)

I. End marks   1. tumblers

   A. The period   2. tap dancer

      1. Sentences   3. singer

      2. Abbreviations and initials

      3. Outlines and lists   4. band

   B. The question mark

   C. The exclamation point

II. Commas

Exercises **Using Periods Correctly**

A. Number your paper from 1 to 10. Copy the following phrases, putting periods where necessary.

1. 4 ft 10 in

2. Washington, D C

3. P O Box 12

4. Bedford Ave

435

5. Aug 30
6. Butterford Chocolate Co, Inc
7. Dr H M Ritchie
8. 500 mi
9. (list) First five presidents
   1   George Washington
   2   John Adams
   3   Thomas Jefferson
   4   James Madison
   5   James Monroe
10. (outline) Super-8 Movie-Making
   I   Major equipment needed
      A   Camera
         1   For silent movies
         2   For sound movies
      B   Projector
   II   Other materials needed
      A   Film
      B   Splicer

B. Rewrite each of the following phrases, using abbreviations where possible.

1. East 126 Street
2. New York
3. Reverend Marsh
4. 4 gallons
5. Platte River
6. Raleigh, North Carolina
7. December 9
8. Benander Game Company
9. 10 square feet
10. Durapools, Incorporated

C. List the abbreviated forms you find on maps in a geography book. Beside each abbreviation, write the word it stands for.

D. List the abbreviations used in measurement problems in your arithmetic book. Beside each abbreviation, write the word it stands for.

The Question Mark

Use a question mark at the end of an interrogative sentence.

An **interrogative sentence** is a sentence that asks a question.

Where are we?

The Exclamation Point (or Exclamation Mark)

Use an exclamation point at the end of an exclamatory sentence and some imperative sentences.

An **exclamatory sentence** is a sentence that expresses strong feelings.

Jackie struck out!

An exclamation point is used at the end of an imperative sentence that expresses excitement or emotion.

Be careful!

Use an exclamation point after an interjection.

An **interjection** is a word or group of words used to express strong feeling. It is one of the eight parts of speech. Words often used as other parts of speech may become interjections when they express strong feeling.

Oh! How beautiful!   Wow! What an ending!

Exercises   Using End Marks Correctly

A. Copy the following sentences. Supply the missing punctuation.

1. Mr and Mrs Gregory go to St Augustine every winter
2. Ouch This pan is hot
3. Dr Evans will be in his office until 4:30

437

4. What circus did P T Barnum manage

5. Ms Carol F Lunt will speak at the N H S commencement exercises

6. My new address is 600 W 24 St

7. Don't touch that broken glass

8. We stopped at an L C Carran gas station

9. How many empty bottles are you returning

10. Good grief My kite got stuck on that tree again

B. Follow the directions for Exercise A.

1. Terrific We got the last four tickets

2. How much does that album cost

3. W E B DuBois, Ph.D, was a writer and a professor of sociology

4. Jump out of the way of that car

5. Mail the letter to Miss Deborah K Sobol

6. Did Vanessa try out for the team last night

7. The poet Hilda Doolittle signed her poems H D

8. Oh, no You didn't forget the picnic lunch, did you

Part 2   The Comma

Commas in Sentences

Commas tell the reader to pause. The pause keeps the reader from running together words that should be kept apart. Commas are a great help in reading.

When you write a series, use commas to separate the members of the series.

438

Two words are not a series. There are always three or more words in a series.

The children entered dogs, cats, and hamsters in the show.

In a series, commas are placed *after* each word except the last.

You can see how important it is to separate the parts of a series by looking at these sentences.

Bob stuffed himself with cheese, pizza, ice cream, sandwiches, chocolate, milk, and peanuts.

Bob stuffed himself with cheese pizza, ice-cream sandwiches, chocolate milk, and peanuts.

Note that both sentences contain the same words, in the same order. It is the punctuation that differs. Both sentences might be right. It depends upon what Bob ate. The writer has to use commas correctly to tell the reader what Bob ate.

Place a comma after *yes, no,* or *well* when these words start a sentence.

Yes, I'm going.   Well, I'll see you there.

When you use *and, but,* or *or* to combine two sentences, put a comma before these words.

We ran fast. We nearly missed the bus.

We ran fast, but we nearly missed the bus.

Exercises   Using Commas Correctly

A. Copy these sentences. Place commas where they are needed.

1. Yes we went to the zoo last summer.
2. You can take a bus to the zoo but we drove out.
3. We took our lunches and we spent the whole day.
4. We saw a hippopotamus a gorilla and an anteater.
5. No you can't feed the elephants.

439

6. Well we liked the monkey house best.

7. There were monkeys of every size color and shape.

8. Two monkeys started a fight and another watched.

9. We took pictures had a boat ride and saw a movie.

10. The movie was good but it wasn't as much fun as the animals at the zoo.

B. Follow the directions for Exercise A.

1. No it's not raining.

2. Karen aimed fired and just missed the bull's eye.

3. Motels are all right but I like campgrounds better.

4. Dawn Ramon and Anna dug a harbor in the sand and Doug and Nancy built a sandcastle.

5. Yes your answer is right.

6. Denmark Sweden and Norway are called Scandinavian countries.

7. Will you drive us or should we take the bus?

8. The spaghetti tomato sauce and spices are in that cupboard.

9. Well what do you think?

10. Donald Duck's nephews are Huey Dewey and Louie.

Use commas to set off the name of a person spoken to. If the name comes at the beginning or end of the sentence, one comma is enough. If the name comes in the middle of the sentence, place one comma before the name and another comma after it.

Please answer the phone, Jim.

Ginny, may I use your pen?

I believe, Mark, that you are right.

440

Set off an appositive by commas. An **appositive** is a word or group of words that means the same as the noun just before it. The appositive gives more information about the noun.

The words in italics in the following sentences are appositives. Notice that they are set off by commas.

Mr. Lopez, *the scoutmaster,* moved away.

Our neighbor, *Ms. Carl,* drives an ambulance.

Separate the parts of a date by commas. If the date appears in the middle of a sentence, place a comma after the last part.

On November 7, 1962, Eleanor Roosevelt died.

We'll expect you on Tuesday, April 4.

Notice that you do not place a comma between the month and the number of the day.

Separate the name of a city from the name of a state or country by a comma. If the two names come in the middle of a sentence, place a comma after the second name, too.

My grandmother was born in Dublin, Ireland.

We left Concord, New Hampshire, at noon.

Exercises   Using Commas Correctly

A. Copy these sentences. Place commas where they are needed.

1. Last summer we went to Phoenix Arizona.
2. Friday May 5 was our opening night.
3. We all met the new principal Mrs. Gomez.
4. At Kitty Hawk North Carolina the Wright brothers successfully flew three gliders.
5. Dad this is Al Cresco a friend of mine.
6. It was hot in Corpus Christi Texas.
7. Hold the line Gerry and I'll ask her.
8. On Saturday January 25 the excavation was begun.

441

B. Follow the directions for Exercise A.

1. Rhonda were you born in September 1970?
2. Albany New York is on the Hudson.
3. No Mrs. Lucas I have never lived in Dayton Ohio.
4. Mr. Gray let's have the exhibit on Friday February 19.
5. The candidate Ms. Wingreen made a speech.
6. On October 7 1943 my father was born.
7. You know Adele I'll be away tomorrow.
8. In Duluth Minnesota there is a statue of Jay Cooke the financier.

Commas with Quotations

Use a comma to set off the explanatory words of a direct quotation.

When you use a quotation you are giving the words of a speaker or writer. You are said to be *quoting* the words of the speaker or writer. If you give the *exact* words, you are giving a **direct quotation.** Usually you include explanatory words of your own, like *Mary Kay said, JoAnne answered,* or *Phil asked.*

Courtney announced, "The movie will begin in ten minutes."

In the above sentence, the explanatory words come *before* the quotation. A comma is then placed after the last explanatory word. Now look at this quotation:

"I want to go home," moaned Lisa.

In the above sentence, the explanatory words come *after* the quotation. A comma is then placed inside the quotation marks after the last word of the quotation.

Sometimes the quotation is separated into two parts.

"One of the people in this room," the detective said, "is the murderer."

442

The preceding sentence is an example of a **divided quotation.** It is called "divided" because it is made up of two parts that are separated by the explanatory words. A comma is used after the last word of the first part. Another comma is used after the last explanatory word.

The quotations you have just looked at are all direct quotations. A quotation can be either *direct* or *indirect.* In an **indirect quotation** you change the words of a speaker or writer to your own words. No commas are used.

Clark Kent said that he had to make a phone call.

Commas in Letter Parts

Use a comma after the greeting of a friendly letter and after the closing of any letter.

Dear Agnes, Sincerely yours,

The Comma To Avoid Confusion

Some sentences can be very confusing if commas are not used in them. Here are two examples of such sentences:

Going up the elevator lost power.
In the grocery bags were in demand.

Now notice how much clearer a sentence is when a comma is used:

Going up, the elevator lost power.

In the grocery, bags were in demand.

Use a comma whenever the reader might otherwise be confused.

443

Exercises **Using Commas Correctly**

A. Copy these sentences. Add commas where they are needed.

1. Benjamin said "I'd like to visit Boston some day."

2. "This cake is delicious" said my father.

3. When Sheila typed the table shook.

4. "It seems to me" Carol said "that this puzzle is missing some pieces."

5. In the story books were forbidden.

6. After we ate the neighbors came to visit.

7. "Who" the caterpillar asked Alice in Wonderland "are you?"

8. According to the paper cups of coffee will cost a dollar each.

9. In the garden flowers were blooming from May through September.

10. "Come here Midnight" Ned called.

B. Follow the directions for Exercise A.

1. While Vickie painted Eric sanded the table.

2. "Tomorrow's weather" the forecaster said "will be sunny and warm."

3. For dinner, Tony had macaroni salad and dessert. (three items)

4. Ms. Gajda announced "The concert begins at seven o'clock."

5. "The radio is too loud" my mother complained.

6. When our team lost the players felt depressed.

7. Coming down the tree snapped telephone lines.

8. Yvette asked "What's on TV tonight?"

9. After Mr. Knowles left his puppy whined.

10. "Three weeks ago today" Meg said "I got my new bike."

Part 3   The Apostrophe

444

Use an apostrophe to show possession.

To form the possessive of a singular noun, add an apostrophe and *s* after the apostrophe.

dog + 's = dog's   lady + 's = lady's   James + 's = James's

To form the possessive of a plural noun that does not end in s, add an apostrophe and an s after the apostrophe.

gentlemen + 's = gentlemen's   geese + 's = geese's

To form the possessive of a plural noun that ends in s, add only an apostrophe.

dogs + ' = dogs'   ladies + ' = ladies'

Exercises   Using Apostrophes in Possessives

A. Make these words show possession. Write the possessive form.

1. island   4. babies   7. goalies   10. children
2. mechanics   5. Chris   8. guides   11. golfers
3. chickadee   6. announcer   9. cow   12. frogmen

B. Make these words show possession. Write the possessive form.

1. hunters   4. women   7. painter   10. cyclist
2. Ms. Smith   5. Louisa   8. cats   11. Dr. Bliss
3. policemen   6. poets   9. horse   12. partner

Use an apostrophe in a contraction.

A **contraction** is a word made by combining two words and omitting one or more letters. The apostrophe shows where a letter or letters have been omitted.

can not = can't   we are = we're

will not = won't   does not = doesn't

you will = you'll   he had = he'd

must not = mustn't   she would = she'd

they are = they're   are not = aren't

445

Exercise **Using Apostrophes in Contractions**

Write the contractions of these words.

1. I am	5. has not	9. we will
2. are not	6. I will	10. is not
3. it is	7. she is	11. that is
4. will not	8. we would	12. had not

Part 4 The Hyphen

In writing, you often run out of space at the end of a line and can fit in only part of a word.

Use a hyphen after the first part of a word at the end of a line.

The second part of the word is placed at the beginning of the next line, without punctuation.

Before you choose a career, inves-
tigate many fields.

Only words of two or more syllables can be divided at the end of a line. Never divide words of one syllable, such as *slight* or *bounce*. If you are in doubt about dividing a word, look it up in a dictionary.

A single letter must not be left at the end of a line. For example, this division would be wrong: *a- mong*. A single letter must not appear at the beginning of a line either. It would be wrong to divide *inventory* like this: *inventor- y*.

Use a hyphen in compound numbers from twenty-one through ninety-nine.

seventy-six trombones   Twenty-third Psalm

446

Exercises **Using Hyphens Correctly**

A. Copy the following phrases. Decide whether you can divide the word in italics into two parts, each part having more than one letter.

If you can, divide the word as you would at the end of a line. Add the necessary hyphens.

Example: the thirty eight *cannons*
the thirty-eight can-
nons

1. forty five *minutes*
2. the fifty ninth *correction*
3. twenty second *Amendment*
4. thirty four *years*
5. eighty one *trailers*
6. seventy nine years *ago*
7. ninety three *skateboards*
8. twenty nine *cents*
9. my sixty fourth *experiment*
10. forty *clarinets*

B. Follow the directions for Exercise A.

1. the eighty fifth *problem*
2. the forty eighth *state*
3. the seventy first *variation*
4. twenty two *classrooms*
5. ninety seven *cups*
6. the fifty fourth *contestant*
7. my seventy nine *marbles*
8. the thirty sixth *card*
9. his ninety third *birthday*
10. the sixty ninth *story*

Part 5   The Colon

The colon has several uses.

Use a colon after the greeting in a business letter.

Dear Mrs. Winter: Dear Sir:

Use a colon between the numerals that tell the hours and minutes.

8:30 A.M.   3:30 P.M.

Remember to capitalize the letters and to use periods after each letter in the abbreviations *A.M.* and *P.M.*

447

Part 6 The Semicolon

There are two ways to combine two related sentences into one. The first way is to use a conjunction, such as *and*, *but*, and *or*, to connect the sentences. When you write that kind of sentence, you use a comma before the conjunction.

Judge Marino announced her decision, and the courtroom emptied quickly.

The second way to combine two related sentences is to use a **semicolon** (;) alone. The semicolon takes the place of both the comma and the conjunction.

Judge Marino announced her decision; the courtroom emptied quickly.

Exercise Using Colons and Semicolons Correctly

Copy the following business letter, using colons, semicolons, and commas where they are needed.

June 1 1986

Dear Mr. Grant
    Our puppet theater in Tyler Texas will present the story "Cinderella" this weekend. Please print the schedule in tonight's paper. The play will be shown on Saturday June 9 at 1100 A.M. and 300 P.M. it will also be shown on Sunday June 10 at 1030 A.M. 230 P.M. and 700 P.M.

448

Sincerely yours
Toy Chest Puppet Theater

Part 7   Quotation Marks

Direct Quotations

When you write what someone has said or written, you are using a **quotation.** If you write the person's exact words, you write a **direct quotation.** If you do not write his exact words, you have an **indirect quotation.** Study these sentences.

> Direct quotation: Steven said, "I will come."
> Indirect quotation: Steven said that he would come.

The quotation marks in the sample direct quotation mark off Steven's exact words. They were "I will come."

Put quotation marks before and after the words of a direct quotation.

Quotation marks [" "] consist of two pairs of small marks that resemble apostrophes. They tell a reader that the exact words of another speaker or writer are being given.

Quotation marks are *not* used with indirect quotations.

Separate the words of a direct quotation from the rest of the sentence with a comma or end mark, in addition to quotation marks.

> Jane said, "The dog is hungry."
>
> "The dog is hungry," Jane said.

Notice that, in the first sentence above, the comma comes *before* the quotation marks. But the second sentence starts with the quoted words, and the comma falls *inside* the quotation marks.

449

Now look at these sentences carefully:

Mom asked, "Are you hungry?"

Bill replied, "We're starving!"

"We're starving!" Bill replied.

You can see that in these sentences the question marks and exclamation points fall *inside* the quotation marks.

Place question marks and exclamation points inside quotation marks if they belong to the quotation itself.

Place question marks and exclamation points outside quotation marks if they do not belong to the quotation.

Did Dad say, "Come home at seven o'clock"?

I was shocked to hear her say, "I'll go"!

Remember to capitalize the first word of a direct quotation.

Exercise   Punctuating Direct Quotations

Copy these sentences. Add all the necessary punctuation marks.

1. Drop anchor bellowed the captain.
2. Don't forget your key Jeff said Nina.
3. The cashier asked Will there be anything else?
4. Call me when you finish said Ms. Walters.
5. Kevin replied I am finished now.
6. His parents have already said that Pablo can't go.
7. Do you really believe in ESP asked Tammy.
8. Did Lillian say I'll be at the pool soon?
9. Ron asked Where are you going?
10. Two eggs, with bacon shouted the waitress.
11. What was that noise asked my sister.
12. Last call for dinner announced the Amtrak waiter.

Divided Quotations

Sometimes a quotation is divided. Explanatory words, like *she said* or *he asked*, occur in the middle of the quotation.

"My favorite movie," Lewis said, "is the original *King Kong*."

Divided quotations follow the capitalization and punctuation guidelines presented already. In addition, these rules apply:

1. Two sets of quotation marks are used.

2. The explanatory words are followed by a comma or a period. Use a comma if the second part of the quotation does not begin a new sentence. Use a period if the second part of the quotation is a new sentence.

   "I believe," said Mona, "that you are wrong."

   "I can't go," Frank said. "My homework is not done."

3. The second part of the quotation begins with a capital letter if it is the start of a new sentence, as in the second example above. Otherwise, the second part begins with a small letter.

Exercises Punctuating Divided Quotations

A. Copy these sentences, capitalizing and punctuating correctly.

1. Are you ready said Bryan I'll time you.

2. The crawl kick isn't hard Judy assured us just keep your knees straight.

3. Take the game home Sally said generously you can keep it.

4. What would you do Mr. Rocher asked if the rope broke?

5. How much does this spray cost Bonita inquired is it guaranteed to repel mosquitoes?

6. Captain Mr. Spock reported the ship was seriously damaged during the attack.

451

7. Where did you go Julia asked I couldn't find you.

8. Look at my watch exclaimed Zane it doesn't even have water in it.

9. You can pat Prince said Linda he won't bite.

10. The other way Hector insisted is much shorter.

B. Follow the directions for Exercise A.

1. Be careful shouted John the canoe will hit bottom.

2. Ask Mrs. Mitchell suggested Maureen maybe we can broadcast the announcement.

3. No answered Seth my jacket is blue.

4. If you need more spigots said the farmer they're in this sap bucket.

5. Fortunately piped up Andrea I've got fifty cents.

6. Turn the box over my brother suggested maybe the price is on the back.

7. Saturday Dora said I'll come about 8:30.

8. I'm getting cold complained Robin let's go in.

Titles

Put quotation marks around the titles of stories, poems, television programs, reports, articles, and chapters of a book.

"Spring Song" (poem)   "Taxi" (television program)

Exercise   Using Quotation Marks with Titles

Copy the following titles, using quotation marks correctly.

1. Fame (TV show)
2. Rapunzel (story)
3. Fog (poem)
4. My Hobby (report)
5. New Bridge Opens (article)
6. The Muscles (chapter)
7. Peacock Pie (poem)
8. The Planets (chapter)
9. Benson (TV show)
10. The Open Boat (story)

452

Part 8 Underlining

Underline the title of a book, magazine, or motion picture.
When you see these titles in print, they are in italics.

Mary Jane by Dorothy Sterling

Exercise **Using Underlining Correctly**

Copy the following titles, underlining them.

1. The Jazz Man (book)
2. Cricket (magazine)
3. Roosevelt Grady (book)
4. Rascal (book)
5. Newsweek (magazine)
6. Annie (movie)
7. Sports Illustrated (magazine)
8. Raiders of the Lost Ark (movie)
9. Freaky Friday (book and movie)
10. The Revenge of the Jedi (movie)

Reinforcement Exercises—Review

Punctuation

A. Using End Marks Correctly

Copy the following sentences. Supply the missing periods, question marks, and exclamation points.

1. The soccer game was still going on at 8:30 P M
2. Does George know what a hobbit is
3. Miguel trained his dog to catch a Frisbee in its mouth
4. Get help fast
5. When is Tara coming
6. Cheryl has an appointment with Dr H P Lewis tomorrow
7. Move to a seat with a better view
8. Wow I never saw such a huge cave before
9. Elena entered her giant sunflower in a contest
10. May I borrow your ruler

B. Using Commas Correctly

Copy these sentences. Place commas where they are needed.

1. A catamaran has two hulls but it has only one sail.
2. Mayor Wilmont a friend of Senator Stevens rode with him in the parade.
3. Charles M. Schulz is famous for drawing Charlie Brown Lucy and Snoopy.
4. Florence are you going to the movie with us?
5. "Satellites" Ms. Lee said "are used for communications weather reporting and navigation."
6. Do you mean Paris France or Paris Ontario Canada?
7. Well Tracy has enough money and she wants to buy the hat.

454

8. On July 20 1969 the United States landed two astronauts on the moon.

9. "You should take an umbrella" Ned reminded his mother.

10. When Gayle moved the street became much quieter.

C. Using Apostrophes Correctly

Rewrite the following sentences. In each sentence make a contraction of the words in italics. Change any underlined word to show possession.

Example: *Let us* go to Valerie house.

Let's go to Valerie's house.

1. *He will* mail Mother letter.
2. *They have* always bought cider here.
3. Bret dog *did not* wake up.
4. I *do not* know how to ice skate.
5. Eddie book *was not* overdue.
6. *She had* already left her grandmother house.
7. You *should not* phone again tonight.
8. Isabelle *will not* copy anyone work.
9. *You are* ready early.
10. The smaller children *could not* see the acrobats stunts at all.

D. Using Hyphens Correctly

Copy the following phrases. Decide whether you can divide the word in italics into two parts, each part having more than one letter. If you can, divide the word as you would at the end of a line. Add the necessary hyphens.

455

Example: fifty-two *papers*
fifty-two pa-
pers

1. the eighty seven *students*
2. my eighty fourth *mistake*
3. sixty five *days*
4. their forty six *members*
5. more than seventy two *dollars*
6. over ninety *degrees*
7. the twenty eighth *caller*
8. only sixty three *cents*
9. the thirty first *section*
10. his fifty ninth *order*

E. Using Colons and Commas Correctly

Copy the following business letter, using colons and commas correctly.

April 14 1986

Dear Mrs. Brink

Here is the information you need for your trip to Cleveland Ohio on June 15 1986.

Flight 340 leaves Boston at 11 00 A.M. there will be a stopover in Rochester New York from 11 30 A.M. until 11 45 A.M. You arrive in Cleveland at 12 55 P.M.

Sincerely yours
Flying Carpet Travel Agency

F. Using Colons, Semicolons, and Commas Correctly

Copy the following business letter, using colons, semicolons, and commas where they are needed.

April 12 1986

Dear Ms. Walker

We are glad you and your class have decided to visit the science museum in San Diego California. The museum opens at 930 A.M. There is an electricity demonstration at 1000 A.M., 130 P.M., and 400 there is also a forty-five minute program in the planetarium at 1115 A.M. and 330 P.M.

We're looking forward to seeing you on Thursday May 3 and hope you'll enjoy your visit.

Truly yours
Sarah Carson

456

G. Punctuating Quotations Correctly

Copy these sentences. Add all the punctuation marks and capital letters that are needed.

1. The pharmacist said I'll show you how to open this bottle.
2. Good morning Mr. Moser Richard called.
3. Janice spoke quickly it must be Marny's parka.
4. Which do you like asked Henry is this photo better?
5. Paul have you ever read about old castles asked Veronica.
6. Well muttered Kim who asked you?
7. I have some money but I'm saving it I told Alonzo.
8. Beat the egg whites well Julia said and then blend in the sugar.
9. Heather asked where is my basketball Terence?
10. Take all the pie you want Conrad's mother urged.

H. Punctuating Titles Correctly

Copy the following titles. Use quotation marks or underlining as needed.

1. Paul Revere's Ride (poem)
2. My Visit to Epcot Center (report)
3. It's Like This, Cat (book)
4. Rip Van Winkle (story)
5. What's Up, Doc? (movie)
6. Heavy Rains Flood Town (news article)
7. Black Beauty (book and movie)
8. Boy's Life (magazine)
9. Homer Price (book)
10. Gilligan's Island (TV show)

Chapter 29

Spelling

You won't wake up one day and find that suddenly you are a good speller. However, you can learn to spell well. It takes practice. It also takes a knowledge of some spelling rules. If you are a poor speller, you don't have to remain one.

There are many ways to approach spelling problems. These ways will be explained in this chapter.

Good spelling skills are valuable. They are important for writing reports in school. They are needed for writing different kinds of letters. They are vital for filling out forms and applications. As you grow older and write more, they will become even more necessary. To show people that you are careful and informed, you will need to be able to spell correctly.

459

Part 1 How To Become a Better Speller

1. Find out your own spelling enemies and attack them. Look over your past papers and make a list of the misspelled words. Study these words until you can spell them correctly.

2. When you speak, pronounce words carefully. Sometimes people misspell words because they say them wrong. Be sure that you are not blending syllables together. For example, you may write *probly* for *probably* if you are mispronouncing it.

3. Make a habit of looking at words carefully. Practice seeing every letter. Store the letters in your memory. Many people see a word again and again but don't really look at it. Then they make mistakes like writing *safty* for *safety* or *sayed* for *said*. When you see a new word or a tricky word, like *necessary*, look at all the letters. To help yourself remember the spelling, write the word several times. You may want to keep a list of the new words for later practice.

4. Find memory devices to help with problem spellings. Memory devices link words with their correct spellings. Below are some devices. They may give you ideas for other words.

> sep**ara**te (*ara*) Only *a rat* makes us sep**ara**te.
> princi**pal** (*pal*) The princi**pal** is my *pal*.
> tra**ge**dy (*age*) Every *age* has its tra**ge**dy.
> spons**or** (*or*) *Oh, are* you the spons**or**?
> **pur**sue (*pur*) **Pur**sue *Sue's purse* snatcher!
> gui**dance** (*dance*) I *dance* with gui**dance**.
> embar**ra**ss (*rr, ss*) I turned **r**eally **r**ed and felt **s**o **s**illy.

5. Proofread what you write. To make sure that you have spelled all words correctly, reread your work. Examine it carefully, word for word. Don't let your eyes race over the page and miss misspellings.

6. Learn the few important spelling rules given in this chapter.

460

How To Master the Spelling of Particular Words

1. Look at a new or difficult word and say it to yourself. Pronounce it carefully. Look at each syllable as you say it.

2. Look at the letters and say each one. If the word has two or more syllables, pause between syllables as you say the letters.

3. Copy the word.

4. Close your eyes and picture the word in your mind.

5. Without looking at the word, write it.

6. Now look at your book or list and see if you have spelled the word correctly.

7. If you have misspelled the word, notice where the error was. Then repeat steps 3 through 6 until you have spelled the word correctly three times in a row.

Part 2   Rules for Spelling

The Final Silent *e*

When a suffix beginning with a vowel is added to a word ending with a silent *e*, the *e* is usually dropped.

make + ing = making	advise + or = advisor
confuse + ion = confusion	believe + able = believable
expense + ive = expensive	fame + ous = famous

When a suffix beginning with a consonant is added to a word ending with a silent *e*, the *e* is usually kept.

hate + ful = hateful	hope + less = hopeless
bore + dom = boredom	sure + ly = surely
safe + ty = safety	move + ment = movement

461

The following words are exceptions:

truly   argument   ninth   wholly   judgment

Exercise **Suffixes and Silent e**

Find the misspelled words. Spell them correctly.

1. Some fameous people are lonly.
2. Why are we haveing this silly arguement?
3. I am hopeing that this game won't remain scoreless.
4. A jack is usful for changeing tires.
5. Ms. Moore's statment was truly moveing.
6. Terence is blameing me for the damage to his bike.
7. We ordered a flower arrangment of ninty roses.
8. The blazeing fire severly damaged the house.
9. The performance of the dareing acrobats was surly exciteing.
10. Good writeing skills are a desirable achievment.

Words Ending in *y*

When a suffix is added to a word that ends with *y* following a consonant, the *y* is usually changed to *i*.

noisy + ly = noisily   carry + age = carriage
happy + est = happiest   fifty + eth = fiftieth
try + ed = tried   heavy + ness = heaviness

Note this exception: When *-ing* is added, the *y* remains.

bury + ing = burying   cry + ing = crying
deny + ing = denying   apply + ing = applying

462

When a suffix is added to a word that ends with *y* following a vowel, the *y* usually is not changed.

joy + ful = joyful   pay + ment = payment
stay + ing = staying   annoy + ed = annoyed

Exercise **Suffixes and the Final _y_**

Add the suffixes as shown and write the new word.

1. employ + er
2. enjoy + able
3. marry + age
4. play + ed
5. carry + ing
6. sneaky + est
7. destroy + er
8. sixty + eth
9. say + ing
10. reply + es
11. hurry + ed
12. holy + ness
13. easy + ly
14. ready + ness
15. boy + ish
16. lovely + er
17. ugly + est
18. relay + ed
19. happy + ly
20. rely + able

The Addition of Prefixes

When a prefix is added to a word, the spelling of the word stays the same.

un + named = unnamed   re + enter = reenter
dis + appear = disappear   un + known = unknown
in + formal = informal   il + legible = illegible
im + mature = immature   in + appropriate = inappropriate

The Suffixes _-ly_ and _-ness_

When the suffix _-ly_ is added to a word ending with _l_, both _l_'s are kept. When _-ness_ is added to a word ending in _n_, both _n_'s are kept.

mean + ness = meanness   practical + ly = practically
open + ness = openness   careful + ly = carefully

Exercise **Words with Prefixes and Suffixes**

Find the misspelled words. Spell them correctly.

1. Luis was imobile in a plaster cast.
2. Carolyn likes this meat for its leaness.

463

3. Sometimes reporters are missinformed.
4. Many students become awfuly unneasy at test time.
5. Mistreating animals should be ilegal.
6. People who write carefuly don't often mispell words.
7. The unevenness of Ken's handwriting makes it ilegible.
8. Idealy, citizens should not dissobey the law.
9. My mother dissapproves of my stubborness.
10. I realy distrust people who are iresponsible.

Words with the "Seed" Sound

Only one English word ends in *sede: supersede.*
Three words end in *ceed: exceed, proceed, succeed.*
All other words ending in the sound of "seed" are spelled *cede:*

concede   precede   recede   secede

Words with *ie* or *ei*

When the sound is long *e* (ē), the word is spelled *ie* except after *c*.

I Before *E*

belief   relieve   yield   fierce   achieve
niece   brief   field   chief   shield

Except After *C*

receive   ceiling   perceive   deceit
conceive   conceited   receipt

These words are exceptions:

either   weird   species
neither   seize   leisure

Exercise   **"Seed" and *ie/ei* Words**

Find the misspelled words. Spell them correctly.

1. Anna recieved an award for her painting.
2. Did the trucker excede the speed limit?
3. Alvarez preceeds Sanders in the batting order.
4. The mayor conceeded that she had been wrong.
5. We saw a breif film about making leisure time work.
6. The criminal yeilded after a feirce fight.
7. The outfielder proseded to snatch the line drive.
8. Weird shadows danced on the cieling.
9. Many people succede because they beleive in themselves.
10. The police cheif siezed the thief.

Doubling the Final Consonant

Words of one syllable, ending with one consonant following one vowel, double the final consonant before adding *-ing, -ed,* or *-er.*

sit + ing = sitting	sad + er = sadder
hop + ed = hopped	stop + ing = stopping
shop + er = shopper	let + ing = letting

The final consonant is not doubled when it is preceded by *two* vowels.

meet + ing = meeting	loan + ed = loaned
break + ing = breaking	train + er = trainer

Exercise   **Doubling the Final Consonant**

Add the suffixes as shown and write the new word.

1. leap + ed	6. hem + ed	11. near + ing
2. fat + er	7. scream + ing	12. trip + ed
3. beat + ing	8. flap + ed	13. swim + er
4. cool + er	9. hot + er	14. leap + ing
5. chop + er	10. hug + ing	15. peek + ed

Part 3 Words Often Confused

Sometimes you make a mistake in spelling simply because of your own carelessness or forgetfulness. Other times, however, your problems are caused by the language itself. In English there are many words that are easily confused. These words sound the same, or nearly the same, but are spelled differently and have different meanings. Words of this type are called **homonyms**. Here are some examples of homonyms:

horse—hoarse   pare—pear—pair   tail—tale   do—dew—due

When you have problems with homonyms, general spelling rules won't help you. The only solution is to memorize which spelling goes with which meaning.

Here is a list of homonyms and other words frequently used and frequently confused in writing. Study the sets of words, and try to connect each word with its correct meaning. Refer to the list if you have further difficulties with these words.

accept means to agree to something or to receive something willingly.

except means to keep out or leave out. As a preposition, *except* means "but" or "leaving out."

My brother will *accept* the job the grocer offered him.
Michelle likes every flavor of ice cream *except* pistachio.

capital means chief, important, or excellent. It also means the city or town that is the official seat of government of a state or nation.

capitol is the building where a state legislature meets.

the Capitol is the building in Washington, D.C., in which the United States Congress meets.

The *capital* of Illinois is the city of Springfield.
The *capitol* of Illinois is a stately building in Springfield.
The senators arrived at the *Capitol* in time to vote.

466

hear means to listen to.
here means in this place.

> Every time I *hear* this song, I feel happy.
> Reference books stay *here* in the library.

it's is the contraction for *it is* or *it has*.
its shows ownership or possession.

> *It's* nearly midnight.
> The boat lost *its* sail during the storm.

lead (lĕd) is a heavy, gray metal.
lead (lēd) means to go first, to guide.
led (lĕd) is the past tense of *lead* (lēd).

> Water pipes are often made of *lead*.
> These signs will *lead* us to the hiking trail.
> Bloodhounds *led* the detectives to the scene of the crime.

loose means free or not tight.
lose means to mislay or suffer the loss of something.

> A rider keeps the horse's reins *loose*.
> If you *lose* your book, report the loss to the library as soon as
> possible.

peace is calm or stillness or the absence of disagreement.
piece means a portion or part.

> A sunset over the ocean is my idea of *peace*.
> Who can stop after one *piece* of pie?

principal means first or most important. It also refers to the head
of a school.
principle is a rule, truth, or belief.

467

> A *principal* export of Brazil is coffee.
> Our school *principal* organized a safety council.
> One *principle* of science is that all matter occupies space.

quiet means free from noise or disturbance.
quite means truly or almost completely.

The only time our classroom is *quiet* is when it's empty.
The aquarium tank is *quite* full.

their means belonging to them.
there means at that place.
they're is the contraction for *they are*.

Our neighbors sold *their* house and moved to a farm.
Please take the squirt guns over *there*.
My sisters have never skied, but *they're* willing to try.

to means in the direction of.
too means also or very.
two is the whole number between one and three.

The surgeon rushed *to* the operating room.
The lights went off, and then the heat went off, *too*.
Only *two* of the four mountaineers reached the peak.

weather is the state of the atmosphere referring to wind, moisture,
temperature, etc.
whether indicates a choice or alternative.

Australia has summer *weather* when the United States has winter.
Whether we drive or take the train, we will arrive in three hours.

who's is the contraction for *who is* or *who has*.
whose is the possessive form of *who*.

Who's been chosen to be a crossing guard?
Whose skateboard was left on the sidewalk?

you're is the contraction for *you are*.
your is the possessive form of *you*.

You're going to the costume party, aren't you?
Please bring *your* sheet music to choir practice.

Exercises Words Often Confused

A. Choose the right word from the words in parentheses.

1. Janie and Alethia built (their, there, they're) own treehouse.
2. The Indian (lead, led) his tribesmen to the hunting ground.
3. (Who's, Whose) bicycle has racing stripes?
4. If I (loose, lose) this dollar bill, I won't eat lunch.
5. A shark is vicious because of (its, it's) double row of teeth.
6. Did Dwayne (accept, except) the invitation to your party?
7. I study best in a well lit, (quiet, quite) room.
8. The (capital, capitol, Capitol) in Washington, D.C., is built on a hill.
9. Are you taller than (your, you're) sister?
10. We will play the game (weather, whether) it rains or not.

B. Choose the right word from the words in parentheses.

1. We had to hunt for the gerbil that got (loose, lose).
2. The (principal, principle) character in *A Christmas Carol* is Ebenezer Scrooge.
3. Jaguars seem fierce, but (their, there, they're) afraid of dogs.
4. A fire engine will (lead, led) the parade.
5. Although bats don't see at night, they (hear, here) where they are.
6. Does your brother know that (your, you're) planning a surprise party?
7. Ceramics is creative, and it's fun, (to, too, two).
8. Eric is the only batter (who's, whose) left-handed.
9. The city of Austin is the (capital, capitol, Capitol) of Texas.
10. Everyone (accept, except) Dawn went down the giant slide.

469

Reinforcement Exercises—Review

Spelling

A. Suffixes and Silent e

Find the misspelled words. Spell them correctly.

1. May I speak to you privatly?
2. Lyn's lovly new jacket is reverseible.
3. Cal's hobbies are bakeing and raceing stock cars.
4. The poor stray dog was namless and homeless.
5. Donna said she was sincerly sorry for leaveing.
6. The summer night was strangly peacful.
7. Raoul's behavior was completly unexpected.
8. Our coach was giveing us guideance in shooting baskets.
9. My relateives held a birthday celebrateion for my cousin.
10. After escapeing from their pen, the cattle came chargeing across the field.

B. Suffixes and the Final y

Add the suffixes as shown and write the new word.

1. fly + er
2. stay + ing
3. funny + est
4. early + er
5. play + ful
6. speedy + est
7. try + ing
8. gray + er
9. copy + ing
10. silly + er
11. deny + al
12. angry + ly
13. city + es
14. portray + ed
15. ninety + eth

C. Words with Prefixes and Suffixes

Find the misspelled words. Spell them correctly.

1. A wolf is known for its meaness.

2. I missunderstood the last question.
3. The new rules are both unnfair and ilogical.
4. My notebook is dissorderly and dissorganized.
5. Kyle's parents were actually shocked by the cleaness of his room.
6. Our teacher dissapproves of imature jokes and fights.
7. Finaly the stagecoach reached the openess of the plains.
8. During the winter, bears are generaly innactive.
9. The trainer cruely whipped his horses for missbehaving.
10. People usualy see pictures in the iregular shapes of inkblots.

D. "Seed" and *ie/ei* Words

Find the misspelled words. Spell them correctly.

1. The tide receeds twice a day.
2. The pass receiver streaked down the feild.
3. Mr. Johnson gave his neice a wierd mask.
4. The Southern states seceeded from the Union.
5. Some people who achieve fame become concieted.
6. Marla feircely defended her beleif in ghosts.
7. The parade proceded to the pier at the edge of town.
8. The fire cheif succeded in controlling the blaze.
9. A detective percieved footprints on the ceiling.
10. An overture preceeds either an opera or a musical.

E. Doubling the Final Consonant

Add the suffixes as shown and write the new word.

1. tour + ed
2. moan + ing
3. star + ing
4. sip + ed
5. seat + ed
6. keep + er
7. slam + ing
8. grab + ed
9. leak + ing
10. mad + er
11. stir + ed
12. troop + er
13. flat + er
14. big + er
15. clap + ed

471

Index

472

477

479

Editorial Director: Joy Littell
Senior Editor: Patricia Opaskar
Managing Editor: Kathleen Laya
Assistant Editor: Elizabeth M. Garber
Director of Design: Allen Carr
Assistant Designer: Mary MacDonald

Acknowledgments

Harold Courlander: For "The Storyteller" from *The Fire on the Mountain and Other Ethiopian Stories* by Harold Courlander and Wolf Leslau, New York: Henry Holt and Co., Inc., 1950, renewed copyright © 1978 by Harold Courlander, Wolf Leslau and Robert W. Kane. Doubleday Publishing Co.: For an excerpt from *The Story of My Life* by Helen Keller. E. P. Dutton: For a selection from *Rascal* by Sterling North; copyright © 1963 by Sterling North. Harper & Row Publishers, Inc.: For "The Cold" (text only, pp. 90-92), from *Whoppers, Tall Tales, and Other Lies* by Alvin Schwartz (J. B. Lippincott, Publishers); copyright © 1975 by Alvin Schwartz. For "Moochie" (text only) from *Honey, I Love and Other Love Poems* by Eloise Greenfield (Thomas Y. Crowell, Publishers); copyright © 1978 by Eloise Greenfield. For "Tree House" (text only, p. 79) and "Spaghetti" from *Where the Sidewalk Ends* by Shel Silverstein; copyright © 1974 by Shel Silverstein. Holt, Rinehart and Winston: For "The Dark Gray Clouds" from *The Sun Is a Golden Earring* by Natalia M. Belting; copyright © 1962 by Natalia Belting. Alfred A. Knopf, Inc.: For "Windshield Wipers Wipe the Windshield" from *Nuts To You and Nuts To Me: An Alphabet of Poems* by Mary Ann Hoberman; copyright © 1974 by Mary Ann Hoberman; reprinted by permission of Alfred A. Knopf, Inc. For "January" from *A Child's Calendar* by John Updike; copyright © 1965 by John Updike and Nancy Burkert; reprinted by permission of Alfred A. Knopf, Inc. For "Dreams" by Langston Hughes, from *The Dream Keeper and Other Poems*; copyright 1932 by Alfred A. Knopf, Inc. and renewed 1960 by Langston Hughes. Little Brown & Co.: For "The Rhinoceros" from *Verses From 1929 on* by Ogden Nash; Copyright 1933 by Ogden Nash; first appeared in *The New Yorker*. The New Yorker: For "Catalog" by Rosalie Moore; copyright © 1940, 1968, The New Yorker Magazine, Inc., reprinted by permission. The New York Times: For "Moonlight" by Maud E. Uschold; copyright © 1951 by the New York Times Company. W. W. Norton & Company, Inc.: For an excerpt from *Those Tremendous Mountains* by David Freeman Hawke; copyright © 1980 by David Hawke. Rand McNally & Co.: For an excerpt from *Benjamin Franklin* by R. Conrad Stein; copyright © 1972 by Rand McNally & Co. Larry Sternig Agency: For "Zoo" by Edward D. Hoch, from *100 Great Science Fiction Short Stories*, edited by Isaac Asimov. A. R. Swinnerton: For "Harry the Heavyweight" by A. R. Swinnerton, from *The Pugnacious Pussycat*. Viking Penguin, Inc.: For an excerpt from *Of Courage Undaunted: Across the Continent with Lewis and Clark* by James Daugherty; copyright 1951 by James Daugherty; copyright renewed 1979 by Charles Michael Daugherty. World Book-Childcraft International: For an excerpt from *The World Book Encyclopedia*, Vol. 14, p. 478.

Photographs

Cover   Photo Researchers: Kjell B. Sandved.

James L. Ballard: 64, 76, 86, 130, 308, 324, 370, 388

The following photographs courtesy of Magnum: Paul Fusco, ii, 28, 276; Dennis Stock, xii, 342, 358; Arthur Tress, 12; Burk Uzzle, 102, 140, 246, 468; Costa Manos, 114, 286; Rene Burri, 156; Charles Harbutt, 184, 198, 432; Burt Glinn, 210, 352; David Hurn, 228; Kryn Taconis, 260; Eve Arnold, 458.

482 ## Illustrations

Len Ebert, 2, 3, 50, 66, 70, 72, 116, 132, 158, 204, 372, 382, 408; Donald Leake, 5, 18, 20, 22, 93, 94, 107, 201, 203, 212, 225, 249, 256, 268, 288, 375, 376, 380, 381; Mila Lazarevich, 6, 32, 39, 89, 90, 91, 98, 104, 117, 122, 125, 127, 149, 166, 187, 201, 264, 293, 326, 366, 368; Bill and Judie Anderson, 69, 238, 397, 399, 400; Bob Masheris, 135, 314, 316, 317, 320, 322, 363; Ken Izzi, 139, 366, 369, 395; Hilary Hayton, 168, 177, 262, 263, 283; Yoshi Miyaki, 189, 230, 231, 241, 252, 270, 391, 392, 393, 394, 402, 403, 404, 411, 412, 413, 414, 415, 416, 417; Michael Deas, 200; Gary Gianni, 296; James Teason, 383; Frank Bozzo, 396; John Walter, 406. Ken Izzi, Jeanne Seabright: mechanical artwork, hand-written letters.